VOICES FROM THE
BACK OF THE BUS

Stewart McKinney is a former Ireland international rugby player who was part of the British and Irish Lions team that was victorious against South Africa in 1974. He played for Ireland for seven years.

VOICES FROM THE BACK OF THE BUS

TALL TALES AND HOARY STORIES FROM RUGBY'S REAL HEROES

STEWART McKINNEY

MAINSTREAM
PUBLISHING

EDINBURGH AND LONDON

First published in Great Britain in 2009 by
MAINSTREAM PUBLISHING COMPANY
(EDINBURGH) LTD
7 Albany Street
Edinburgh EH1 3UG

ISBN 9781845965921

A catalogue record for this book is available
from the British Library

Typeset in Bembo and Century Gothic

5 7 9 10 8 6

Printed and bound in Great Britain by Clays Ltd, St Ives PLC

ACKNOWLEDGEMENTS

I would like to dedicate this book to my children:
Sam, Kathleen, Jamie and Joseph

And also to the surgeons, doctors and nurses at St George's Heart Hospital, Tooting, and Moorfields Eye Hospital, St Ann's Tottenham.

There are many people who have helped me make this book a reality, but there are also a few without whose support this book would not have happened. They are: Siobhan McKinney, Ray, Dessie and Bernadette O'Rourke, Steve Cork, Claire Evans, Liz Fay, Bill Campbell, Suzanne Milligan and Nick Hague.

I must also thank everyone who has contributed a story to this book. These stories have come from my friends, but that each has been so happily and freely given is a measure of these players. I have been delighted by every story – and the excuse it has provided to renew old friendships.

There have also been friends whose efforts in helping me compile this book deserve special mention, and they are: <u>from Ireland</u>: Carmel Dwyer (IRFU), Cavor Drudy (IRFU), Syd Millar, Jim Stokes (BBC Sport NI), Jim Neilly (BBC Sport), Victor Scarlett, Dungannon FC), Ken Nelson (Newtownards Round Table), Joe McKinney (my brother), Mick Fitzpatrick (IRFU Golf Society); <u>from Wales</u>: J.J. Williams, Medwyn Parri, John Evans; <u>from England</u>: Peter Jackson (*Daily Mail*), Mike Burton, Nigel Davies, Alan Hunt, Mark Hudson (Front Row Events), David Willis (National Sporting Club); <u>from Scotland</u>: Sandy Carmichael, Andy Irvine, Ian McLauchlan; from New Zealand: Derek McKeen (Dungannon FC); <u>from South Africa</u>: Choet Visser Rugby Museum (Nico Du Plessis Jnr), Nico and Veronica Du Plessis and family, Jack and Marcia Van der Linde and family.

Liz Fay – Stills Research. Photographs kindly lent from the Choet Visser Rugby Museum (3 Innes Avenue, Bloemfontein, Free State, South Africa).

British Heart
Foundation

Greater London House
180 Hampstead Road
London
NW1 7AW

24 August 2009

Dear Stewart

As the Chief Executive of the British Heart Foundation, I'd like to extend a huge thank you for making a donation of 50 per cent from all the royalties from the sales of your book *Voices from the Back of the Bus*.

I am a rugby fan myself and the stories have given me great deal of pleasure, as I'm sure they will to many others.

The British Heart Foundation is the nation's heart charity. With around 2.5 million people living with heart disease in the UK, it is extremely important that we continue with our life-saving work.

Your extremely kind donation will support our vital and life-saving work to fight heart disease. With donations like yours, we can provide specialist care from BHF heart nurses to improve the physical and emotional health of heart patients and their families, and fund research which could lead to a cure or improvements in treatment.

It is only through the wonderful generosity of supporters like you that we are able to continue with our vital work, making a huge difference to those affected and their families.

Thank you once again and I wish you every success with this endeavour.

With best wishes

Peter Hollins
Chief Executive

CONTENTS

FOREWORD BY SYD MILLAR

*Sydney 'Syd' Millar CBE (born in Ballymena, 23 May 1934)
is the outgoing chairman of the International Rugby Board. He
played for Ballymena RFC and represented Ireland in the pack,
winning 37 caps as a prop. In addition, he played nine times for
the British and Irish Lions, in 1959, 1962 and 1968. Millar also
coached the successful 1974 British Lions tour to South Africa and
managed the tour there in 1980. He served as manager of the Irish
national side at the 1987 World Cup and as head of the IRFU.
On 12 December 2007, he was awarded the Légion d'honneur
by Bernard Lapasset, his successor as IRB chairman.*

The game of rugby football has changed radically since the contributors
to this book played. The stories originate in a different era. An era when
the game was amateur but 'professional' with a small 'p' at the higher
levels, and Test matches and international matches particularly were
played with no less intensity than today. It was an era before high-tech
was available and before there was a proliferation of coaches and advisors
to coaches, etc., etc.

Rugby football, once sampled, becomes addictive and many of us
have been addicted for most of our lives. It's hard to let go, and once
the enjoyment of playing is over people tend to stay on in various
capacities. Some continue to play as Golden Oldies, others coach,
manage, administer, comment and write, happy to remain in a game
that has given them so much pleasure. Rugby football generates a
camaraderie that is unique; friendships develop and last a lifetime.

I am fortunate to have had a long playing career followed by coaching,
managing and administering, and it is a privilege to have been allowed
such a long involvement.

Rugby football has given me and many of the other contributors an
opportunity to travel the world, to play with and against some of the
great players of the game and to meet people from various walks of
life, but above all it has given me the valued friendship of many.

Lions tours were, and still are, unique, where four countries come
together to take on the might of the southern hemisphere. Tours were
longer in my time, for instance in 1959 we played thirty-three games,
six in Australia, twenty-five in New Zealand and two in Canada; in
1962, in South Africa, we played twenty-five games. My son was born
during that tour and he was three months old before I saw him, so

wives were very long-suffering. I was fortunate to have such a wife, in Enid, who despite my time devoted to rugby is still there as a great support and has been over the years.

Lions tours are where players from England, Ireland, Scotland and Wales come together to make up the touring party. Players who have played against each other in the Six Nations become teammates and a loyalty to each other develops. This was especially true when the tours were longer and we had more time to enjoy the game, the country and each other's company. Lifelong friendships were made with teammates and some of the opposition. Many of the stories told in this book originate in Lions tours and when we players meet, as we do from time to time, the 'craic is mighty'. Stewart McKinney is performing a service to the game, ensuring these stories are put into print for others to enjoy and are not lost. Stewart – great player, hard man – who played at the highest possible level, is demonstrating the caring side of rugby football and deserves our thanks and support for producing *Voices from the Back of the Bus*, royalties from which will go to the British Heart Foundation.

Well done, Stewart, and everyone who has contributed their story to this book.

Syd Millar
September 2009

FOREWORD BY TERRY O'CONNOR

Terry O'Connor has been the rugby correspondent for the Daily
Mail *for 31 years and has covered internationals since 1949. He
first toured with British and Irish Lions in 1962 and then went
on a further ten trips. He does not believe the invincible record of
the 1974 team will ever be eclipsed.*

This book proves that rugby union towers over other sports when it
comes to creating friendships that last a lifetime. That is why Stewart
McKinney, an Ireland and Lions forward, was inspired to capture the
views of legends from amateur rugby and their memories of overseas
rugby tours and record them for posterity.

Prompted by hearing the stories told at former Ireland coach Jimmy
Davidson's funeral (May 2007) – and worried they might be lost or
forgotten – McKinney has devoted the past two years corresponding
with and telephoning famous players (some opponents but all friends)
throughout the world in memory of Davidson, a fellow Ulsterman with
whom he played for years, including an Ireland trip to New Zealand
in 1976.

McKinney has brought together well over 100 players from all over the
world, and the great majority of them enjoyed international status. Two
of the most famous, Willie John McBride and Gareth Edwards, toured
together three times with the Lions and every year found themselves
opponents during the then Five Nations Championship – now of
course Six. Gareth writes that some of the Wales–Ireland games were
rough and intense, even for him. The memory of competition still burns
bright all these years later.

During my time reporting on matches from 1962, there have been
many changes to the sport. Rugby ceased to be an amateur game in
1995. This has led to shorter trips abroad and possibly compromised the
intense camaraderie so evident among the amateurs – an unfortunate
casualty of the demands of professionalism. Thus the winning 1997
team in South Africa did not have the same pleasure of visiting the
famous Kruger National Park, with its vast array of wildlife, particularly
jungle animals. The 1974 team were able to benefit from R & R in
this spectacular venue as a respite from training. As a result, midday
training runs in the sun, warthogs and other encounters make up
many of the yarns fondly remembered by those tourists.

VOICES FROM THE BACK OF THE BUS

On reflection, the two Lions centres in the 1974 Tests, Dick Milliken of Ireland and Ian McGeechan of Scotland, did not receive the praise they deserved. Sadly, injuries shortened Milliken's playing days, but he has no regrets, only great pride in having played a major part in the golden era of British Lions rugby. Andy Irvine was one of the superstars of the amateur game in 1974, and he nostalgically recalls what conditions were like for touring teams in the now distant past – more than 35 years ago. Clive Rees reflects on the personality of a fellow teammate, a side not usually seen by the public, but one that his fellow players came to know and one of the reasons why they loved him so.

There are many tales of players taking medical risks to ensure they could play when team doctors would have ordered a rest. Misunderstandings and mistaken identities, pathos and high jinks, flashes of brilliance and regrettable disasters all have their place in this collection of stories. The different sections cover touring, coaching and selection, South Africa, New Zealand, administration, and general miscellaneous anecdotes and hoary tales from around the world.

The recollections in this book have brought back many fond memories of the game, both on and off the pitch, and of the players from that era of epic battles and performances of unparalleled genius for me. What this book does most of all, though, through the pithy, self-deprecating modesty of its contributors, is prove that rugby is a 'game for thugs played by gentlemen' – truly gentlemen.

Terry O'Connor
September 2009

THE CONCEPT

The memorial service to celebrate Jimmy Davidson's life was held in the orchard in the beautiful grounds surrounding his home. He had a wonderful send-off, and as I was leaving, heading for the Maze Golf Club for 'refreshments' with a host of other rugby folk, I ran into Tommy Doyle, who had played for Ireland in 1968.

'Bejaysus,' said Tommy with a mischievous twinkle in his eye. 'All the great Irish back-row forwards are dying, McKinney, but you and I needn't worry, as we were never that good!' I laughed, but unknown to Tommy I was struggling with a heart problem of my own so was also a little anxious about my future.

In the golf club we recounted many rugby tales, and Charlie Murtagh remarked that as we were from a different era it would be a great pity that our little escapades would be lost for ever.

On the way home I thought of those players of my vintage, unique characters who had passed away: Shay Deering, Terry Moore, Ken Goodall, Jimmy D. and Tom Doyle's brother Mick, killed in a tragic road accident outside my home town of Dungannon. And I thought of Gordon Brown – what a man. That's what hatched the plan. I would write anecdotes and collect stories from players of the amateur days. It started off as a hobby, but it developed into a worldwide project, with contributors from far and wide.

The most wonderful aspect of the undertaking was the confirmation that rugby friendships forged all those years ago still remain. We had a unique bond. The greatest flanker I ever played against, the All Black Ian Kirkpatrick, talked for half an hour on the phone, and I hadn't been in his company for 34 years!

Nearly all of the contributors are internationals – All Blacks, Springboks and Lions – but I also have included some players who were great clubmen whose attitude to our game was typical of true rugby men.

Stewart McKinney
September 2009

TOURING

TOURING PREFACE

Touring was part and parcel of an amateur-rugby player's life. At club level it might have been a pre-season tour to build team spirit for the coming year. Easter heralded a great exodus to all parts of Britain and Ireland, and many of those tours were traditional, going back many years. The most famous Easter tour in my day was the Baa-Baas' to South Wales – four games in five days: Penarth on Good Friday, Cardiff on Easter Saturday, Swansea on Easter Monday and Newport on Easter Tuesday. The Baa–Baas were a club without a home, so a Porthcawl base was set up in the Esplanade Hotel, and photographs and memorabilia were hung up in the team room. Nothing was free: ties and scarves were paid for, and woe betide anyone who tried to steal a jersey. (No replica stores in those days!) There was no training or practice, as the lyrics of the club song explained: 'For it's the way we have in the Baa-Baas, and a jolly fine way, too.'

The Irish on club jaunts tended to dress more formally, with club ties and blazers for the Easter tours. But one Easter Monday I happened to come upon a Welsh rugby team, I think it was Tredegar, in Moony's bar in Belfast, dressed in garish Bermuda shorts and dummy teats stuck in their mouths. It made me think that perhaps we Irish weren't so daft after all.

Four rugby aficionados in Bermuda changed the face of Easter tours for ever. Pat O'Riordan, John Kane, Tom Gallaher and David Lunn, four Irishmen collectively known as the 'Bermuda Murphia', secretly invited a ringer, none less than Tommy Kiernan the Ireland captain, to play in the annual Irish v. the Rest of the Island game. There was great protest from the Rest, so the next year Gareth Edwards guested for them, but the Murphia kept the balance in favour of the Irish by importing Ken Kennedy and Mike Gibson. By the time I played in the game in 1978, it had been switched to Easter Sunday, was called the Bermuda Classic and 11 international players were involved. Later, the Murphia – I think the year was 1989 – organised the first Golden Oldies Festival, which has developed into the famous Bermuda Is Another World event, and many of the stories in this book originate from the island.

Stewart McKinney

SHIP'S RATIONS

JACK KYLE
FLY-HALF Queen's University, NIFC, Ulster
IRELAND 1947–58, 46 caps
LIONS TOUR '50, 6 Test matches

Tom Clifford was the first rugby player from Limerick to be made a member of a Lions side. He had a wonderful send-off from the town and from his club. He was renowned far and wide as a man who enjoyed his food, and his mother was worried that he might be going to countries that would not be able to cater for his appetite. There was also a ship journey from Liverpool to Wellington of more than a month. It was not on a passenger liner, but on one that brought lamb and sheep from New Zealand and carried about 90 passengers, so it was important Tom didn't go hungry.

On board we were told that all large trunks were to go to the ship's hold, but Tom insisted that one huge trunk of his go to his cabin. We found out the reason for this when after a few days at sea, and just before bedtime, someone remarked that he was hungry, as it was quite a few hours after dinner. Tom invited us to his cabin, where we likely imagined that he had a bar of chocolate or some other small titbit. He proceeded to pull a huge trunk from under his sleeping berth and opened it. It was filled to the brim with cakes and various durable foodstuffs. Mrs Clifford must have been cooking for at least a month to provide Tom with such nourishment. Tom invited us to help ourselves, which we did that night and on other nights until the trunk was empty.

One night someone suggested that we write a thank-you note to Mrs Clifford, and we all scribbled a line or two to her. 'Dear Mrs Clifford, Just enjoying a piece of your excellent cake. Many thanks.'

To give some idea of Tom's appetite, we had an eating competition at dinner one night on board the ship. Tom was a clear winner, eating every one of the eighteen courses on the menu. Bill McKay was runner up with thirteen, and the rest of us could only manage the usual three or four.

Sadly, Tom is no longer with us, but this is one memory I have amongst others of a wonderful character and a remarkable man.

BRITISH LIONS: ANCIENT AND MODERN

ANDY IRVINE
FULL-BACK Heriot's FP
SCOTLAND 1972–82, 51 caps
LIONS TOURS '74, '77, '80, 9 Test matches

Having been a member of the victorious 1974 squad to South Africa and now currently chairman of the British and Irish Lions board, I was very much involved in the preparation of the 2009 tour, and I thought it might be quite interesting to compare the make-up of the touring party of 1974 v. 2009.

The 1974 tour lasted three months and comprised twenty-two games, of which four were Test matches, and the total touring party amounted to thirty-two people (thirty players, one manager and one coach). All the players were strictly amateur, and the daily allowance that each player received was £1.50. That may not seem a lot, but as all accommodation, food and travel were free, the daily allowance was really just used for socialising and a few beers in between games.

The training in 1974 was pretty simple, with sessions from 10 a.m. every morning until 12 noon. We then had lunch together, and our afternoons and evenings were free so that we could go golfing, sightseeing, shopping, and to the beach and local nightspots. Also, there were no distractions or diversions from communication technology and gadgetry. This was an era before mobile phones, iPods, Game Boys, laptops, etc. The height of sophistication and high-tech machinery was probably a cassette player; otherwise, the players interacted with each other and the people whom they met.

Moving on 35 years, and things are very different. Obviously, the most important difference is that the game is now professional. All the players are elite athletes, and whereas we trained for just two hours a day, the current squad started in the gym most mornings at 7 a.m., had breakfast around 9 a.m., trained between 10 a.m. and midday, had a specially prepared lunch and then trained again in the afternoon. Many evenings, they watched videos and went over tactics at team discussions.

The intensity of the games is now, of course, much greater, and players have to endure a much longer season. In 1974 all of the players were requested to rest for the whole of April. Some of the 2009 squad played right up until they left the British Isles. Whereas in 1974 we took thirty players, the squad this time was thirty-seven, even though the number of games played was only ten.

Ultimately, there was nearly double the party for less than half the matches. The total tour party was sixty-three, and in addition to the players included perhaps a dozen or more 'ancillary staff': four or five coaches, doctors, physios, masseurs, lawyers, specialist chefs, a manager, assistant manager, baggage men. The medical back-up was second to none, which provides an interesting comparison with '74, when we had no doctor, no physio, no nothing! I don't even recall a water boy. (Taking fluids on board was regarded as unmanly . . . and we were *never* sissies.) Apparently, a half-time orange quarter was sufficient to replace lost fluids, salts and electrolytes in those days.

As chance would have it, we were fortunate to have two doctors with our touring party – players! Ken Kennedy was a practising doctor and was very approachable, but he had limited time, as he was committed to keeping pressure on Bobby Windsor to win a Test spot. J.P.R. would tell you to take a gin and tonic – and if that didn't work, you were told not to be a wimp!

The other huge difference between then and now is the amount of support and media coverage that a British and Irish Lions tour generates. In 1974 there were possibly as many as 1,000 fans supporting the team, and most of those only for the third and fourth Tests, whereas on the 2009 tour it was estimated that as many as 25,000 supporters flew over from the British Isles, and the worldwide television audience was huge.

All in all, it was a great tour, but I just wonder if they had as much fun as those of us involved in '74.

SOME GUYS HAVE ALL THE LUCK!

PETER BELL
FLANKER Blackheath
ENGLAND 1968–9, 4 caps

I was lucky enough to go on tour with Jeff Butterfield's ex-international side to Jamaica, the Cayman Islands and the Bahamas. Tony O'Reilly was supposed to have joined the team in the Cayman Islands but only arrived by private plane with a few friends in time for the last game in the Bahamas.

In the evening there was a huge party in the clubhouse, with its obligatory swimming pool, which made for a superb setting. At about 8.30 p.m. 'Golden Boy' Tony O'Reilly turned up in his Ireland tie,

Lions blazer and, as far I know, sporting his Barbarian underpants – ever the model of understated sartorial elegance! Tony was the centre of attention, as he had scored the first try of the game, which seemed to stir up Dickie Jeeps, who was not at all happy that Tony had arrived for the last match only and was now being hailed the hero of the hour. Such is hero worship (fickle at times) that there was a feeling that Tony should be thrown into the pool. It seemed only right. Four of the players grabbed him by a limb each and began to swing him backwards and forwards to get the best possible heave. As the final fling was about to take place, Tony said, 'I thank you, on behalf of Kerrygold, for throwing me into the pool!' And, splash, in he went!

After a considerable amount of time, he eventually resurfaced and paddled up and down the pool with his blazer like a halo around his head, whereupon the best-looking woman at the party, in full evening dress, jumped in to join him. They swam up and down for about 20 minutes and then disappeared, never to be seen again, much to our frustration and annoyance. It just goes to show that some guys do have all the luck.

ACROSS THE MILES – RUGBY FRIENDSHIPS ARE FOR EVER

STEWART McKINNEY
FLANKER King's Scholars, Dungannon, London Irish, Ulster
IRELAND 1972–8, 25 caps
LIONS TOUR '74

King's Scholars, my college side, toured Cowichan in 1969. We stayed in hotels in Calgary, Vancouver and Victoria on Vancouver Island, but when we travelled farther up the island to Cowichan we were billeted out for our stay in that beautiful part of the world. Much to the disgusted envy of the rest of the team, big Hammy Moore and I were assigned accommodation with a lumberjack called 'Goody' Gumundseth. He looked after us royally in his shack, way up a mountainside. He was a horse of a man and ate like a horse, too – six eggs and T-bone steaks for breakfast. Hammy and I thought we'd found heaven.

We played and beat Cowichan then had a magnificent salmon barbecue outside their clubhouse, surely one of the most beautiful settings on God's earth. Of course, the only fitting way to finish off the evening of triumph and celebration was to drink them out of beer . . . so we did.

I often wondered about Goody over the years. I only knew he had gone on to play for Canada. Twenty-five years later, my fond memories probably sold the NIFC (North of Ireland Rugby Club) on a tour to Canada. We took in Vancouver Island, as my college team had done, and I happened to be with the front-row union – Scottie (David Scott), Hutty (Stephen Hutton), Davy Jordan, Brian Berry and Simon Crawford – in a restaurant overlooking a lake in Cowichan. The barmaid asked me if I'd been in this part of the world before. I told her I had stayed with a wonderful rugby player called Goody Gumundseth 25 years previously. 'That's him sitting in the corner with his wife, Angie,' she said.

And there he was, that great bear of a man. Like me, greyer, more stooped, plumper. 'Goody!' I said. 'Stewart McKinney, King's Scholars. I stayed with you 25 years ago!'

'Yes!' he replied. 'And you young bastards drank us out of beer after the game!'

Goody and I attempted over the next three days to drink Cowichan out of beer again. These things have to be done.

TORTURE! IT'S CHARACTER BUILDING

TERRY KENNEDY
WING St Mary's, Leinster
IRELAND 1978–82, 13 caps

Touring is everything that's good about rugby – it's your reward for all your efforts on and off the rugby pitch and the bonus for all the work done on the training ground. I have had many adventures, and along the way I have encountered marvellous characters. The Mary's heroes of my day, such as Fitzy (Ciaran Fitzgerald), Rods (Rodney O'Donnell), Deano (Paul Dean), Chetts (Paul Andreucetti), Gracer (Tom Grace), Noel McCarthy and fab Vinnie Cunningham, the unsung heroes, such as Franko (Frank Kennedy), J.B. John Boy, the Fanjos (not so young Declan and Joe Fanning), Moss (Moss Keane), Deero (Shay Deering) – wonderful tourists one and all. I was fortunate enough to travel on dozens of tours, be they three-day weekend trips to Waterloo or Amsterdam or five-week trips to Australia or South Africa. I forged lifetime friendships, and through my friendship with the 'Stoat' (Stewart McKinney) I'll tell you now of some of my favourite memories from my travels at home and abroad.

St Mary's tour to Russia, 1977 – Sean Lynch (extremely pacey for a prop!) knocked over the corner flags one by one on a punishment run inflicted upon us by John Moloney for the team breaking curfew the night before. A one-mile leisurely run turned into two miles of torture – the day before playing the Russian national team, whom we went on to beat 38–21, a scoreline that remained in the *Guinness Book of Records* for over twenty years as the biggest win for a club team against a national team.

The night before my first cap – against New Zealand, 1978 – training had gone well and everything was tipping along nicely until the Friday evening at around 9.30 when the old nerves started jangling, badly. I mean really badly, so badly I felt completely numb. There was no feeling whatsoever in my legs. As luck would have it, Mick Quinn and 'Gentleman' John Moloney entered the room I shared with Freddie McLennan and enquired about my well-being. I informed them about my predicament, and although there was concern in their voices they assured me that this was totally normal and that there was a simple cure (old wives' tale) that would set me right – nothing to worry about. All I had to do, apparently, was to immerse myself in an ice bath for approximately one hour to rectify the ailment. They diligently set about providing the necessaries, with probably more ice than was actually 'required'.

I submerged into the icy depths and wallowed for over an hour, thinking 'more is better', when into the bathroom marched the three musketeers, camera in hand, saying, 'What the fuck are you at? Are you mad in the head?' Surprisingly enough, my brain hadn't been numbed, and the realisation that I'd been 'had' hit me. I hadn't a leg (metaphorically and possibly quite literally at that stage) to stand on. I was like a frozen prune with wrinkles carved on my stones. The subsequent photo could not have been a pretty sight! I eventually thawed out at about four o'clock in the morning.

Ireland's tour of Australia, 1979 – Freddie McLennan got chased by a kangaroo and Noel 'Noisy' Murphy caught Colin Patterson and me after we'd visited every disco/nightclub in Perth on the first night of the tour. Noisy explained to us both quite calmly, in a tone more commonly reserved for small children and the intellectually feeble, that it was a five-week tour not a five-day tour, thus emphasising that we didn't need to pack everything into the first week. We did go on to beat Australia, in both Tests, under the wonderful captaincy of Fergus Slattery and the brilliance of Ollie Campbell, with thirteen others probably playing the most organised and inventive rugby of their careers.

Ireland's tour of South Africa, 1981 – I was suspended, not from the squad or by some committee but from the window of the hotel we were staying in. I guess that needs some explanation. I was fondly known as the 'Rat', a moniker bestowed upon me that Stewart McKinney correctly took as being a reference to the character from *The Wind in the Willows*. It was an affectionate nickname that associated me with such attributes as loyalty, fun, 'messing about in boats', etc. Somewhere along the way it became linked with just the messing about part. I liked to get the *craic* going, and I loved to talk. According to some, I talked too much – far too much. Apparently, my gregarious nature and witty repartee were, on occasion, simply overwhelming for the company I was in.

I've always loved a wind-up and a bit of mischief, but the lads must have decided that they weren't up to the scintillating conversation I had initiated and reckoned that a quick dunk in the pool might shut me up. The pool, however, was 17 storeys beneath us! Their reasoning was full of flawless logic. I should fall like a cat with nine lives (cat/rat . . . hey, they rhyme!) into the pool below, and, unlike a cat, I would scurry rat-like through the water and come out unscathed but quieted.

I was mighty scared, I can tell you. John O'Driscoll had been known to do a bit of a Spiderman thing in his time, but that was of his own volition. Being dangled by the ankles from 17 storeys sets the brain racing in contemplation of one's fragile mortality, and, more importantly, it shuts you up! My silence saved me. Relief washed over me when I realised they weren't going to test their theory. My mood had been metaphorically dampened, so the lads didn't need to dunk me to keep me quiet, and, mercifully, I was hauled back into the room, stunned, somewhat subdued and glad I was sober. Squealing like a girl could have been disastrous!

Animals featured largely on this tour. Nobody quite knows why Ginger McLoughlin and Brendan Foley felt compelled to bring a penguin, which they claim they rescued from a marine reserve in Cape Town, to a black-tie alickadoos reception in our hotel. I guess the fact that none of the Ireland team had been invited might have had something to do with it.

Having recovered from my dangling ordeal, I was up for the challenge of riding an ostrich, totally against the instructions of our coach, Tom Kiernan. The Rat and the ostrich! Getting on was easy enough, getting off was another matter. I stayed on the back of the great feathered bird in a pen full of ostrich droppings and around 40 other birds. The Rat astride an ostrich provided great giggles to the onlookers. Tom Kiernan insisted I dismount, but this was proving problematical, and he had no advice to assist me. Michael Kiernan and Keith Crossan came to my 'rescue' by providing a distraction with loud, fervent hand clapping, thus scaring the bejaysus out of the assembly, people and birds alike. My mount reared up like a bucking bronco and threw me a terrific height. Painfully sailing over his spine tore the inside of my thighs and my number-two trousers to pieces. (Needless to say we haven't kept in touch.)

Covered in ostrich dung and feathers, I was relegated to the back of the bus alone for the return journey back to our hotel.

(By the way, thanks for the decorated ostrich egg, Ollie. Very thoughtful!)

CHARLIE'S PHONE CALL

GRAHAM PRICE
PROP Pontypool
WALES 1975–83, 41 caps
LIONS TOURS '77, '80, '83, 12 Test matches

One of the benefits of being an international rugby player is that you are given the opportunity to travel the world. The Pontypool front row's (i.e. my, Charlie Faulkner and Bobby Windsor's) first international tour was on the Wales trip to Japan in 1975. The cost of the international flights and internal transport, hotel accommodation and meals was paid for. There was even a stock of free beer kept in the team room. About the only things we had to pay for were phone calls home, and after sharing a room with Charlie for three weeks I knew this was really bugging him.

After a particularly heavy night out in Tokyo, we arrived back at our hotel in the early hours of the morning. We subsequently decided to finish the night off by having a few beers in the team room with the rest of the team. Within a few minutes, Charlie realised there was a telephone in the room and said to us, 'Do you think I could get away with making a phone call home on that phone without having to pay for it?'

Back in 1975, it was not possible to make a direct-dial phone call from a hotel. It was necessary to speak to the hotel's switchboard operator first and, therefore, Charlie would have to give his personal details. He would, consequently, have to pay for the phone call, because they could trace it back to him.

Of course, Charlie was not prepared to leave it at that, and with a measure of lateral thinking (well, as much as we could come up with at two o'clock in the morning after a skinful of beer) we soon devised a plan to allow Charlie to avoid paying for his phone call home! We eventually came to the conclusion that when he gave the details of his phone call to the switchboard operator, he should tell her his name was John Dawes, the Wales team coach, because he didn't have to pay for his calls.

Charlie picked up the phone, and the conversation went like this:

SWITCHBOARD OPERATOR: 'Hello, sir, how may I help you?'

CHARLIE: 'Hello, my name is John Dawes. I'm the Wales team coach, and I want to make an international telephone call to Newport in South Wales. The number is . . .'

SWITCHBOARD OPERATOR: 'Thank you, sir. The international lines are quite busy at the moment. It will probably take about 20 minutes, but if you put the phone down, I will call you back when I have managed to make the connection.'

So Charlie put the phone down, and we carried on drinking and chatting about all sorts of nonsense, as you do when under the influence of alcohol, especially the amount that we had put away! After about 35 minutes, the phone rang and Charlie picked it up.

CHARLIE: 'Hello.'

SWITCHBOARD OPERATOR: 'Hello, sir, I've got an international call to Newport, South Wales, for Mr John Dawes, the Wales team coach.'

Charlie looked around the room and said, 'Has anyone seen John Dawes? There's an international call for him.'

We told him that we hadn't seen him, and Charlie told the switchboard operator, 'Sorry, love, he's not here!' and promptly put down the phone!

WHAT MORE COULD I HAVE ASKED FOR?

IAN McCALLUM
FULL-BACK Natal, Western Province
SOUTH AFRICA 1970–4, 11 caps

I was privileged to play in the Test match at Lansdowne Road commemorating the 100th year of rugby in Ireland. It was in October of 1974. Normally a full-back and one-time aspirant fly-half, I was chosen to play at centre for the game. It was only when I was on the field that I realised I was marking the legendary Mike Gibson. While I don't remember missing any tackles in the 17–17 draw, I do remember that Gibson scored two tries. Stewart McKinney and Fergus Slattery were in the back row for Ireland, and while I didn't see them, they certainly saw me – gaps were hard to find, let alone negotiate.

What a wonderful way to end my rugby career, I thought, especially having played against those mentioned and also with the likes of Gareth Edwards, Phil Bennett, Ian 'Mighty Mouse' McLauchlan, Bobby Windsor, Andy Ripley and Tony Neary (all members – with McKinney and Slattery – of the successful British and Irish Lions side that I faced in two Tests in South Africa that year), as well as the French stars Roland Bertranne and Victor Boffelli for the Invitation XV. But there was more to come. I will undoubtedly remember what followed as me 'having my cake' with the added privilege of being able to 'eat it'. I went on tour with the Wolfhounds. Phil Bennett was unavailable – I was the fly-half!

The tour took in some wonderful 'outback' venues in Ireland and was managed by the late Dr Karl Mullen. (Thank goodness he saw Ireland win another Grand Slam before he departed.) A prominent Dublin gynaecologist and a former Lions hooker, it was his welcome speech that I will never forget. Unlike anything I had ever heard before from a rugby coach, what he had to say put this great game into its ultimate perspective. 'Gentlemen,' he said, addressing the stew of international players before him, 'on this tour I will not be telling you how to play rugby, but I will insist on one important matter – that you have social stamina!'

It was a powerful reminder that rugby, everything said and done, is about people and about knowing how fortunate we were to have played this game at a high level. In other words, as players we had an obligation – to reach out and to give back to those who were perhaps not as fortunate as we had been but who loved the game as we did.

I came back from that tour wearing Victor Boffelli's France blazer. Victor returned to France wearing a leaping springbok. There may have been times on that tour when the pubs were closed, but, as they say in Ireland, they were never shut. What more could I have asked for?

BAA-BAA BLACK SHEEP

STEWART McKINNEY

Jimmy Davidson was a great motivator and an inspiration to his students and his players. He wanted the best for you and settled for nothing less. I played alongside him at Dungannon, and he saw potential in me that he was damned sure wasn't going to be squandered. I had already represented Ulster and Ireland, but Jimmy was certain there could be bigger and better things for me if I applied myself with the rigour and vigour he espoused.

We turned out for a match against Belfast Royal Academy FPs in March 1973. It wasn't a heavy-duty game, more of a friendly encounter not to be taken too seriously. I played my usual game, nothing exceptional, and after the match Jimmy took me aside and berated me for cruising, sitting on my laurels and not pushing myself to the limits. He continued along this track, giving me a dressing down and a general bollocking, citing that I had done nothing of import or consequence yet. I hadn't played for the Barbarians or the Lions, and the way I was going I would be unlikely to.

The following week, after the 'dismal' performance I had put in for the BRA match, I received a letter from the Baa-Baas inviting me to play for them. One for the little boy who lived down the lane! With great delight I made my way to the Dungannon v. City of Derry fixture and secreted the letter in the pocket of my shorts. I managed to contrive a kick that sent the ball into a hedge, thus delaying the lineout and giving me enough time to produce the letter for Jimmy to see. His congratulations were delivered in true J.D. style. A big smile crossed his face as he realised the contents. 'You bollox!'

FEAR OF FLYING

BOBBY WINDSOR
HOOKER Pontypool
WALES 1973–79, 28 caps
LIONS TOUR '74, '77, 5 Test matches

I don't like flyin'... no, I don't like flyin'. When I flew to South Africa in '74, I was very unfortunate because I'd had a prawn cocktail in the hotel before and on the flight... well, it was food poisoning I had (that's what I found out after). I was taken very ill and I was laid out flat at the back of the plane, cos I was absolutely pouring with sweat. A nurse on the plane came up and put some ice cubes in my mouth to try and cool me down. Ken Kennedy came up and put the – er, what d'you call it? – the thermometer thing in my mouth, not knowing I'd ice cubes in there. When Syd Millar come up, he said, 'How is he, Ken?'

Ken took the thermometer out and said, 'I think he's dead!'

I was carried off the back of the plane when we got to South Africa. It's lucky I wasn't in a box! I didn't mind that flight too much, though, cos I didn't know much about it.

PINK SANDS AND BLACK SEAL RUM

CHARLIE FAULKNER
PROP Pontypool
WALES 1975–79, 19 caps
LIONS TOURS '74, '77

I don't want to sound like a sad old bastard sucking on sour grapes through my ill-fitting dentures but rugby has changed, and I don't think it's all been for the best. Back in the day, Bobby Windsor, the rest of the Pontypool team and I had to face club training sessions under the watchful eye of Ray Prosser, and he knew a thing or two about rugby and what was required to become the fittest fighting machine an opposition side would despair to see.

After a hard day's physical work in the steelworks – no nine-to-five cushy office number, let me tell you – we faced the 'ski slope' at Pontypool Park at full pelt and ten laps as a warm-up before we even began any of the serious training in our two-hour sessions. Scrummaging sessions on the beach at Aberavon in sand that shifted underfoot weren't for sissies either. Nature has a mean way of getting you fit, unlike the manufactured players who only ever train with machines.

Through my rose-tinted NHS prescription spectacles I recall when players with innate ability and no taste for training but possessing natural talent could display their genius on the park – players such as Derek Quinell and Barry McGann. They didn't come through any academy (how would a late developer make it in the modern game today? Here I think of the great Willie John), and they were mentally tough and match fit through playing many, many games without rest periods in between. They played their hearts out, sang their souls out and often drank the bar out of spirits while they reviewed the game with their opposite number, probably sporting a bruise or two if they were in the front row. Forwards were immensely strong and backs were immensely fast.

These same spectacles allow me to look back fondly to an occasion when one of the perks of rugby gave me occasion to attend a party in fine surroundings in Bermuda. The pink beaches and postcard sunsets were the backdrop to a good gathering of players from all over the UK, and, as was the custom, the obligatory 'Dark and Stormy' cocktails were taken on board.

Now, for those of you who don't know what a Dark and Stormy is, it is dark rum mixed with ginger beer – not ginger ale, mind, ginger beer. Gosling's Black Seal Rum is legendary in Bermuda. It is used for 'roof wettings' of new houses and instead of champagne to christen ships. According to the blurb, when Sir George Somers was on his way to rescue the colony at Jamestown in 1609, his ship the *Sea Venture* came dramatically aground on the deserted islands of Bermuda, but the whole party managed to survive, and many took solace in a dram of celebratory rum – or, as it was recorded, 'comfortable waters'. (I believe that fellow William Shakespeare wrote a play called *The Tempest* that was partly based on this event.) In its raw and more potent state it was said that the drink could 'light ablaze' and 'provoke rumbustious behaviour', soon becoming known as 'rumbullion' and hence 'rum'. I admit I read some of the information off the label – there's a lot of education there.

Anyway, as you will now appreciate and understand, it would have been insulting to refuse the national drink of the island, and I was never one to cause offence – not off the pitch, anyway. My wife, Gillian, left early to return to our lodgings in Southampton, which meant I was left to take care of myself on the way home. There was no 'rumbustious' behaviour from me. It had a more mellowing effect, like the comfortable waters, so when it was time to leave I straddled my moped (obligatory mode of transport on the island, with a speed limit of 20 mph), snatched the helmet from the pillion and duly stuffed the lid on. I had been pootling along at a pretty safe speed, certainly within the limits, when a member of the local constabulary pulled up alongside me and indicated that I should pull over. Being a law-abiding type, I did, though I was concerned about what had attracted his attention to me. I had been driving sensibly, was in control of the moped and most definitely within the speed limit. What could be wrong?

'What's wrong, officer?' I asked, bewildered. He said nothing but tapped my helmet. I thought that perhaps I was supposed to have removed the item as a gesture of respect or something, and that didn't suit me at all . . . I had done nothing wrong.

I looked at him, and he tapped my helmet again, then removed it from my head, telling me, 'You've got your helmet on the wrong way.' I felt an utter fool, but there was nothing I could do as the kind officer replaced the helmet correctly on my head and wished me on my way with kind regards. I love Bermuda.

BEDTIME STORIES

MERVYN ELDER
WINGER King's Scholars, Malone, Instonians

Dublin 1968

Stewart McKinney and I were members of Stranmillis College, Belfast, basketball team, which had arranged to play a few matches in the Dublin area over the same weekend as the Ireland–France rugby international. As tour manager, I had arranged very modest B & B accommodation in a none too salubrious part of the city. The rationale for that was quite simple. Being in receipt of a daily allowance from the college authorities for sports tours, the less paid out for food and accommodation, the more left for the 'devil's buttermilk': Guinness.

The accommodation fulfilled our cheap expectations – not great! Indeed, we had to share a large double bed in a fairly small room – neither a suite nor en suite! After a first night out on the tiles in Dublin, we slept soundly only to be wakened early the next morning by a knock on the bedroom door. The large Dublin landlady entered, carrying a great tray upon which were two full Irish breakfasts – which would have choked a donkey. 'Jesus! This is great,' Stewart said. 'Breakfast in bed!' I nodded agreement as I finished off my black pudding.

The door was knocked again, and the landlady returned for the empty tray. 'Will you lads ever be gettin' up?' she enquired.

'Ah, missus,' I said, 'sure, it's only eight o' clock yet. We might have a wee lie in.'

'Not today, lads!' she said in a firm tone. 'My permanent lodger, who stays in this room, will be back from the night shift just after nine o'clock, and I have to make the bed for him.'

Well, for twenty-five shillings a night for a room for two with breakfast in bed we couldn't complain!

Victoria, Vancouver Island, Canada 1969

In 1969 King's Scholars, the rugby club of Stranmillis College (Belfast), went on a summer tour to Canada, where we were to play seven matches. After our first game, against Calgary Irish, we flew to Victoria on Vancouver Island and booked into our hotel. As students with a limited tour budget, we were staying in large, multiple-occupancy rooms. Four of us were sharing: Stewart McKinney, Jim Neilly, Scott Kelso (tour captain and scrum-half) and me.

I had learned from Calgary that the first to the room got the best bed and the last got what was left. I was first and Stewart was last. I got the best double bed beside the window, and Jim and Scotty got the other two double beds, which left a fairly modest single bed for the big man.

'That's not fair, Kelso. You're only a wee runt!' Stewart raged. 'You should be in the wee bed!'

'Bugger off, McKinney,' said Scotty. 'I'm not for moving!'

'We'll see about that,' said Stewart, the threat unspoken but left hanging in the air menacingly.

Later that night – well, early the next morning – having returned from the official civic reception followed by a private players' 'cultural tour' of downtown Victoria, and feeling no pain at all, we returned to our hotel room. Jim, Scotty and I were soon tucked up under our covers. 'Well, Kelso, are you for swapping beds?' demanded Stewart.

'No way!' said Scotty.

Unperturbed by the response, Stewart stripped ready for bed and, clad only in his birthday suit, jumped in beside Scotty. Vain protestations from Scotty and threats of all kinds of nocturnal delights from Stewart finalised the rooming arrangements to the Dungannon man's satisfaction. The number 8, the prop forward and the bulky centre three-quarter got the double beds and the team captain, scrum-half, the single bed. Proper order! And everyone's virginity stayed intact.

FREE DINNERS

STEWART McKINNEY

My teaching career began in January 1969 in Abbotts Cross Primary School, which was the largest primary school in the UK. It was streamed, four classes per year, thirty-six pupils to each class, a thousand pupils in total. Jim Kennedy, the principal, Mrs Davison, the vice principal, and all the staff were so kind to the rookie teacher. I was assigned a 'D' stream primary-six class, the supposed 'hard lot', but I loved them, and discipline was never a problem.

I was picked for Ulster later that year, and once the press photographers began to call in periodically those kids began to feel famous, as their faces would appear in the *Belfast Telegraph* or *The Newsletter*.

There was great excitement when I was selected for the 1974 Lions, and after the press had interviewed me and taken photographs the questions began – the class were concerned about my welfare and their own, too. 'Who's going to teach us when you're away, sir?' someone asked.

'A supply teacher will come in. You'll be all right,' I replied.

'Will you be paid, Mr McKinney?'

'Yes, the school will still pay me.'

'Will you have to pay for your hotels, Mr McKinney?'

'No, the hotels will be paid for.'

'Will you have to pay for your food, Mr McKinney?'

'No, that's all taken care of.'

And so it continued until they were satisfied that I wasn't going to miss out on any of my entitlements and that they would be taken care of in my absence. With such a buzz generated, I took advantage of the situation – I suppose modern educators would refer to it as utilising a spontaneous opportunity – and asked the kids to write about my selection. This school was in a soccer-mad area, with little understanding of rugby. One composition contained the following sentence: 'Our master has been picked for the British Lions because he is very good at the tripping up, and when he is in South Africa he is on free dinners.'

Quite a few of the kids whose parents were out of work or on benefits received free school dinners. Those dinner tickets were yellow and the others were brown. To this day I laugh as I imagine Big Willie John, Fran, Burto and company queuing up in a five-star hotel with yellow tickets to receive a free dinner from the dinner ladies!

HUMBLED

WILLIE JOHN McBRIDE
LOCK Ballymena, Ulster
IRELAND 1961–75, 63 caps
LIONS TOURS '62, '66, '68, '71, '74, 17 Test matches

Many years ago, after I stopped playing international rugby, to maintain my fitness I regularly went with a group of friends to play touch rugby at Ballyclare Rugby Club, Cloughan Lane, Ballyclare. One training night in the middle of a particularly nasty Ulster winter it was pouring with rain when I went down to the clubhouse. Usually there was a group of us who were strongly committed to our touch sessions – they were always good craic – but this night there was only one other person there, a fellow called Will McKee. Understandably, neither of us was too keen to go out and face the elements, but we went anyway, thinking the others would surely be bound to show up soon. As we squelched over the pitch, through the mud, the intensity of the rain increased. It was now coming down in stair rods, bouncing off the ground.

To avail of some shelter, we jogged over to a tall hedge where we thought we could huddle from the torrent. By now we were soaked through to the skin and shivering pathetically as the rain and the wind continued to lash and bluster around our sodden bodies. We stood for some time in miserable silence, getting wetter and wetter, our kit sticking to our arms, legs and torsos as we waited disconsolately for the others to arrive, when suddenly Will turned to me and said through the rain, 'Willie John, you know you're famous all over the world as a great rugby player and have played in some of the biggest stadiums with the best facilities in the world.'

'Yes,' I agreed, 'some wonderful places, sure enough.'

Will wiped his face with the back of his soaking sleeve and continued with a broad smile. 'At the height of your fame, did you ever think you'd end up under a hedge in the Cloughan Lane?' What was there I could say?!

IMPRUDENCE IN PROVIDENCE

DESSIE McCANN
PROP Portadown, Dungannon, Ulster
IRELAND B 1977

In 1979 the Dungannon tour was to Providence, Rhode Island. The players didn't stay in hotels but were hosted by the club. Andy Crawford, who was later to become Irish Rugby Football Union president, and I were billeted together. Our host was a huge man who'd played American football and was also rumoured to have been a contender for selection to the American Olympic team for shot-putting. 'Panda' was a stereotypical American sportsman: huge (beastly huge), competitive, confident and brash. His house was surrounded by plants, which I think were some sort of dietary aid or supplement, for when they were cooked and prepared the leaves of the herb increased the appetite, essential for maintaining a gigantic frame.

Chatting over a few beers, he promised we'd have a good time, 'one helluva match' and that he would prepare for us his legendary beef fillet for breakfast. Eventually, the talk came round to rugby, and he asked who we would be playing at loose-head prop. I was delighted to claim my position and with great pride told him that it would be me wearing the number 1 jersey.

Now, I know I'm not the tallest, nor the stoutest player – some people even refer to me as 'Wee Dessie' or 'Wee McCann' – but despite my diminutive stature I made my place on teams through merit. I didn't like it when he gave me the once-over with a glance that sneered 'thirteen-and-a-half-stone midget!' He gave a big intimidating smile and puffed himself up so that his shoulders grew broader and his chest grew bigger. If further motivation had been needed to come out hard in the match, Panda had just provided it.

On the day of the game I was fired up and ready to face the mighty behemoth. It might have seemed a mismatch, but I knew the story of David and Goliath. The scrum went down, our binding was tight and we were solid. Determined to overpower the opposition, the shove was on. Panda was puffing and groaning, and it wasn't until John McDonald hollered out, 'He's enough snow on his arse, Dessie. Let him down now!' that I relaxed my effort. The big American's game was over. He didn't better me and was taken off injured and substituted, which sadly meant that we never did get the fabled fillet for breakfast.

THE MAGIC OF THE LIONS

HUGO MacNEILL
FULL-BACK Blackrock, London Irish, Leinster
IRELAND 1981–8, 37 caps
LIONS TOUR '83, 3 Test matches

The Lions have always been special to me. I remember being on holiday in Bettystown and watching the great 1971 side winning in New Zealand, with my hero J.P.R. playing a starring role, as he did three years later with Willie John's giants in South Africa. (I just missed playing against J.P.R., as his last game for Wales was in 1981 just prior to them playing us at Cardiff in what was my second cap.) I can still see the look of disbelief on Fergus Slattery's face as the referee disallowed his try that would have given the Lions an unbelievable 4–0 series victory over the Boks in 1974. (They still won the series with three victories and a draw.)

In 1977 I had just left school and was working for the summer in Nuremberg. I used to go to the train station to read the English newspapers for details of the series in New Zealand. I remember reading about Terry Cobner (the pack leader) on the eve of the second Test (having lost the first one) demanding a huge performance from his fellow forwards, as he wanted his 'family to be able to walk the streets of Pontypool with their heads held high'. They did win the next day but were to lose the series.

And then in 1983 it was my turn with the Lions in New Zealand. On the eve of the first Test Ollie Campbell and I stayed on after training to practise drop goals. We got most of them and left feeling good. The next day it was the Test. In the dying minutes the Blacks led 13–12. We were on their 22. Ruck ball. We won it. Roy Laidlaw fired the ball to me. I shaped to drop a goal. But it had rained overnight. As I kicked, my left leg went from under me. Still, I didn't miss by much. Sickening. The Blacks went downfield, Alan Hewson dropped a goal and they won 16–12.

A couple of days later I got a letter from my brother Eoin. He described setting his alarm clock for 4 a.m. In those days the matches were played mid-afternoon in New Zealand and were not live on TV, and I imagined alarm clocks going off around England, Wales, Scotland and Ireland. Instead, he listened to the match on the radio, disappointed with the outcome of the late drama. As the match finished, day was dawning in south Dublin, and he took our dogs for a walk along the coast. Then he went home and watched the match on TV.

Fast-forward a couple of weeks. We were on the bus to Wellington for the second Test. I took out Eoin's letter. All around the bus was silence, the guys deep in their own personal thoughts. Then, suddenly, one of the Scots quietly started to sing 'Will Ye Go, Lassie, Go', the Scottish melody sung by the Clancy Brothers and one of the songs of the 1974 Lions. Gradually, it was picked up by other voices, English, Welsh and Irish, and soon the whole bus was singing . . . quietly, thoughtfully. We went into the Test and played into a gale-force wind, strong even by Wellington standards. We held the All Blacks to 9–0 in the first half. We were pretty pleased, as we were turning over with Ollie Campbell, the best kicker in the world. But the Blacks gave a master class in keeping possession and that coupled with our mistakes meant they won 9–0. We went on to lose the third Test 15–8 and then were well beaten in the fourth.

But I will never forget that bus, that atmosphere and the unique spirit of the Lions, which brought all the home unions, former adversaries, together as one. Special. Very special.

HE'S GOT HIGH HOPES

STEWART McKINNEY

My last year at college was the 1967–68 rugby season, and during the first week of the autumn term Ian McIlrath approached me to enquire about my availability to play for his home-town side Ballymena, who had an early September tour to South Wales. They had a Saturday game against Abertillery, who were the strongest of the valley sides, boasting three British Lions in Alan Lewis, Haydn Morgan and Alan Pask, and a Monday match against Newbridge, who had a very strong back row, notably the brothers Hughes – Arthur and Dennis.

I had played some games for my own home side Dungannon on

Easter tours to Cork and Limerick, but this was to Wales! An overseas tour! I was thrilled at the prospect and beside myself with excitement. Syd Millar and Willie John, those great Ballymena Lions, were travelling, and I was so keen and honoured to have the chance to play on the same pitch as those two giants of Irish rugby.

There was one obstacle, however: the King's Scholars coach, Jos Lapsley. So, Ian and I went to Mr Lapsley to ask permission to miss the college game the following Saturday and travel instead with Ballymena to Wales. 'Of course, Mr McIlrath and Mr McKinney [he called everyone 'mister'], you must go. What a wonderful opportunity! You will only improve with that kind of experience.' Little did he know . . .

We flew to Cardiff and checked in to a small hotel – more of a guest house, actually. I was rooming with Jimmy Wilson, an alickadoo who owned the local Ballymena nursery, which was pretty ironic when I recall the events of the coming Saturday night. There was a connecting door between our bedroom and the adjacent one, where Syd Millar was rooming with Wallace Ewart. We were talking to Syd, who was sitting on his bed rooting through his bag, when I sensed the first sign of trouble. The landlady appeared, a battleaxe of a woman, and told Syd in no uncertain terms that the beds were for sleeping in and not for sitting on. Syd gave her a look as if to say that he had travelled the world and had sat on hundreds of hotel beds from Durban to Dunedin. He said nothing, but I had an uneasy feeling.

The game against Abertillery wasn't high scoring – they won 5–0 – but it was wonderful to play for the first time in Wales and in such a beautiful setting before a partisan crowd. I was determined to shove as hard as I could at number 8, as I didn't want any complaints from Willie John in the second row that I wasn't pushing my weight. Now, he didn't grumble, instead paying me a great compliment when he told Ian McIlrath that I had pushed so hard that I'd hurt his arse! If I'd known then one of Willie's party pieces, I'd have told him, 'Better a sore arse than Old Smokey Blue!' (From a bawdy Australian rugby song.)

The hospitality after the game was first class. Haydn Morgan, who wasn't playing, came to see Willie and Syd, and I therefore met another of my heroes. Both teams had a mighty sing-song around a piano before Ballymena set off by bus to our hotel/guest house, where we planned to have a few quiet drinks in the bar before retiring. That plan was immediately thwarted when the battleaxe landlady shut the bar and told us that we should all go to bed. No amount of cajoling, persuasion or quoting of the law that as residents we should be allowed to drink

– in fact, we should have a night porter to cater for our needs – would melt that stony heart. 'No!' She locked the bar and off she went. What could we do? Idle hands and all that . . .

Cardiff in 1967 wasn't the buzzing metropolis and centre of nightlife that it is today. We wandered around, but the bars were all shut. The only place open was a sub-standard Chinese restaurant. What a sad end to a wonderful day.

But not quite! Back at base, while playing some silly alcohol-free games, word got around that I had a penchant for eating flowers and that I was rooming with Jimmy Wilson, the local nursery man. Daffodils were out of season, and the battleaxe hadn't decorated the hotel with any feminine floral touches, so I resigned myself to a blossom-free weekend. Peter Torrie, the prop, noticed a rubber plant in the corner and bet me that I couldn't eat it. Challenge? If daffodils were Eleven Plus material and chrysanthemums A levels on the flower-eating scale of difficulty, a rubber plant should merit a Master of Arts. So I ate the rubber plant.

The next morning, when the team assembled for breakfast, not only was the bar shut but so was the kitchen. Battleaxe wanted £40, which was a fortune in 1967, for her precious rubber plant before she would fry an egg. A pint of beer forty years ago was two shillings, or ten pence, so factoring in inflation, with a pint now being around £3, the calculation requires a multiplication of thirty times the original amount – £1,200!

I don't to this day know what negotiations went on, but I'm sure Jimmy Wilson the nursery man was involved, as he knew the value of plants. Eventually, we were served breakfast and drew 6–6 with Newbridge on the Monday night.

Yes, Mr Lapsley, it was that kind of experience.

P.S. A word of warning: be very careful when eating flowers. Willie Anderson followed in the tradition and one night at a college reunion gathered 200 daffodils so that a group of us, including Jimmy Neilly of BBC fame, could have a feast. We were all violently ill, as the gardener had sprayed the borders with weed killer, and I suppose some of the spray had landed on the petals. It was all very funny when the first person was sick, attracting much cheering and comments such as, 'You can't hold your drink, and you can't hold your daffodils!' However, when the assembled group quickly followed, spewing up in rapid succession, we realised we'd had a lucky escape.

DARK AND STORMY

IAN McCRAE
SCRUM-HALF Gordonians
SCOTLAND 1967–72, 9 caps

My tale takes you to the beautiful island of Bermuda, which, as it happens, is where, in the space of a few short days, I became a boon companion of Stewart McKinney. We were there to represent our respective countries at the 1988 Bermuda World Rugby Classic, a stage on which a hundred or so ex-international players from the four home countries attempted to prolong adolescence beyond all previously known bounds.

We met in the Mariners club, where we discovered an interesting selection of whiskies but also became devotees of the local favourite, the Dark and Stormy, and that hostelry became our regular haunt until the night I sampled another Bermudian experience known as 'road rash' (a euphemism for the resulting cuts and grazes when naked sunburned skin makes contact with the tarmac) when I came to grief whilst riding home on my hired moped – a common occurrence at the Bermuda Classic. As my mishap occurred at some ungodly hour, I left it until the following day to visit the hospital to have my injuries treated, whereupon I was informed that another rugby player with a Scottish-sounding name had been admitted during the night. My consternation that we might be two players short for our next game was soon allayed by the revelation that the other patient was my erstwhile drinking crony but consternation quickly returned when it was explained to me that he had not, in fact, fallen off his bike like I had gleefully assumed but had suffered a cardiac episode. I don't know if the two were definitely connected, but 'road rash' and 'heart trouble' became associated with Dark and Stormies, and I vowed caution regarding their consumption thereafter.

One year later I returned to the island determined to be more circumspect when attending any festivities. By this time I had become a close friend of an expatriate Scot called Tom Watters, who put a huge amount of time and energy into the organisation of the Classic and was president of the Bermuda Rugby Football Union. At one of the many outdoor functions held for the touring teams, Tom said to me, 'Don't spend your money on drink tonight, Ian. I know one of the bar tenders, and I'll keep you well stocked.' True to his word, he did. The Dark and Stormies kept coming, and whilst I may have been vaguely aware that they appeared to be getting darker as time progressed it didn't occur to me that each successive Dark and Stormy contained more rum and less ginger beer. Tom confessed the next day that he'd wanted to see if he could make me fall off my bike again (he probably had a bet on it). I was never sure if it was just his mischievous sense of humour or an attempt to nobble the opposition, as we were due to play the Bermuda team in a couple of days. This competition had to be taken seriously.

In the course of the evening Tom's wife Eleanor had asked me if I'd seen her husband recently, to which I replied in the affirmative, adding with a glance at my half-empty glass that I would almost certainly see him again shortly. 'Good!' she said. 'Then tell him that I'm taking "Hovis" [Scottish full-back Arthur Brown] home in the car, as he isn't feeling too well.'

An hour or two later, when the crowd was dispersing and Tom approached with what would be his last handout of the evening, he asked if I had any idea where Eleanor was. 'Sorry, Tom,' I said. 'I forgot to tell you. She left a couple of hours ago to take Hovis home – he was feeling poorly – and she's not coming back.'

'So how am I supposed to get home?' the prankster asked peevishly.

'All taken care of,' I said, smirking. 'Eleanor left Hovis's helmet so I could take you home on the pillion!'

The phrase 'hoist with his own petard' springs to mind, and I thought Tom was going to trip over his own jaw. However, he accepted his kismet with fortitude, no doubt supported by the free Dark and Stormies he too had been enjoying all evening. The next day he was rather contrite when he called to enquire if I had managed to get home safely after dropping him off but admitted the bike ride had been 'exhilarating'. I'm not sure if that was another euphemism or not. He had been particularly impressed with my negotiation of the steep brae just outside the stadium. Unable to generate enough speed for the approach, I used my mountaineering experience and followed a zigzag pattern to complete the climb. He was, however, none too comfortable with the manner in which I kept turning around to ask for directions whilst on the seriously inclined gradient. Served him right!

THE TRUTH ABOUT THE OMELETTE

BOBBY WINDSOR

Favourite Food

Well, I'm not going to say, 'egg omelette'. After being in hospital with the food poisoning, the boys picked me up and the Springboks, or the people of South Africa, were taking the mickey, cos they said I had 'Bok Fever', meaning that I was shitting myself about playing the Springboks – oh, they were taking the piss.

Some of the boys stopped at a restaurant on the way back. I was still a bit dickey in the old guts, like, so I thought I'd just have an omelette. Now, I'm an ordinary working man so when the chap came up and said, 'What sort of omelette do you want?' I thought he was taking the piss again.

'I want a bastard *egg* omelette, don't I!' I said. I didn't know you could get mushroom omelette or Spanish omelette. I'd only ever had an omelette – the one you make with eggs! So that was a big laugh amongst the boys. No, I wouldn't say omelettes are my favourite. Mine is a Sunday roast: roast lamb. I don't mind if it's Welsh lamb or New Zealand lamb.

Just one more thing about food. When Charlie Faulkner came out to New Zealand in '77 as a replacement on the Lions tour, I went out with some of the boys to pick him up. He came out of the airport after travelling about 40 bloody hours and said he was starving. So we pulled in to get him some food, and he said to the girl serving, 'I'll have some bacon and eggs.'

The girl said, 'We haven't got no bacon.'

Charlie looks at her and says, 'I've just landed in a country with five million bastard sheep and you got no bacon?'

I had some of the boys looking at me as if to say, 'Who the bloody hell is this idiot? You'd think a Welshman woulda known sheep from pigs!'

NO SEAT BELTS

STEWART McKINNEY

I believe the Bermuda Golden Oldies Festival is now a very serious affair and that the All Blacks even hold trials, such is the competition for places. J.P.R. Williams was manager of the Old British Lions Team last November! It wasn't like that for the first event, 20 years ago. Then it was strictly for over 35s. I was 41 and the elder statesmen were around the 50 mark. Some hadn't donned boots for at least 15 years.

Everyone flew to New York to catch a connecting flight to Bermuda. The Irish boys had arrived earlier. I could hear them in the bar, and it sounded as if they had been at it for quite a while. I could hear them but not see them because living in London I had flown out with the Scots, Welsh and English lads from Heathrow and had been arrested on a passport irregularity by the most humourless Customs officials – of Puerto Rican origins, I believe – I'd ever met. This wasn't going to be a problem, though, for when they were distracted by some other matter I made my escape to join the craic at the bar with everyone else. (This had serious repercussions on the return journey when I was held for 12 hours!)

Over one hundred ex-internationals boarded the plane for Hamilton, and what a mixture they were. All the notorious hell-raisers were there: Peter Bell, Robin Challis, Sandy Carmichael, Moss Keane, the Rat Kennedy, Charlie Faulkner, et al. This was not going to be a peaceful flight. I absolutely detest flying, so I strapped myself in for the duration, working on the Bobby Windsor theory that walking about the plane could disturb its equilibrium.

Once the seat-belt lights had been extinguished, the other 99 or so didn't give a fig about the equilibrium being compromised so stood around in groups, drinking and recounting old stories. Props who had never had the ball in their hands their whole rugby career were now sprinting 90 yards to score tries. The second rows were jumping like stags in some game 30 years ago, forgetting that nobody jumped in those days, they just pushed each other around. It got noisier and noisier. Turbulence caused much cheering and hilarity from the assembly as I stayed belted in, white as a sheet, knuckles turning a deathly lavender shade. I could have killed the Rat Kennedy, who was loving my growing discomfort.

The stewardesses dispensed the beer with wonderful patience as they squeezed between, under or around the mass. The noise was now deafening. And then I heard it! 'Cabin crew, ten minutes to landing.'

Nobody else heard the announcement, neither players nor stewardesses. I'd been to Bermuda many times previously to play in the Classic game, and I picked out the landmarks as we passed over the American Air Base. I knew we had about 30 seconds to landing, but the boys were all standing, and the beer was still being distributed.

As the wheels touched the concrete, the stewardesses threw themselves on the floor – that must have been the procedure in such an emergency. It was a perfect landing, and, amazingly, no one fell over. The cabin crew, although somewhat embarrassed, saw the funny side.

There were a lot of casualties during the following week, as there were no safety belts on the mopeds or on the counter of Casey's Bar – but that's another story.

RAVENHILL, REDCLIFF AND ROMANIA

STEVIE SMITH
HOOKER Ballymena, Ulster
IRELAND 1987–93, 25 caps
LIONS TOUR '89

I don't go to Ravenhill much these days, but when I do I can't help but cast an envious eye over the player car park. It's an impressive sight all right, a myriad of luxury marquees no less, with sponsors' names emblazoned on their sides. When I think back to my playing days, the car park more resembled an 'Arfur' Daley car lot, with battered Ford Fiestas and Escorts. The only writing on the side of my car was 'Wash me please, you lazy bastard'!

I see the players now prancing about off the field in the best kit money can buy. So far down the food chain were we during my days with Ulster that we used to get Notts Forest hand-me-down gear – I still have a tracksuit at home to prove it, with the red hand superimposed over the Forest logo! Nor was there any concession for size – it was either Willie Anderson XXL or Rab Brady XS. Half the team had sleeves trailing the floor, the other half sleeves halfway up their arms.

Ironically, on one occasion we happened to be travelling on tour to Milan, the fashion capital of the world, where 30 pale-skinned Ulstermen in cheap, ill-fitting polyester tracksuits with a red hand screen-printed on the front, representing our province, looked for all the world like the UDA on tour!

I remember our official post-match gear was a green V-neck sweater with the Ulster logo on it and cheap polyester slacks. Bin bags full of these sweaters live in the attic at home. I don't know what to do with them . . . I think they're starting to breed! At one point I had considered giving them to one of those African charities, but I was scared of turning on the TV news some night to see a band of Congolese rebels waving AK-47s resplendent in their Ulster Branch V-neck sweaters chanting 'Freedom to da Ulster Branch! Whoever de fuck dey be.'

Talking of Africa, I remember touring with Ulster to Zimbabwe in the mid '80s. It was a fascinating time, as Mugabe hadn't long been in power but already cracks were starting to appear and a lot of the whites were leaving the country and there were shortages. I remember drinking rum and Coke in a Harare nightclub out of a jam jar because there was a lack of proper glasses. It was at that precise moment I first realised I had a drink problem!

Also on that tour we had the opportunity of going up country, a lost delight of modern rugby. We ended up in a place called Redcliff, and none of us who were there will ever forget it. Redcliff basically consisted of a smelting plant and a hotel in which we were the only guests. Recalling this, the lyrics from the Eagles' 'Hotel California' – 'you can check out but you can never leave' – always spring to mind. Nothing but bush surrounded us, and I still wonder if this might have been part of some bizarre social experiment as we slowly went insane in the isolation under the heat of the African sun. However, these were the character-building aspects of touring that have perhaps been somewhat lost nowadays – different people react and respond to adversity in different ways.

Travelling across the highlands on another interminable bus journey we occasioned upon an army roadblock in the middle of nowhere. Being from the North, we were well used to this but, nevertheless, in a foreign country . . . you never quite know. There was a definite air of tension as an Idi Amin-like officer boarded our bus, demanding to see our papers. To his eternal credit, Jim Stevenson, our tour manager, leaped to his feet and welcomed the officer on board, presenting him with a tour brochure and commemorative plastic key ring – a must for any modern-day Marxist freedom fighter! To this day it intrigues me what might have happened to that key ring. Did the officer throw it away, show it to his mates in the pub or is he perhaps still driving around Bulawayo with it dangling from his ignition? Sadly, we will never know the answer to that one.

Perhaps the most infamous bus trip I was part of was on tour again with Ulster, this time to Romania in the early '80s. Again, all of us who were on that tour will never forget it. If ever a country exemplified the bankruptcy of communism, Romania was it. One particular Sunday our perfidious hosts, in an attempt to fatigue us completely, subjected us to a ten-hour bus journey taking in the delights of the Transylvanian monasteries (of all things). The *pièce de résistance* of this particular trip was a lunch served by Trappist monks, consisting of fish-head soup with a dollop of sheep's cheese on top. The appearance of the cheese suggested that the fermentation process had taken place within the sheep itself. As most of us politely pushed our plates aside, the sight of Davy Wallace, our prop forward, voraciously tearing the flesh from the fish head is indelibly inked upon the memory. Funnily, looking back, that tour was so bad it was good, and of all the tours I was on it is the most memorable. Humour and team spirit helped us through and arguably laid the basis for the success of the Ulster teams of the next few years.

Perhaps the most striking example of the difference in the game then and today took place before the first match of every Ulster season. The president of the day would enter the changing-rooms with a large cardboard box and proceed to give us an impassioned speech, reminding us how privileged we were to be playing for Ulster and to think of all the great players who had gone before us. Just as we were about to fall into a bored slumber the president would then empty the contents of the box onto the changing-room floor. Our eyes lit up, for there in front of us were 22 pairs of brand new Ulster socks, pristine in their cellophane packaging. For an instant there was hesitation, a hiatus until a primeval survival instinct surfaced and players dived in to claim their pair. You knew if you didn't retrieve your spoil from the ensuing scrum, you didn't get a pair for the rest of the season. Can you imagine today's players suffering such humiliation in the cause of Ulster – I think not . . . and rightly so.

But who am I to complain? Would I change a single thing about my rugby career? The answer is: not one! Thinking about it, though, maybe just one. The quarter-final of the 1991 World Cup, Ireland v. Australia . . . after Gordon Hamilton's historic try, we as a group were on the cusp of doing something no other Ireland side had done before or has done since – namely, reaching the semi-final of the World Cup – and in true Irish fashion we contrived to snatch defeat from the jaws of victory! I've consigned my entire rugby career to history, but that game still creeps out of the vault to haunt me, as I'm sure it does the other guys who played that day. It's only a game, I know, but these opportunities come along only once in a lifetime.

It angers me, I must admit, to see the amount of money poured into the national team nowadays compared with in my time. A whole generation of Irish players was wasted because of the Irish Rugby Football Union's refusal to accept the changes that were happening in the world rugby scene at that time, and we were dragged kicking and screaming into the professional game. Despite this, for a small country – the 2007 World Cup excepted, it has to be said – we've punched well above our weight. Long may it continue and rugby as a game prosper!

I WANT TO GO ON TOUR!

PHILLIP MATTHEWS
FLANKER Queen's University, Ards, Wanderers, Ulster
IRELAND 1984–92, 38 caps

It's Monday, 23 March 2009, and I'm sitting down to write this piece, but I can't ignore what happened at the weekend. Last Saturday evening Ireland won their first ever Six Nations Grand Slam, their last Grand Slam being the old Five Nations version in 1948, 61 years ago.

For this Grand Slam the pre-match mind games included Wales coach Warren Gatland telling the press that, of all the Six Nations teams, the Welsh players hated playing against the Irish the most. He subsequently tried to play down these comments, but anyone who watched the game could see that there was no love lost between the two sides as tempers on both sides threatened to ignite the already gasoline-fumed atmosphere from the pre-match pyrotechnics. Things were very different in the amateur days. The occasion and the fact that they had to defeat Wales in Cardiff reminds me of a very different time.

Rugby 'officially' went professional in 1995, but in truth the writing had been on the wall since New Zealand's dominance of the first Rugby World Cup in 1987. This first World Cup put Ireland and Wales in the same group, and it seemed that not only did we go head to head on the pitch, but my memory has it that (training aside) we seemed to spend a lot of time with them off the pitch as well – socialising. Things were very different then, and for many players it was their first experience of 'touring' with an international rugby team. And for one player in particular, it seemed he'd found nirvana.

VOICES FROM THE BACK OF THE BUS

Not everyone will remember Glen Webbe's relatively short international career. He won ten caps on the wing between 1986 and 1988, but I and most of the Ireland and Wales players who played in that World Cup will remember him for capturing the spirit and ethos of rugby tours in those times in one simple statement. But before I tell you what he said, I should give you a flavour of what it was like in that era, a flavour that you will undoubtedly get from the numerous other stories in this book.

So much of the experience of touring in those days was centred around the craic with the locals and the opposition. I'm not sure that it's quite the same these days. Anyone who played in that first World Cup will remember the complimentary crates of Steinlager from the sponsors greeting you in your hotel room, and one team had a particularly 'entrepreneurial' use for them. The Scots (ringleaders being the Hastings brothers) collected all their free crates together, booked a room in their hotel and sold tickets around town to the locals for their post-match party. They always seemed to be one step ahead of us in those days, on and off the pitch!

We had our moments too, I guess, although sometimes we took a few 'shortcuts' to get the girls' clothes off! I'll never forget a game of 'strip bunnies' in Tokyo (on tour in Japan with Ireland) with a group of Irish models and a few unfortunate locals. It's pretty much the same as strip poker only we had total control of the rules, and needless to say the locals and the models couldn't quite get the hang of it. I'll leave the rest to your imagination . . .

Anyone who has ever toured has stories, and my favourite is from a Wanderers FC tour to Amsterdam. Our fly-half (we'll just call him John) was getting off the tour bus at the end of the evening, and some helpful teammate chucked his gear bag down a grass bank onto what in the dark looked like a footpath. So John ran down the bank and leaped the last few feet, expecting to land on the path, only to find it was a very dirty canal. He completely disappeared before emerging like a monster from the deep. Even now the memory of that image brings tears of laughter to my eyes.

You may be thinking that much of touring craic is rather . . . boyish? And you'd be right. But more than that, seeing the world, being treated like a king and playing the sport you love is . . . well, as Glen Webbe put it, 'When I die, I don't want to go to heaven. I want to go on tour!' I wonder if today's players would say the same?

THE ADMINISTRATORS

THE ADMINISTRATORS PREFACE

International rugby players love a good moan about the committee members, alickadoos and treasurers. Some players continue contributing to the game in what is an essential if often-maligned role. Many players mock the administration but few take on the mantle once they have retired, and those that do have a rude awakening when they discover just how much work is done in the background so that players, kitted out and catered for, can walk onto the park at their own club or international venues.

Just as with any performance there is a backstage crew (physios, sponge boys, water boys, etc.), a technical team (groundsmen and caretakers) and the front-of-house team who work to get the performers an audience, a platform on which to perform and all the permissions regarding insurance, indemnity and eligibility. We couldn't play without them, no matter how much disdain and contempt we often pour upon them.

Looking back, gripes about travelling expenses and disgruntlement regarding charges to rooms were all part of the experience, and we would all do it all over again on the same terms just to wear the beloved shirt of our country once more.

Stewart McKinney

A STITCH IN TIME

KEN KENNEDY
HOOKER Queen's University, CIYMS, London Irish, Ulster
IRELAND 1964–75, 45 caps
LIONS TOURS '66, '74, 4 Test matches

In today's world of professional rugby, with players supplied with all their kit, both training and match jerseys, it is interesting to reflect a bit on the past. In the amateur days the committees were fond of first-class travel for themselves and tourist/economy/cattle class for the players. This foible extended to the allocation of hotel rooms and menus: à la carte for them and table d'hôte for the boys. They expected the players to use the jersey and socks provided in their first game for the whole of the season. This led to the ludicrous situation in Cardiff in 1969 of an Irish team taking the field with several different colours of green jerseys, due to some being washed with varying kinds of other laundry while others looked pristine and new. Talk about the 40 shades of green! (Check it out. It's not poor film production, lighting or camera angles that give the range of hue.) Not only that but in the dressing-room before the game two of the jerseys had to be repaired by the team doctor with surgical silk, as the armpits of the hooker's and loose-head prop's jerseys had been ripped in the previous match by tight binding in the scrum. Can you imagine having to consider saving your jersey or saving the match? What did the committee expect players to do?

Two years later on the same pitch, due to a wayward boot, the same surgical silk was sewn into a scalp laceration of the Ireland hooker. Medical staff had cut off the jersey before suturing, and to rub salt into the wound a week later the player concerned received a bill for the jersey, which had not been returned after the match! Changed times indeed, but we would not swap them!

HAND ON HEART/HAND IN POCKET

STEWART McKINNEY

When a team has finished playing and the dinners are over, the debriefings are done and the excitement of the competition has dissipated, players are suddenly thrust back into their own individual environments. A plane touching down on the tarmac indicated a return to everyday normality and wrenched players from the comfort of camaraderie and sacrifice selflessly displayed on the pitch and in the changing-room and hotel room. Flankers, props, fly-halfs: whatever the position, the players resumed their places in society as hard-working tradesmen, teachers and businessmen. The amateurs returned to their professions, the occupations that paid their mortgages and allowed for little luxuries. Back in reality, players had to make their own way from the band of brothers and manage life just like everybody else.

After a game in either Cardiff or Edinburgh the plane flew into Aldergrove and from there players made their own way home, with a petrol allowance of 10p per mile. The official route from Aldergrove to Jordanstown was recorded as 18 miles, thus permitting a claim of £1.80. Being a teacher, there weren't many perks of the job, and the salary in those days was but a pittance. Training and preparation for selection incurred many unseen costs at a personal level, such as gym membership, dietary supplements and other incidental out-of-pocket expenses directly related to rugby.

I decided to chance my arm and submitted a claim for £2.00 to the frugal Bob Fitzgerald. By return of post, he wrote back and informed me that I had overcharged the union by 20p. It had become a matter of honour now, so I responded to his letter by telling him that his map might well have indicated a journey of 18 miles; however, with the Troubles affecting traffic routes in many areas, barriers and blockades necessitated diversions, which brought the total journey length up to 20 miles and thus justified my claim for £2. Bob got back in touch with me immediately and said that the union ('tight as') had accepted the explanation and that the extra 20p had been OK'd on this occasion!

The union never really appreciated how much it cost a player to represent his country. After my first game against England, the reception dinner was held in the ballroom of the Hilton Hotel, Park Lane, which had to be cleared of tables for the post-dinner dance. The players were ushered out to the foyer bar whilst this took place. I didn't know that the foyer bar wasn't free, which ordinarily wouldn't have been a problem to me. I like to think I am known for getting my round in, but London hotel prices are exorbitant if not extortionate. Fergus Slattery, my teammate and a guy who loves a gag, was a well-travelled and experienced international who did know the form. On seeing me he hailed me to him and after a hearty slap on the shoulder sent me up to the bar for four large G & Ts. I only had £10 for the weekend, so when the barman asked for £12 for the four drinks I had to think on my feet and pretty damn quick!

Luxury hotels credit themselves with being able to meet all of their clients' needs, no matter how strange or peculiar their requests might be. Taking advantage of this, I asked the barman for a bottle of Blue Bass. Only a few select bars in the north of Ireland stocked this, so it was unlikely they'd have any on the shelf here. He looked around, but no such drink was in view. He apologised to me and said he'd go and look in the cellar to see if he could find some. I remained at the bar until he disappeared through the door then I bolted with the four G & Ts never to return!

I think Slats was quite impressed with my quick thinking, but I suspect it only served as a spur for further challenges each time we met subsequently.

GOOD OLE AMATEUR DAYS

GORDON HAMILTON
FLANKER NIFC, Howe of Fife, Blackheath, Ballymena, Ulster
IRELAND 1990–1, 10 caps

I start with one wee story that will always stick in my mind. The 'senior players' in Ireland's 1991 World Cup squad were looking for some dosh, as they used to say, in exchange for signing the Rugby World Cup participation contract. Noel 'Noisey' Murphy just could not get his mind around the fact that players were looking for money to play for Ireland. 'Look, lads,' he exclaimed in that lovely squeaky Cork lilt, 'sign the bloody contracts, for fuck's sake!'

Of course, Noisey had played for Ireland with distinction for many years and more recently had given up a lot of time to help with the Irish Rugby Football Union – a pure amateur! He went on to explain to the squad, 'Look, lads, when I played against Wales and was checking out of the Cardiff hotel the next day I had to pay for an extra fucking sausage I had on the morning of the game! Come on, lads, catch yerselves on and sign the bloody contracts.'

Professionalism was on the move during the 1991 Rugby World Cup, and it was clear the southern-hemisphere players were making money. Senior Ireland players were understandably keen that they should get something back if the others were, while us young whips just wanted to get the green jersey on as often as possible.

I am not sure a contract was ever signed, but at the end of a reasonable campaign, ending in that famous quarter-final defeat (professional defeats aren't famous), the Irish Rugby Football Union buckled and sent us to the final in London with 2,500 Irish punts!

I put what money was left in a Dundalk bank account to avoid bringing it north and having to pay UK tax and hoped for a few nights out with the lads in Donegal or something. Of course, my girlfriend, later to be my wife, found this out, and I ended up blowing it on an engagement ring in Dublin!

I had so much fun playing rugby, whether it was for school, university, Howe of Fife, Blackheath, NIFC (often for fifth XVs on an afternoon off), Ballymena, Ulster or Ireland, it didn't matter to me I wasn't paid. I even paid club subs!

Of course, rugby is a very different ball game now and offers our best players so many opportunities. I do worry, however, about opportunities lost for those guys who either sacrifice an alternative professional career to play rugby or by choosing an alternative career lose the opportunity to play for their province or their country. In my own case, on the one hand I would have loved to have seen how I could have improved my game as a professional player but on the other hand I wonder if I would have survived the physical rigours of the modern game or indeed been good enough in the competitive environment to have been selected for Ulster or Ireland.

One thing is for sure, some of my best days were my club days and playing for NIFC and that big bollox of a coach, Stewart McKinney.

THE KNEE TEST

STEWART McKINNEY

I often wonder how much a professional international rugby team is insured for. Certainly, when professional careers are at stake, a situation similar to that when Ireland played France in February 1978 at the Parc des Princes would not have arisen.

It was an absolute disgrace, and it was pure luck that no one was seriously injured. The pitch was badly frozen over – not just in patches, but completely. Everyone was going out to inspect the pitch, but Willie Duggan told me not to bother. 'Stewie, this game will be played regardless, believe you me,' he said dismissively. So we stayed in the dressing-room changing studs, thus missing the ridiculous sight of the committee members rolling up their trousers and gently lowering themselves to kneel on the frozen turf. There's a bit of a difference between a gentle and deliberate genuflection and being tackled or tipped unexpectedly on a neck or a shoulder!

Injuries are an unfortunate legacy of a contact sport, and normally the only considerations are fair play from the opposition, good management of the game by the referee and good technique in the execution of skills by the players. Perhaps a gum shield and shin pads (optional) as protective wear, maybe a scrum cap or a bit of tape to flatten down protruding ears or support a dodgy joint might be worn, but the condition of the pitch should be safe. There are enough health and safety issues to contend with without having to worry about the elements.

Unsurprisingly, the pitch was declared playable, vindicating Willie's prediction and choice of stud, which allowed him to move with great speed over the ice rink to clatter Jean-Pierre Bastiat from the kick-off. I often wonder if the France and Ireland committees could have lived with their consciences if someone had been seriously hurt that day.

HOW THINGS HAVE CHANGED

WALLACE McMASTER
WING Ballymena, Ulster
IRELAND 1971–6, 18 caps

I am sure that those who played rugby in my day are amazed by how things have changed as compared to how they were in the 1960s and '70s. I do not refer to the muscle-bound forwards whose level of fitness allows them to gallop around the pitch like backs until the coach sees any sign of fatigue and promptly replaces them. Nor do I refer to the forwards' 'keep-possession' tactics, resulting in the wide players and spectators alike seeing little of the ball.

No, I refer to the attire of the modern player! Base layers? Body armour? And on top of these a skin-tight, non-rip, non-slip jersey. Apparently, the jerseys are changed several times per season to ensure that the sponsors' names are fresh and easily read by spectators. Well, I guess they need something to look at when the ball spends most of the game hidden away.

It was not like that in my day! Oh no, things were very different back then when it came to kit. The backs were easily distinguished from the forwards, as they were much more smartly turned out: collars were turned up, socks neatly pulled up and shorts snug fitting. Forwards, on the other hand, were usually a scruffy lot, with little apparent thought put into their appearance.

As a winger spending most of my time strolling up and down the touchline in the hope that the ball, usually in error, might come my way, I felt it should be incumbent on me to keep the dress standards up. I tell you this in order to help you understand the situation I found myself in before and during a game playing for Ulster versus Australia. I believe it was around 1975 at Ravenhill.

When we arrived at our changing-room, we were told that the Ulster Branch of the Irish Rugby Football Union, in their wisdom, had splashed out on a new set of jerseys. Normally, this only happened every three years or so, but as this was a special occasion it was felt that the extra expense was warranted. The Ulster secretary proudly went round the changing-room handing each player his numbered jersey.

Now, most players have their own routine when changing before a match. Some put their jerseys on first, some their shorts, etc. I always went shorts, then boots then jersey last. Those of you from my era will also remember the rugby jersey named Bukta Superscrum. I am convinced that they made these jerseys from the same material that was used to make the sails for the old tea clippers. The new jerseys were, you guessed it, the aforementioned Bukta Superscrums.

Looking across the changing-room, I noticed Willie John McBride had pulled his jersey on, and it appeared to be a more than ample fit. I shouted over to him, asking what size he had been given. The secretary overheard me and explained that the forwards had size 44 while the backs had a size 42. Being 5 ft 9 in. and around 12 st. 8 lb, I was somewhat concerned as to how my jersey might fit, especially having seen how large the size 44 was on Willie John. I held mine out in front of me, and it appeared so large I checked the size. To my horror, it was size 46!

Kick-off was only ten minutes away, and when I pulled it on I discovered it hung well below my knees. Well, there was no way I could get it to fit inside my snug-fitting shorts. Urgent and drastic action had to be taken. I grabbed a pair of scissors from the first-aid kit and cut a good foot off the bottom of the jersey. This done, it was still a struggle to get the wide jersey stuffed inside my shorts. The result gave the impression I was wearing an oversized nappy. I then rolled up the sleeves to allow my hands to appear just as the referee called us out. Too late now!

Thinking the worst was over, I jogged out only to find there was a strong wind blowing straight down the pitch. The jersey billowed out like a kite, making progress into the wind difficult. I looked across at my opposite number – yes, he was wearing his collar turned up and his jersey was the perfect fit.

Luckily, I only received the ball a few times in the first half, discovering that my best strategy to make progress over the ground was to zigzag forward like a yacht tacking in the breeze. In the second half, my opposite number must have been totally surprised at my new turn of speed. In fact, I am convinced to this day that if I had held my arms out I could have taken flight and soared like a hang-glider past or even over him!

I am sure you can imagine my annoyance when two weeks later I received a bill from the Ulster Branch to replace the jersey that I had, and I quote, 'destroyed'. Yes, things have certainly changed!

TAKEN TO ACCOUNT

TONY WARD
FLY-HALF Garryowen, St Mary's, Greystones, Munster
IRELAND 1977–88, 19 caps
LIONS TOUR '80, 1 Test match

It's a funny thing, but if there's one promise I made myself before finally hanging them up and calling it quits, it was that I would never resort to the 'Ah, but in our day' line of reminiscing. Sadly, here I am some 20 years on and guess what? Ah, but in our day it *was* different.

I suppose were I to sum it up I would say that where the game went following the Paris Accord in '95 made me envious, although never, ever begrudging, of today's rugby-playing generation. Their hobby truly is their livelihood – and lucky them. It is a different game in almost every technical respect. Players are bigger, fitter and stronger. They are more skilful, too, as they should be given that it is indeed their daily bread.

Numbers on shirts are now rendered meaningless, as forward and backs interchange seamlessly. It is high octane, high intensity, but whether it's a better end product I'm not so sure. Like rugby league when it took off all those years ago, rugby union has become a game of massive mobile bodies and minimal space. In many respects it is a cross between gridiron minus the gear and league minus the space. The Northern Union addressed that issue many, many moons ago when removing the flankers and making its version of the game 13-a-side – take it as read that union and the International Rugby Board powers that be will never go a similar route.

Where that leaves an electric Gerald Davies or a dancing Phil Bennett I'm not too sure. To his credit, Shane Williams keeps that creative light flickering, but he is a one-off in a time of claustrophobic defending, where ex-rugby league coaches are king. If wall-on-wall defending and recycling, or, to borrow from the jargon of the modern game, 'going through the phases', is your thing, then fair enough. Personally, it drives me to distraction, but clearly there is a market for it, placing former league defensive gurus at the top of each new season's union shopping list. Sad but true.

If this 'once was' sounds bitter and resentful, with hand on heart it is not intended as such. I envy today's pros their lot and know I speak on behalf of so many of my contemporaries when emphasising what we would have given to have had their opportunity. That said, technological advances and increased (full-time) demands allowing, on behalf of previous generations, I do not concede an inch in terms of passion and commitment.

Rugby then was every bit as all-embracing – particularly to those privileged enough to make the representative elite – as it is now. The difference, however, is in the respect and treatment today's pro generation so take for granted. As a very simple and obvious case in point, pre-professionalism, when players cost the individual unions not a bean to take on tour (time off in terms of compensation to the employer was the sole concern of the player), travel was cattle class. Now, when they cost top dollar, they travel top of the bus.

It is but one of a raft of practical improvements to the well-being of the modern-day international. Not that long ago, with the Grand Slam-winning Welsh on the receiving end of a thumping from the Springboks in Bloemfontein, Warren Gatland's charges were up in arms because 'a logistical cock-up' the following day resulted in both squads having to travel on the same flight to Pretoria for the second Test and, worse still, actually share the same airport space. God forbid.

There was a time when home internationals in Dublin meant both teams sharing the same (Shelbourne) hotel from Thursday to Sunday. It wasn't comfortable dodging each other in the lifts, but that was the way it was, with no questions asked and every one of us naively and foolishly 100 per cent happy just to be on board. On a personal level, I found some of the goings on degrading in the extreme. Can you imagine Brian O'Driscoll, Ronan O'Gara, Paul O'Connell or anyone else you care to name on the receiving end of this?

This letter was addressed to 'Mr A.J.P. Ward' from the Irish Rugby Football Union, 62 Lansdowne Road, dated 4 November 1978:

REFERENCE: Ireland v. New Zealand, 4 November 1978

Shelbourne Hotel Account

Dear Tony [a rare personal address; usually it was 'sir'],

I have deducted £2.66 from Colin Patterson's claim for travel expenses in respect of 50% cost of telephone calls and papers left unpaid on your hotel account. Please let me have remittance of £2.66 in respect of the other 50% and arrange adjustment with your roommate if necessary.

The 'Shop' charges were 37p, 49p and 46p. The phone calls cost 95p and £3.05.

I would again ask that such personal expenses should be paid at reception before departure from the hotel.

Yours Sincerely,
R. Fitzgerald
Secretary

These account-settling notes from the clearly 'cash-strapped' governing body were standard currency of the time. We all got them, although I think the one to Michael Kiernan and Mossie Finn when they were rooming together prior to a Five Nations match in 1982 took the proverbial biscuit. One of them was guilty of going down for a haircut and charging it to the room, for which each got a subsequent bill for half a haircut!

I recall another from around that same time underlining the extent of union suffocation. Bear in mind that their take on me was that I was a jumped-up superstar out of control. It concerned an International Player of the Year award and read:

Dear Tony [well, it might have been 'sir'],

It has come to the notice of the Irish Rugby Football Union committee that you have been in London as recipient of an award as an Ireland international rugby player. I have to ascertain from you, for the information of my committee, details as to what organisation was responsible for the award in question and also the nature of the award.

In future if you should receive offers of similar awards the union committee would like you to kindly seek its approval before your acceptance.

Yours Sincerely,
R. Fitzgerald
Secretary

Let me emphasise that Bob Fitzgerald and Harry Booker were the employed go-betweens and inherently decent people charged with carrying out what many people felt to be the dirty work of a faceless committee. I think the gist of this sample correspondence captures in essence the dictatorial flavour of union workings at the time.

But they were good times, and far be it for me to suggest otherwise. We played a game we loved for no other reason. I hope I am wrong, but I fear the camaraderie we so took for granted and the rugby friendships we still enjoy to this day might not be of the same substance, say, in 20 years' time.

Rugby has long broken down barriers on the island of Ireland, and none more so than during the 30-plus years of the Troubles. Well do I recall Ciaran Fitzgerald (then a captain in the Irish Army and aide-de-camp to the president) and his opposite number for Dungannon (covered from shoulder to wrist in Loyalist tattoos) rag arsed in the Stevenson Park clubhouse, arm in arm and in full voice until well after midnight.

And post-match Ravenhill (interprovincial) revelry included a guided tour in the company of Johnny McDonald and Jimmy McCoy (both members of the Royal Ulster Constabulary) through otherwise no-go areas on both sides of the then sectarian divide. How can you put a monetary value on those experiences? You can't.

In some ways players now have the best of everything, but for those of us who went before, while poorer in the pocket, I think it is fair to say we are, deep down, fully signed-up and committed members of the 'Ah, but in our day' club. No doubt we too could have hacked professionalism, but, with hand on heart, given our lot, would we have wanted it any other way?

THE MEDICS

STEWART McKINNEY

Bobby Windsor told me that the opposition at Pontypool required so many stitches that they kept a Singer sewing machine in the tunnel, and I've no reason to doubt him!

When I played for London Irish we had five doctors (Ken Kennedy had retired), and although they were great for the likes of dislocations they weren't what I would call 'blood' doctors. So, if you needed stitches, you hoped Ken Kennedy was at the game or there was a medic in the crowd. Dr Pat Parfrey was the coach, and his answer to any complaint was, 'It's only pain!' even if a leg was hanging off. Mossie Finn, a fellow international of Pat's from Cork, would announce every Saturday, an hour before kick-off, that his hamstring was playing up and that he felt he couldn't play. 'It's only pain,' Pat would reply, 'but I'll give you a jag in the back of the leg anyway.' Mossie would lie upon the table and Pat, with a wink to us, would jag him with nothing in the needle.

'Jesus, Pat!' Mossie would say. 'That's great now!' (Funny people, those Cork boys.)

The Ulster team doctor was a great character called Stym Smith, and he liked to sink a few brandies before he started stitching. He stitched Dessie McCann one day, and Dessie reckoned he had hay fever for months afterwards, as there was a big tuft of grass left in the wound.

In my first game for Ireland in Paris the French gave me the treatment, but Victor Boffelli miskicked at one point and snapped his shinbone on my head! Cliff Morgan was the match commentator for the old *Rugby Special* programme, and he said, sympathetically, that it was so sad to see a player carried off on a stretcher writhing in agony. Not a word about the big lump on my head was spoken, nor speculation made about any possible concussion I might have suffered from such a whack. I didn't need any stitches, though.

Moss Keane needed them two years later on his debut in Paris when, trapped in a ruck, a boot opened him badly. As it was his first cap and he was a bit shy, he didn't tell the rest of us the name of the bastard who'd stamped him. *Quel dommage!* Jamesy Maher was our Irish team doctor, a really placid gentleman – unless there were Germans around and he'd had a few drinks. Jamesy was good with the suturing needle, but as it was such a horrific cut I thought I'd try to take Moss's mind off the pain. 'It could have been worse, Moss,' I said.

'What could have been worse?' he asked, puzzled.

'They could have kicked you up the arse and damaged your brains!' We had a good laugh as Jamesy continued with his embroidery.

Now Moss should have remembered my distraction tactics when his international colleague Mickey Quinn was badly gashed on the forehead during a Lansdowne club game. Mickey was lying on his back, and all he could see was a red mist as the blood ran into his eyes. Player after player attempted to comfort and reassure him that it wasn't too bad and that help was on its way. Then Moss took a look and announced in horrified tone, 'Jaysus, Mickey, you're totally destroyed!' Mickey fainted.

When I split my right eye in an Ireland squad session the Sunday before the England game in 1976, it required six stitches. It made the papers: 'Injury scare for Ireland. McKinney splits an eye.' I cursed the press as I had three very good friends in the England front row – Fran Cotton, Peter Wheeler and Mike Burton – and I knew the eye would be tested. I cunningly trimmed back the superfluous little bits of thread from the stitches over the offending eye, applied mascara to the eyebrow and stuck a big plaster over the uninjured brow. Sure enough, Franny tested the protected eye early on, but the resulting shiner was worth it, as my stitched eye remained intact for the duration.

Ronnie Lamont returned from the 1966 Lions tour to New Zealand as the only player, in the Kiwis' opinion, who would have won a place in the All Blacks Test side. What a wonderful accolade – that would have made Ronnie the best openside in the world. Unfortunately, he also returned with a ghastly shoulder injury and didn't play for two years. During that time, he received neither medical advice nor help from the Irish Rugby Football Union . . . what shabby treatment for such a heroic player.

Willie John had his own medical wizard, and he wasn't National Health. Many regarded him as eccentric, and perhaps he was, but to me he was a man of magic, a genius. His name was Jack Nixon. I pulled a hamstring (perversely, I had always secretly wanted to sustain such an injury, as it was only fast players who were supposed to suffer from them) and Willie told me to do everything exactly as Jack said, for he'd kept him right over the years. However, he also warned me that Jack was very deaf. I duly agreed to abide by his word.

When I explained that I'd pulled my hamstring, Jack started to poke at the back of my neck – deafness, I thought. He got out some electrodes and produced some cotton wool dipped in a foul-looking yellow mixture, redolent of the sulphurous rotten-egg mixture from the school science laboratory. He placed the impregnated cotton wool under the electrodes and turned on the power. I kept protesting that it wasn't my neck but my hamstring, but he wasn't listening or couldn't hear, as he took no notice and left the room. After half an hour, he returned. By then, I could smell burning flesh as well as the rotten egg – hellfire and brimstone, perhaps. Unfazed, he turned off the instrument of torture. 'Imbalance,' he kept saying. 'The neck is out of line, and you're running out of line, too, so you pulled the hamstring. Come back in three days, and you will play in a week.'

I wasn't totally convinced by Willie's alternative medicine, but, of course, as usual, he was right. I played in a week, and from that day on I placed my strains and pains in Jack's capable healing hands. I never did find out what the noxious yellow concoction was, though – just as well, maybe.

SAMMY BOYD – AN UNLIKELY ULSTER RUGBY LEGEND

JIM NEILLY
PROP King's Scholars, Instonians
BBC broadcaster

Above the hatch through which the pre- and post-match drinks are dispensed in the committee room at Ravenhill Park in Belfast is a plaque bearing the legend 'Sammy's Bar'. This was placed strategically and lovingly, not as a memorial to some Ulster player past or an administrator of note or a coach of great renown but in memory of Sammy Boyd, who served alcohol and vitriolic comments in equal measure.

Having spent many years admitting spectators and their vehicles through Ravenhill's main gate, Sammy, in his latter days, was moved inside and took upon himself the role of 'mine host', engaging the good and the great of rugby in Ulster and beyond with his unique blend of familiarity and disdain.

Sammy was a member of Malone Rugby Club (located less than half a mile away from Ravenhill) and a lifelong supporter of Linfield Football Club. He would make it very clear that once he had provided the rugby hierarchy and their guests with an adequate quantity of refreshment (all gratis, it must be mentioned), he had other places to go where he could enjoy his own evening, making this point with uncommon brevity on Friday nights or Saturday afternoons.

When Sir Ronnie Flanagan, a former Ulster hooker and for several years the chief constable of the Royal Ulster Constabulary and then the Police Service of Northern Ireland, looked as if he was settling in for the night in the company of friends with whom he was enjoying a few drinks, Sammy inquired of Northern Ireland's top policeman, 'Hey, Flanagan, have you no bloody home to go to?'

Ulster made unprecedented progress toward a European Cup victory in the 1998–99 season, so business was brisk, and Sammy was forced to work overtime in order to cope with the ever-increasing numbers of so-called 'VIPs' who had pitched up to his hatch in search of Ulster

Branch largesse. As the queue for drinks grew longer, Sammy's temper grew shorter. Politicians in Northern Ireland, from all sides, had begun to appear out at Ravenhill (some having to ask directions to the Ulster Branch HQ!), and on a memorable Friday evening in December 1998, following Ulster's thrilling victory over Toulouse, Sammy had gotten himself into a considerable lather while being acutely aware that the standard of clientele had increased in terms of status. David Trimble, Northern Ireland's First Minister (teetotal and strongly religious), was doing his best to keep up with the subtleties and nuances of a game and surroundings that were palpably alien to him and cut a forlorn figure as he sipped his orange juice while all around him pints were being quaffed with gusto. Blasphemy and insult aside, Sammy barked, 'Jesus, Davy! Would you not get a pint of stout down your neck and maybe we might get a smile out of you?'

Nobody knows quite when or how Sammy acquired his official Ulster garb or, to be accurate, an Ulster badge that had been none too carefully attached to the pocket of a blazer. Still, he looked the part and wore it with pride behind his bar at Ravenhill and also on those few occasions when he ventured outside of Belfast. Ulster officials were astounded on arrival at Vicarage Road for a Heineken Cup game against Saracens when they were informed that one of their party had already been shown to the directors' lounge and were even more amazed when they were met by Sammy, resplendent in Ulster blazer and tie, flat cap on his head and pint firmly in his hand.

Alas, Ulster went down, not helped – they will claim to this day – by some iffy refereeing from a relatively inexperienced Italian official. Sammy was staying with one of his sons in London but was outside Vicarage Road as the Ulster party boarded their coach to Heathrow. Realising that Sammy had spotted the referee, I urged him to be diplomatic and restrict his conversation to the finer points of rugby law. 'Don't worry, big lad,' he said to me. 'I'll not let the side down.' However, he turned to the bemused Italian and declared, 'See you, Corleone, you should stick to selling fucking ice cream!'

It became apparent after a few years that whenever Sammy was in charge of the main gate at Ravenhill, the match takings and the expected revenue from the number of cars and their passengers admitted by the philanthropic Mr Boyd never quite tallied. Indeed, there was great benefit in being a member of the Malone Club at the time, since Sammy would have popped into Gibson Park (Malone's ground) well in advance of his stint at Ravenhill and let it be known that he was on the gate.

On the morning of Saturday, 30 January 1999, as all of Ulster waited for the European Cup final, Sammy was the first Ulsterman to gain admittance to Lansdowne Road. Bedecked in his full official Ulster regalia, Sammy had inveigled his way into the ground and was given a personal VIP tour by the chief steward, an obliging and innocent soul. Sammy was suitably impressed with the oldest international stadium in the world, since despite its modest capacity and mediocre facilities, it was positively palatial in comparison with Ravenhill or even Sammy's beloved Windsor Park in Belfast. 'How many will you get in here for the game?' Sammy asked the chief steward.

'Oh, there'll be close to 50,000,' he replied with a fair degree of pride.

'See if I was on the gate,' said Sammy, 'there'd be closer to 70,000!'

A MASSIVE

STEWART McKINNEY

By the time I was first selected for Ulster in the 1969–70 season, Ken Goodall was not only a seasoned interprovincial but had become the star of Irish rugby. We were the same age and had played against one another throughout our school days – he'd attended Foyle College and I was a pupil of Dungannon Royal. We knew each other very well.

After my debut in Connaught, the reception was held in Glenina, the home of Galwegians Rugby Club. Ken decided that we would go on a 'massive' and that he would look after the rookie who was absolutely unknown in those parts of the Emerald Isle.

Ken was very popular due to his exploits with Ireland. 'Would you like a drink, Ken?'

'Large gin and tonic and one for my friend.'

'Who's yer friend, Ken?'

'Stewart McKinney. You'll be hearing about him!'

'Would you like a drink, Ken?'

'Large gin and tonic and one for Stewart.'

'Stewart who?'

'Stewart McKinney, my back-row colleague!'

God! The whole of Ireland knew the man and wanted to buy him a drink. I was now his 'back-row colleague'. I was so proud. I never, ever forgot Ken's kindness and how he had looked after me in Glenina.

THE ADMINISTRATORS

Three days before St Patrick's Day 1970, I watched the massive man score a massive individual try to deny Wales the Triple Crown. Ireland won 14–0, and Ken Goodall was the toast of the country. By the time I played against Connaught the next season, Ken had become an outcast, a pariah, the Huckleberry Finn of Irish rugby. His crime? He joined Workington Rugby League Club. He had 'gone north', as they said then.

It beggars belief in today's world of commercially driven professional rugby, money-saturated corporate hospitality and commonplace celebrity greed that this great man of Irish rugby, who will for ever be a true legend, could have been unwelcome in rugby clubhouses in Ireland, unclean like a latter-day leper, because of personal choice and circumstances.

Ken's rugby-league career didn't last too long because of injury. When I'd meet him in the Shelbourne Hotel in Dublin after I'd represented Ireland, I was still very proud to have played with Ken, even though it was for only one season at Ulster level, as his back-row colleague. He was still the warm, caring man from the Glenina clubhouse.

'If you're seen drinking with me, Stewartie,' he'd say, 'it could go very badly against you,' meaning selection-wise. So, we would have our massive in some secluded nook away from the prying eyes and prejudice of the Irish committee members . . . what a ludicrous situation!

SOUTH AFRICA

SOUTH AFRICA PREFACE

In 1974 I was privileged and honoured to be a member of the Lions tour to South Africa on what is regarded as the greatest tour of all time. Lifetime friendships were forged during those three months among a disparate group of very special men. There were many rough, tough games, but we were to experience wonderful hospitality and kindness from the people of that great rugby nation. It was an experience that today's Lions will never be able to replicate and enjoy because of the way the game has developed and changed.

The Kruger National Park, the Kango Caves, the Victoria Falls, the trip up the Zambezi River, the vintage car parade in Bloemfontein, the visits to schools and hospitals were experiences that are still treasured. We trained and played hard but toured in the true sense of the word. Thank you, South Africa.

Stewart McKinney

THE TRUE SPIRIT OF RUGBY

HANNES MARAIS
PROP Eastern Province
SOUTH AFRICA 1963–74, 35 caps

My first exposure to Lions rugby, in fact to Test rugby, was in 1955 when Robin Thompson's Lions played the fourth Test in Port Elizabeth. I come from Somerset East, a farming district about 200 km from Port Elizabeth. On the day of the Test I got up early, stood for many hours in a long queue and ended up standing on brandy bottles (empty, of course) behind the posts, a 14 year old amongst a capacity crowd. This was at the old Crusaders ground. The Springboks won that day, and I remember Theuns Briers's tackle that dislocated Tony O'Reilly's shoulder.

Touring sides later played at the larger Boet Erasmus Stadium, where many fierce battles were fought. The deciding third Test against Willie John McBride's '74 Lions was no exception. Our selectors picked two meanies at lock not renowned for their jumping abilities: Moaner van Heerden and Johan de Bruyn. Physically, they could stand their own against the toughest opponents.

The game was fierce, and when Willie John made the infamous '99' call (the secret signal for his troops to engage in extended fighting), we were caught by complete surprise. We did not comprehend what was happening when the free-for-all broke out. At best, I thought it was a Lions ploy to break our concentration, since we were on their goal line.

Be that as it may, in the ruckus that followed Johan de Bruyn got hit in the face, which caused his glass eye to pop out and disappear in the grass. When normality returned, we hunted for the eye and eventually found it. Johan licked it clean and returned it to its socket.

At the celebration dinners in the UK 21 and 25 years after the historic efforts of the '74 Lions, Gordon Brown often told his version of this particular incident. He maintains that in the lineout following a penalty awarded to the Lions, he looked up at the towering figure of Johan de Bruyn marking him. He had never in his life seen a bigger or more mean-looking figure. To his amazement he saw a blade of grass sticking out from underneath the replaced eyeball. He recounts that for the first time in that series he was worried. Should he bend over and pull the blade from Johan's eye or should he tap him on the shoulder and inform him of the situation? He was worried because he feared that this giant would mistake either action as hostile and thus did neither!

When Gordon was terminally ill, suffering from cancer, and on his deathbed, he invited Johan to visit him. I believe he got a friend to sponsor the trip. This spirit of friendship between rugby opponents is what makes the game so special and what I would like to take with me to the end of my days.

COUNTERING CHALLENGES

NELIE SMITH
SCRUM-HALF Orange Free State
SOUTH AFRICA 1963–5, 7 caps (coach 1980–81)

I met Stewart in 1974 when the Lions played the Free State in Bloemfontein. J.B.G. Thomas said in his book *The Greatest Lions*:

> Choet Visser, the South African liaison officer, lived in Bloemfontein, and he was immensely proud of his fellow citizens for turning up in such force and providing a fleet of vintage cars to drive the visiting heroes from the airport to the hotel, a trip that was much enjoyed by all. I was soon at work at the previews and other items all prepared with a note of caution, because

one felt there was to be a real challenge from the Vrystaat. This was due to Nelie Smith and Sakkie van Zyl, two of the most enthusiastic of the younger coaches in South Africa; they had done their homework and studied closely most of the Lions' matches on tour and films of each of the home countries in action. In fact their ambush was perfectly prepared and even the sayings of the modern maestro, Carwyn James, had been incorporated in the Free State drill and nothing, but simply nothing, had been left to chance.

As far as the match itself was concerned, Syd Millar, the coach, and Willie John McBride, the captain, realised that in order to survive in South Africa you had to survive in the scrums. We as Free State coaches concentrated on our scrummaging strategy, and we were confident that our eight forwards would not surrender in this important facet of the game. When Jackie Snyman, our number 10, dropped a goal with ten minutes to go, it seemed as if a miracle could happen at the Free State stadium. From the kick-off and the score 9-8 in favour of the home team, Stoffel Botha, our lock forward, collided with his captain, Jakes Swart, and the former was concussed. In those days the team doctor had to certify that the injured player could not continue before a replacement could appear on the field.

The last scrum of the match was five metres from the Free State goal line. The Free State had the put-in, but they only had seven forwards. With Botha leaving the field on the far side, there was no way that the doctor could certify the injury to bring on the replacement. The Lions won the heel, and Gareth Edwards went blind side for J.J. Williams to score the winning points. I tried to get the replacement on the field without a note, but the Lions complained, and the replacement had to leave the field. It was the first time in my coaching career that I was out-foxed by a greater fox, Willie John McBride, and we lost this prestigious match 11–9. That particular day I realised that a dead lock was better than no lock in a vital situation!

Before the match, I'd observed that from kick-offs and dropouts Mervyn Davies, with his tremendous flexibility, would jump high and deflect the ball back to Gareth Edwards. Three Lions players would form a wall behind Mervyn in case the ball was dropped. Therefore, I instructed Johan de Bruyn, our heavy lock forward, to stand ten yards back from our ten-yard line. I also pointed out to Johan that he was the one player in South Africa at the time who could go for the man and not the ball, because he only had one eye and everyone was aware of it. Harold Verster, the openside flanker, and Jakes Swart, the blindside flanker, were to harass Gareth Edwards behind the wall, which they did superbly. Mervyn survived, showing the character of the Lions – they could take anything thrown at them. Stewart McKinney was one of the stars of the match and was also trusted with the goalkicking. Stewart succeeded with one penalty, which saved the day for the Lions.

I have many happy memories of coaching in Ballymena. The hospitality and friendships were tremendous. For each victory I was rewarded with a chocolate cake. Sometimes, after a vital away game, I'd return home to find three cakes at my doorstep from three different people. When I was in Ireland, I was also delighted to meet up with Stewart in Belfast, where he was a key rugby figure, ploughing back a tremendous amount into the sport.

TAKE ME BACK TO THE OLD TRANSVAAL

CECIL PEDLOW
WING Queen's University, CIYMS
IRELAND 1953–63, 30 caps
LIONS TOUR '55, 2 Test matches

If only we could turn back time. Although I am extremely proud to be an Irishman, I was so enamoured to be part of the British and Irish Lions tour to South Africa in 1955 that I kept a journal for every day of the three months of that magnificent experience. Don't worry, I shan't subject you to the minutiae.

The flight in those days took 28 hours, and when we landed 1,500 people were eagerly awaiting our arrival at the airport. Our choirmaster, the wonderful Cliff Morgan, led us in singing the popular patriotic Afrikaans tune 'Sarie Marais' . . . in Afrikaans! It was a stroke of genius, a fantastic piece of public relations, and we were welcomed and feted like film stars. It set the mood for the tour, and we were exceptionally well received.

I was young and impressionable, only 21, and my fellow wing and countryman Tony O'Reilly was just 19. We were friends even before we were selected for the tour – he'd umpired tennis matches I'd played in at Fitzwilliam. Early on in the tour we were roommates, and like the other players we were loaned cars for getting about midweek. Dressed up to the nines in our tour blazers, we cruised the length of the very salubrious Jan Smuts Avenue, looking for driveways with several cars parked in them and in the road as a means of identifying a good house party in full swing. We'd knock at the door, claim we were lost and looking for directions, then because we seemed so respectable we'd be asked in to enjoy the party, taking full advantage of the marvellous hospitality extended to us.

Being his roommate meant we shared a letterbox for our mail. He received plenty of fan mail from the local schoolchildren, but I was always pleased with the two or three addressed to me out of the twenty or thirty that regularly stuffed the pigeon hole.

Tony's good looks and natural charm guaranteed plenty of invitations. His magic wasn't limited to the rugby pitch, though. The first match, in Johannesburg at Ellis Park on 6 August 1955, was close, with the score sitting at 23–22 in the Lions' favour as we awaited the result of the Springboks' conversion in the dying minutes. Prayers were being muttered by all the players: from us that they would not score; from them that they would succeed. We won! But you don't gloat even if you are elated. You have to be magnanimous in victory and gracious in defeat.

South Africans take their rugby terribly seriously, and in the bar afterwards Tony noticed an old man in his 80s slouched in a chair, totally dejected, so contrived an introduction. Tony shook his hand enthusiastically, congratulating the old man, telling him that he had read of a winning try the octogenarian had scored for the Springboks back in the day. The former Bok beamed with pride, and despite his age he drew himself up to his full height and a sparkle returned to his eyes. Even his walking stick seemed superfluous. He was enchanted by the humbleness and modesty of one so young (you might have imagined he'd be arrogant, such was his talent), and Tony's respectful recognition was affirmation of all that is best about rugby. I could see then he had the skills that would take him far.

At a reunion some four or five years ago it was fantastic to meet up with the players from the tour – neither geography nor distance had changed the camaraderie we shared back then. Age and ill-health had caught up with a few of us, and when I met up with Cliff Morgan (who unfortunately can't speak because of throat cancer) and Jack Kyle, I said, 'How're you doing, Cliffie?' He obviously couldn't reply clearly. All that could be heard was a rasping noise. I turned to Jack, outraged, and said, 'Do you know what Cliff just said to me? He told me to fuck off!' He hadn't, of course, but he couldn't defend himself. He looked perturbed although he was feigning the slight, of course.

The next morning when we met on the stairs, he looked at me, smiled and covered his throat before rasping, 'Fuck off!' He'd been practising all night to be able to take the wind out of my sails. It was his way of saying, 'Touché!' Of course, I wasn't insulted – it was just banter and a reminder that he wouldn't be beaten.

THE QUICKEST SPRINT

SANDY CARMICHAEL
PROP West of Scotland, Glasgow and District
SCOTLAND 1967–78, 50 caps
LIONS TOURS '71 and '74

The 1974 tour had reached Durban, with three games to go: Natal, Eastern Transvaal and the final Test. I was rooming with Stewart McKinney, and we had become great friends, borne out of respect and a mutual Celtic heritage, I suspect. I was in charge of rooming arrangements and had made sure we roomed together. (It was in our room in Port Elizabeth that the party was held after the series was won . . . no room had ever taken such punishment.)

The success of the tour had made things claustrophobic for the team. Springbok supporters were still buttonholing us and saying, 'Wait till you play Natal,' or 'Wait till you play Eastern Transvaal,' but now with little conviction. A large number of Lions supporters had also arrived from home in anticipation of witnessing further victories, and although well meaning they too added to the smothering atmosphere. Stewartie had the solution: escape! Not far, not for ever, just for a bit of peace and space away from the circus that followed us. Of course, I had to go along with him: he was my roomie and my mate.

To make sure we wouldn't be collared by eagle-eyed Lions or Springbok supporters, he decided, in his wisdom, that we should abandon our Lions uniform and dress down in jeans and T-shirt to go 'incognito' to the Durban docks. The idea had immediate appeal, and I asked a taxi driver to drop us off at the roughest pub he could find. There'd be no hassle there.

We were in the southern hemisphere: everything was upside down; not everything was as it seemed. The seasons were the wrong way round, the constellations above us were strange, and under the light of a full moon we made our way into The Smugglers. It was satisfyingly rough, full of ladies of the night and Korean sailors dressed in white uniforms. Perfect! We could have a few beers in peace, no rugby heavies. We were just sipping our first beers when a huge bouncer approached us and asked if we were enjoying the tour. Damn! Our cover was blown. We explained the purpose of our visit, and he promised not to talk rugby.

Not long into the conversation in the salubrious establishment, Stewartie was poked in the back by one of the Koreans, a mean-looking wee bastard who said two words, 'Geisha Boy!' Stewartie glared but wasn't too riled and told him to clear off before returning to the conversation with me and the bouncer. He hadn't seen the pile of South African rands that had been placed on the table behind his back, the stack of which the bouncer had slipped into his own pocket. It didn't mean anything to me at the time. What the bouncer did for his payment, as far as I was concerned, was his own business, so I didn't mention it.

Some time later the little sailor returned and said, 'You take my money, Geisha Boy. We go back to ship!' Stewartie protested that he was no Geisha Boy and that he hadn't touched his bloody money nor was he going back to any ship. Before it dawned on me that the bouncer had nicked the money meant for Stewart's services, the Korean, now agitated and aggressive, became forcefully insistent that Stewartie go with him and foolishly grabbed him by the arm. Stewartie gave him a bit of a dig, and the bouncer threw his remains out. (Stewart packs a legendary punch!) Too late to say anything now!

When we emerged from The Smugglers, we were met by an awful and terrifying sight. The little sailor had gone back to his ship and rounded up a posse . . . a large posse of around 100 crewmates, as mean and ugly as their leader, all armed with urban missiles. Now, J.J. Williams and Fergus Slattery were fast, phenomenally fast, but Stewartie and I would have given them a run for their money. No '99' call, no getting stuck in. With the quickest sprint our bodies and souls could muster, we legged it out of Durban docks, fearing for our lives as bricks and bottles rained down upon us. Still, it was an interesting night, and we had found peace away from the hotel.

TENNIS, J.P.R.-STYLE AND AMBULANCE RIDE, SOUTH AFRICAN-STYLE

ALAN OLD
FLY-HALF Middlesbrough
ENGLAND 1972–8, 16 caps
LIONS TOUR '74

Tennis, J.P.R.-Style

On the Lions tour to South Africa in 1974 we spent the first week getting used to the altitude around Johannesburg (around 3,000 ft above sea level, if I recall correctly). We were staying in a small mining town called Stilfontein, whose mayor assured us that every facility in the community was available to us. Taking advantage of this offer, J.P.R. Williams rang the tennis club to see if they could arrange for him to play against a local star. It should be noted that some years previously J.P.R. had won Junior Wimbledon – no mean feat!

Anyway, the telephone conversation between J.P.R. and the secretary of the exclusive Stilfontein Tennis Club went something like this:

> J.P.R.: Hi! I'm with the British Lions and would like to play tennis with one of your local stars. Can you arrange this?
>
> SECRETARY: Sorry, this club is 'members only'.
>
> J.P.R.: But the mayor said that all facilities were available to us . . . and I play for Wales!
>
> SECRETARY: Yes, *that's* why you are on the tour.
>
> J.P.R.: No, I play for Wales at *tennis*!
>
> SECRETARY: Sorry? Wales don't play much tennis, do they?
>
> J.P.R.: OK, I won Junior Wimbledon five years ago. Does that count?
>
> SECRETARY: Oh yes, sir, we'd be *honoured* to have you play – I'll make the arrangements.

So, one evening a couple of us accompanied J.P.R. to this exclusive tennis club – we had trained all morning and played soccer and various other games all afternoon. Not surprisingly, we were all a bit sweaty and dirty and still in our training gear.

When we got to the court, the local champion arrived . . . absolutely immaculately kitted out in cream sweater and shorts, a freshly pressed white Fred Perry shirt, sparkling-white Dunlop Green Flash shoes, white socks carefully folded over and a shining white Frew McMillan cap. He carried a pristine green towel, six Dunlop Maxply racquets and three boxes of new tennis balls. J.P.R. was wearing: blue Adidas training shoes, red Wales socks, faded blue shorts, a red Adidas T-shirt and, adding to the sartorial elegance of the outfit, a muddy white knee bandage and headband. The single dark brown racquet with no name on it, which he carried casually, had obviously seen better days!

The result: J.P.R. won 6–1, 6–0, 6–0. With true J.P.R. magnanimity, he then thanked his opponent for the game and apologised for not playing very well because he was a bit rusty!

Ambulance Ride, South African-Style

On the Lions tour of 1974 I had the misfortune to be badly injured in a game being played on the outskirts of Cape Town. As it was a game involving the Proteas from the Cape Coloured community, the medical arrangements were rather basic, and after being helped from the field and carried into the dressing-room by other Lions players I was left with Phil Bennett to await an ambulance that was to take me to Cape Town for treatment. A local doctor had splinted my right leg, because he had diagnosed severe damage to the right knee ligaments.

Whilst we waited, there was no real discomfort, but the wait was over half an hour. Eventually, St John Ambulance arrived. The doctor came in with the ambulance crew and explained what to do with me and where to go in Cape Town. He asked them if they were familiar with the Medicentre building, to which they said that they were. They were to take me to the 16th floor, where arrangements had been made for me to see a consultant. I should add that the crew was one very small, nervy male and one large, confident female and that Phil Bennett was to accompany me to the hospital.

So, I was carried outside to the ambulance and placed on my back onto a platform down one side of the ambulance. Phil had to travel up front. Now, the car parking at the stadium was chaotic, and many latecomers had just gotten as far into the car park as they could and had then abandoned their cars. Therefore, despite setting off for the most convenient exit from the car park, we soon had to abandon that route.

This required the male driver to reverse about 400 yards, and we appeared to be making reasonable progress when the female said, 'You're a bit close on this side!' The driver maintained he was OK, and to prove it reversed a little bit faster – crash! – straight into the back of a big truck. I was immediately catapulted into the air, off the platform and onto the floor. You can probably imagine the pain as the splint came off. There ensued some unpleasant words between the driver and crewmate before I was hauled back onto the platform and the splint reset.

Phil Bennett then insisted on getting out and guiding the driver the remaining 50 yards to a point where we could turn and head to the main exit. Successfully negotiating the 50 yards, Phil got back in. However, the driver decided he would give himself a bit more space to turn round so backed up even further – crash! – straight into another parked van. The result was the same: me on the floor, splint off and pain as bad as the initial injury.

Once again, I was placed on the platform, the splint was tightened and we set off on the 30-mile journey to Cape Town. We met with no further incident until we approached the outskirts of the city and the driver said to his mate, 'Do you know where this place is?'

'No!' she answered. 'Do you?'

Then Phil reminded them that they had told the doctor they knew where it was.

'Oh, I wasn't going to let him know that we didn't know. He would think we are amateurs.' No comment!

The farce continued as we drove along the ring road of a very large city, keenly looking for a building with 'Medicentre' on it. After a while, the driver gleefully said, 'There it is!' despite Phil pointing out that this was the Medipark. Regardless, we parked, and they put me onto a trolley, wheeled me in and went up to the 16th floor in the lift. On arrival we walked about 50 yards to a reception desk, where the female crewmate triumphantly announced that they had brought the injured rugby player as arranged. This news was met with confusion and astonishment, as no rugby player had been expected and, indeed, people with such injuries were normally sent to the Medicentre. Phil then took over and got directions to the correct destination, ensuring that the remainder of the journey passed without any further mishaps. Fortunately, as soon as we arrived at the Medicentre there was a professional crew on hand to facilitate a safe and effective transfer.

Just think, if I hadn't suffered a serious injury, Phil and I would not have had this glorious, memorable experience!

LIONS: BIG CATS AND LITTLE CATS

CLIVE REES
WING London Welsh
WALES 1973–83, 13 caps
LIONS TOUR '74

Andy Ripley: what a player, what a giant of a man. Known for raw power on the rugby pitch, his tall frame all knees and elbows, the ball tucked under one arm, he used to burst through tackles with an awesome aggression that intimidated and usually overcame the opposition . . . if they could catch him in the first place! No wonder he was selected for the Lions tour in 1974. Andy had spirit in abundance, driven from a fire within, piercing intellect that questioned everything around and beyond him, and was oft-times a bit of a philosopher, pondering and contemplating complex issues with a compassionate soul and a heart full of humanity. He is also the softest, nicest person I ever shared a room with.

At our training village in Stilfontein, Andy, the tough-minded, self-composed, committed athlete, took time out from the strict discipline of training and preparation, not to break free from the pressure cooker of competitive rugby in an indulgent recreational binge but to adopt an abandoned, blind kitten. He admits that he really should have drowned it, but being the big softie that he is he decided to take the little cat on tour with him.

His room was chaos! Saucers of milk and cat scat were everywhere, and he had a special compartment made in his kit bag for transporting the tiny creature. After a few days, W.J. McBride discovered that Andy was intending to increase the touring party to 31! He fixed Andy with his legendary Ballymena glare, a scowl that conveys exactly the measure of disapproval it intends, and told him that the cat would *not* be a member of the party. This was a Lions tour!

Reluctantly (captain's orders had to be followed), Andy advertised the forlorn little animal in the local paper and interviewed dozens and dozens of people to secure the best home for the kitten. What a lovely man.

THE LEADER

STEWART McKINNEY

Among my many captains I had two great ones: Tom Kiernan followed by Willie John McBride. When I was first capped, the back of the bus was dominated by Willie John, Sean Lynch, Ray McLoughlin and Slats – the hard core. Once Willie became captain, he moved up to the front of the bus, probably because he felt that to remain at the back might be viewed as cliquish.

Willie was a charismatic leader, and he also led by example. I had spent days with him digging turf and clearing trees at the back of his house and was very aware of his huge natural physical strength. I wouldn't like to have argued with him.

On the '74 tour his leadership was never more needed than during a vital period in the match before the third Test when it seemed our unbeaten record was under threat. Call them foolhardy, daring, brave or stupid, but the Orange Free State had put their bodies on the line and killed every loose ball. You'd have almost thought the referee was in on the act, allowing them to do so, and with a minute to go they looked like a front-line casualty station at the Somme, as we had shoed and raked them all afternoon. They didn't look like they minded. The pain was a worthy price for our scalp on which they had claims.

Enter Willie John. A penalty to the Lions. 'Give me the ball,' he ordered and set off with great malice in his heart towards their biggest forward, a giant called Stoffel Botha. He knocked him over, and the seven of us rucked him out. Botha tried to get up, but his legs wouldn't work, and he wobbled and wobbled like a punch-drunk boxer. 'This man is not fit to continue,' declared Willie, and he dragged him quickly towards the touchline, where the Free State bench were frantically trying to get a reserve ready. In those days a doctor had to do an examination before the substitute could go on, but nevertheless in those last few desperate moments we needed to lessen the odds to eight forwards against seven.

Down to the last scrum – one point in it – Free State, with their seven-man pack, put in, won the ball and kicked it into touch – game over, the Lions lost.

It couldn't happen.

Free State put in, their seven-man pack was hurtled back and the Lions won the ball. Mervyn Davies picked up and fed Gareth Edwards on his outside, who ran diagonally towards the touchline and threw the ball over his shoulder to J.J. Williams, who scissored in to score.

Willie John went straight to the referee. 'You can bring that man back now if you like,' he said, 'because the game's over.'

What a leader!

LIONS OR WARTHOGS?

MIKE BURTON
PROP Gloucester
ENGLAND 1972–78, 17 caps
LIONS TOUR '74

Each and every one of the characters on a rugby tour has a side to him that the public rarely sees. So, apart from the lasting friendships that are conceived on these tours, there is always a cupboard full of memories (some printable, some not!) to cherish.

On the 1974 Lions Tour to South Africa I became firm friends with Stewart McKinney, a rambunctious back-row forward for Ulster and Ireland. We were often paired together for the daily training routine, and more often than not enjoyed one another's company during the evening.

The tour lasted for three months, and we played twenty-two matches, including four Tests. Between the second and third Tests, the management, in their wisdom, decided that the team should take a short break in the Kruger National Park for relaxation and recuperation. We did our bit of elephant spotting from the back seat of a Land Rover driven around by one of the game wardens, who seemed to know every inch of the wilderness. Although we saw rhino, buffalo and giraffe, there were no sightings of any lions, despite our guide assuring us that they were there in abundance.

After a couple of days, McKinney became bored with the daytime game-spotting activities and playing cards with the rest of the team. The evenings were more eventful, however. We had dinner on our laps around a camp fire, and things usually deteriorated into playing the silly drinking games that rugby teams are famous for. No one could escape, and only a sissy would refuse to play. As a result, some of the team members would wake up the next morning feeling less than pristine.

We all slept in rondavels. As the name implies, they are round buildings with a thatched roof, and they were situated just around the open area and the camp fire. One morning McKinney declared his intention to 'run off' the excesses of the previous night with a long jog in the midday heat, outside the safety of the compound, which housed the rondavels. 'You could do with a run, Burton. Do you want to come with me?'

I looked around for support from the captain. Willie John McBride sat comfortably in his chair and shook his head. Willie came from Ballymena in Northern Ireland, which was not very far from McKinney's home in Dungannon, and he knew that running in the midday sun was not for him – or any other sensible man. Significantly, no one else volunteered.

McKinney, unperturbed by any sort of logical argument, set off towards the huge wire exit gates, which were designed to keep out the dangerous wildlife that lived in the nearby wilderness. In that climate, everyone lives in shorts and trainers, and there was no excuse for me in trying to claim that I was not suitably attired to go running. So it was that I set off with him, the two of us running through the gate, up the hill, onto the cobbled road (until such time as the cobbles petered out) and then onto the red dust that led away from the safety of the compound and out into the wilderness.

McKinney, as a back-row forward, was always a little bit quicker than me. I, like most uncomplicated props, was built for comfort not speed. The pace did not worry me at first, but I later began to struggle. Words of encouragement from McKinney did nothing to make me feel any better, and I began to wonder if this was a world-record attempt or the gentle jog he had promised.

McKinney was now uncompromising. 'Come on, Burton. It will do you good.'

The relentless pace continued, until I was distracted by rustling in the nearby undergrowth. Just a few yards from the track I saw a patch of brown beast that was certainly a lion. My vocal cords deserted me as I tried to call out to McKinney, by now running 40 metres ahead of me. I turned back and ran as fast as my legs would carry me. On stopping to steady myself, a backward glance saw McKinney still heading away from the compound.

I called, 'Stewart, a lion,' and pointed to the undergrowth that he still had to pass on the return run to the safety of the compound. The track back was slightly downhill, and once he had become alerted to the desperate situation he set off on his toes back in my direction.

Within a few yards of the compound gates, I felt sufficiently confident to stop and look back. I saw McKinney pass the point in the undergrowth where the rustling had been heard. The change in his facial expression was discernible from a distance, and his pace quickened.

Now past the undergrowth and running downhill towards the camp, a male warthog burst onto the road behind him. The beast was slightly darker in colour than a lion but was big enough to be mistaken for one in the undergrowth. It was accompanied by a 'wife' and several small piglets. None of them gave chase, but McKinney had no time to look back.

I was doubled up with laughter and still standing outside the compound gates when he arrived back, blue in the face and breathless. I put my hands on his shoulders, turned him around and pointed up the track. He saw the offending warthogs grazing on the roadside as if nothing had happened.

McKinney staggered back to the seclusion of his rondavel, convinced I had planned the whole thing and swearing revenge at the first opportunity.

MUD HUT MADNESS

FERGUS SLATTERY
FLANKER Blackrock College, Leinster
IRELAND 1969–84, 61 caps
LIONS TOURS '71, '74, 4 Test matches

The South African Rugby Board arranged a midterm break for the most successful side to have visited their shores to a beach resort on the Indian Ocean . . . WRONG! They sent us to the Kruger National Park to view 'Ellie the Elephant' in the wild with no clothes on . . . EXCITING!

Day 1: viewing Ellie with no clothes on.

Day 2: viewing Ellie with no clothes on again (optional) or 11 a.m. to 11 p.m. beer, lots more beer, even more beer, beer again, beer and perhaps too much beer.

Fuck it, have another beer and another beer and another and then . . . no more beer, aargh! Then there were two – me and McKinney. It was dark, very, very dark, and Ellie wasn't about, so the long trek to the mud hut commenced with great reluctance and considerable difficulty. Mud huts in the Kruger all looked the same, even more so in the dark and particularly when vision was blurred by alcohol. The only difference between them was what was inside: biped Lions.

McKinney spotted a mud hut, remarkable given the darkness, inhabited by 'Killer' Tommy David. Hmm! Without slurring, a suggestive and seductive whisper with an Ulster accent sighed on the night air. 'See that dead tree there? Wouldn't it look a lot better inside that mud hut?' It was like a siren's song. Acting upon the suggestion, the campaign to transplant the dead tree began in earnest. But? Hesitation, deliberation, inspiration and then another slowly revealed thought expressed itself, 'First, let's scratch the door!'

Scratch! Scratch!

Silence.

Scratch! Scratch!

'Who's there?' Killer's voice enquired.

Silence.

Assembly at the launch pad. Countdown . . . ten, nine, eight, seven, six, five, four, three, two, one. We have ignition and . . . lift off! The tree sailed majestically though the air, seemingly in slow motion, its trajectory true to target: the window of Killer's hut and hopefully onto the floor, missing the player.

SHIT! We'd forgotten that Gareth was sharing with Killer. Too late now! CRASH! SMASH! SPLINTER!

Barely seconds elapsed before Killer burst through the door. 'Who the fuck? What the fuck?'

And the moral of the story is . . . don't go to bed before McKinney!

THE '99' – FIGHTING IN SOUTH AFRICA

BOBBY WINDSOR

The one who started the tour off on the right foot was Stewart McKinney when he walked back and laid out that bastard Springbok – that's what set us all off in the right fashion. He walked back, rounded a lovely hook and dropped the fella stone dead. [Laughter.] And he just walked back to the lineout. [Laughter.] That was the best one!

SOUTH AFRICA

DISAPPOINTED? I WISH I'D NEVER BEEN BORN

TOMMY DAVID
FLANKER Llanelli, Pontypridd
WALES 1972–6, 4 caps
LIONS TOUR '74

My mother was proud of me, my father was proud of me, my whole family and village were proud of me. I had made selection for the British and Irish Lions 1974 tour! I was going to South Africa with the greatest players in the world. Legends of the home nations would be my teammates. I too was filled with pride. I worked hard to ensure that my selection was justified and that I would give a good account of myself. Tears, sweat and bloody-minded determination were grist to the training mill in readiness for the battle on the 'Dark Continent'.

I bonded with my fellow players, gave 100 per cent in training and prepared myself mentally for the challenge that lay ahead, despite the negative press and anti-apartheid demonstrations. Millar and McBride drove us hard, and we responded with commitment and honesty. I was to play in the first match against Western Transvaal, donning the red jersey of the Lions (such a lovely Welsh red), ready to contribute to a historic contest.

The team with the first points on the board would most certainly take the psychological advantage. If the Lions could get the points up there, it would be a blow to the arrogant confidence of the partisan Western Transvaal. From the first scrum we knew it was going to be tough. When Gareth Edwards had asked whose ball it was and the ref had replied, 'Our ball' – meaning Western Transvaal's – it was clear that we were in for a hell of a tour and that this match would be a defining moment.

We were ten minutes into the game, with either side yet to score. The Western Transvaal number 10 kicked a high ball towards our posts. Anticipating a scoring opportunity from the opposition, I did my defensive job and ran back to cover when the ball bounced in front of me and went between my legs and over the try-line. To my shame and horror, the number 10, having charged the length of the field to follow up his kick, touched down and scored. A successful conversion followed: Lions 0, Western Transvaal 6.

Returning to the halfway line disconsolate, humiliated and angry with myself that I'd let such a stupid error result in a soft try, I turned to Willie John McBride and said, 'I've let the players down. I should have closed my legs. The number 10 wouldn't have scored then.'

87

McBride glowered at me with fury and frustration etched into his face and retorted, 'Your mother should have closed hers – 26 years ago!'

RUGBY IN SOUTH AFRICA

ROY McCALLUM
SCRUM-HALF Western Province
SOUTH AFRICA 1974, 1 cap

Our father Jim, a Glaswegian, always wanted to play for the Jags (Partick Thistle) and then Rangers. This did not happen, but he did end up in Northern Rhodesia and captained Northern Rhodesia against FA Cup-winners Newcastle United in 1952. Jackie Milburn, Joe Harvey and Frank Brennan played for the Magpies at that time, and Ian and I got to keep the FA Cup in our bedroom for a few days. We both played football at junior school until we started commuting to boarding school at Rondebosch Boys School in Cape Town. I took an instant shine to this game called rugby. The teachers who coached me were of a very special breed, and I think the grounding they gave us, including guidance on attitude and sportsmanship, was of the highest quality.

After school I spent a year at Stellenbosch University, where the great Danie Craven had a huge influence on all who played under his guidance. With Dawie de Villiers away with the Springboks in New Zealand in 1965, I was able to tour with the Stellenbosch first team to West Transvaal and Natal, my introduction to senior rugby, where I had to learn very quickly. In 1966 I returned to Zambia and played for Diggers RFC, which was comprised of some of the toughest miners you could ever hope to meet and play with. We had a great tour to Ireland with a side from the copperbelt region of Zambia that was virtually a full national team, as most of the players had represented Rhodesia. I had just turned 20, and what a privilege it was to tour with that team. We played Munster, University of Cork, Galway, Blackrock and Ballymena, meeting Willie John for the first time, and Queen's University, where Roger Young's brother-in-law Dennis Scott and I played together. He took good care of me.

After two seasons at UCT in Cape Town under Dr Cecil Moss, a great coach and friend, I took to the USA, where I studied at Palmer College of Chiropractic and graduated in 1971. Fortunately, rugby was growing in the Midwest, so we played many tournaments all over the States from Chicago to New Orleans and California. Talk about demanding, playing no less than five games in one weekend.

UCT invited me to tour the UK and Europe with them in 1968–9. What a great tour and such a great opportunity to meet wonderful folk. My brother Ian was playing full-back, and it was special for us to tour together. J.P.R. Williams played against us for London Welsh, and we could see already what a great talent he had. My highlight was playing against Barry John at the old Cardiff Arms Park. At one point, I tackled him, holding onto his right foot to prevent him drop-kicking when he casually dropped with the left foot. It was a marvellous tour – other than tearing my medial cartilage, which was my first real casualty relating to the game. I stopped counting the broken nose scenario after ten.

In 1972 I joined Villagers RFC, where I got to play alongside and get coached by the likes of John Gainsford, Dave Stewart, H.O. de Villiers and Lionel Wilson, who were all mentors of mine, where I am still an old crock. I think H.O. de Villiers was one of the most exciting players I ever played with. He captained me for a number of seasons, and with his astuteness, cunning and understanding of the game he was streets ahead of anyone who thought they knew the game. I think he would have been one of South Africa's best coaches if the game had not been so political.

My brother's last game for Western Province was my first, against Northern Transvaal at Loftus Versfeld. We won 14–12, with Ian scoring in the last minute, another great highlight. (Ian moved up to Natal to do his housemanship at Maritzburg Hospital.)

Playing for Western Province with Morne du Plessis as my captain was such a privilege. Despite him being a gentleman of note, you could go to war with this man, who was always ready to put his body on the line.

In 1974 my childhood dreams came true when I got selected along with Ian to play in the first Test against the Lions. It was rather a sad series for the Springboks, as the selectors lost the plot a bit. Nevertheless, the Lions were a well-drilled side, having beaten the New Zealand All Blacks a couple of seasons before. Willie John, with his great experience, and legendary stars such as Gareth Edwards, Phil Bennett, J.P.R. Williams and Fergus Slattery gave the Boks a lesson in teamwork, skill and passion.

The game has changed a bit as it has moved into the professional era, but my adrenalin still pumps when I go to Newlands or any of the other rugby stadiums to watch a Tri Nations or Super 14 match.

How blessed we have been to play this game and make lifelong friends. There is no truer saying than that of the old brigade when they get together: 'The older we get, the better we were.'

THE HARDEST SCRUM

STEWART McKINNEY

Springbok rugby had, down the years, prided itself on the scrum, and that's where Syd Millar, the most astute of coaches, decided to attack. 'If we destroy their scrum, we will destroy South Africa,' he stressed. We worked at the scrum from the first day at our training camp in Stilfontein. 'We will scrum, scrum and scrum,' said Syd, 'and when you're sick of scrummaging, we will scrum some more!'

God, it was hard! There was no scrummaging machine, so it was all live stuff – eight against eight, fifty scrums a day. If there was a forward short, that masochist J.P.R. Williams would rush to get into prop. The best full-back in the world relishing scrummaging practices – wouldn't happen today!

Port Elizabeth, 12 July 1974. The last scrummaging practice before the team had a chance to make history the following day in the third Test. A win and the series would be won. Our scrum was a bit higgledy-piggledy due to the fact that Roger Uttley, originally picked as a second row, was playing flanker on the Test side and Franny Cotton, selected as a loose-head, was packing down at tight-head. The dirt trackers' (those not selected for the Test side) scrum was, therefore, as follows: Sandy Carmichael (out of position at loose-head), Ken Kennedy, Mike Burton, Chris Ralston, Andy Ripley (out of position in the second row), Tom David, me and Tony Neary (out of position at number 8).

Willie John took the Test scrum to one side to issue final instructions while Ken Kennedy announced to us that it was our duty to make life as difficult as possible for them. We weren't going to be cannon fodder.

The two packs faced each other. 'Test side's put-in,' said Syd. Gareth put the ball in and, because we got all the basics right, the impossible happened! The Test side shot back, something that had not happened in the two previous Tests or any of the provincial games, in which the Lions' scrum had dominated. Willie John was incandescent with rage. I had never seen him so angry. He took the Test eight away for a good five minutes of McBride's own special brand of psychological therapy – and that meant big trouble. I wished that Kennedy had shut up.

Back they came. 'Reserves put-in,' said Syd – he didn't call us dirt trackers. John Moloney put the ball in. They destroyed us! Franny hit Sandy, and as the scrum disintegrated Ralston fell and got the full Pontypool and Jordanhill treatment. As he lay there in agony, holding his shoulder, he moaned that the pain was 'excruciating'. 'Get up, you bastard!' said Bobby Windsor, with his Welsh snarling sneer. 'If you can get a big word like that out, there's fuck all wrong with you!'

SAVED BY ERIC THE VIKING

ANDY RIPLEY
NUMBER 8 Rosslyn Park
ENGLAND 1972–6, 24 caps
LIONS TOUR '74

'The objective of rugby football is to produce a race of robust young men with active habits and manly sympathies,' said Rev. W.W. Ormonde, one of the three umpires (flags, no whistles) at the after-match function following the first rugby football international between Scotland and England in 1871. (Scotland won, four goals to three.)

Baby-faced Stewart Alexander McKinney, the Lions' blindside flanker and currently on a GBH charge following a fracas in a Belfast pub toilet, was five sheets to the wind at the after-match function in Pretoria. 'So you think you're hard, McKinney?' someone said as he reached out and took the gun from the sweet young Afrikaner's twin sister's handbag and roamed about the marquee in the grounds of the Union Hotel in Pretoria in a sort of 1974 Ulster Protestant way. No one was remotely interested in Stu's behaviour. It was just Stu, and that's what he did.

'Why does your sister carry a gun?' asked Christopher Wayne Ralston to the other identical twin. Chris and I had gone to an ice-skating rink with them earlier that morning, before the match.

'Because her boyfriend has just got out of jail on a dog-napping charge and blames her for him being sent to jail. He is looking to kill her, and that's why we were at the male strip club on Sunday at the Xanadu Hotel, when and where we met you, because we were too frightened to go home.'

This is at least what I think she meant to say, but it probably isn't word for word, as her English was as rubbish as my Afrikaans. But the sentiment is at least a sort of holding-pen for the truth. Chris said nothing, although he never said much. This was his ploy to attract attention, and it didn't usually work especially well, particularly with sommeliers. They just thought he was mute and teetotal. (Anyway, Chris can't even spell sommelier, let alone play one.) I had told Chris till I was blue in the face that 'deep' and 'brooding' might work, but that it was a long con when you were so big and obviously not blessed with a face like Tony Neary, who had perfected the silent, smouldering approach. For Nero, this non-speaking approach to human relations worked, as he had the basic requirement of actually being good-looking and desirable. For Chris, the same ploy was spectacularly unsuccessful but doubtlessly character building.

By this time, Willie had given Stu a bit of a stare, and the gun, safety catch back on, had found its way back into Margarita's handbag. Just another after-match function. The Saturday side had earlier that 6 July afternoon smashed Northern Transvaal 16–12.

To roll back a bit – well, a lot really – the 1974 tour was twenty-two matches and lasted about three months. Our first stop at the Union Hotel in Pretoria had been way back on 10 May, following our ten-day acclimatisation on the Highveld in Stilfontein. After dinner on Sunday, 12 May, Chris and I had decided to wander out of the hotel in the warm, still capital of Afrikanerdom, expecting to find, maybe, a post-service tea-and-cakes do at the local Dutch Reformed Church. I had, because I am extremely annoying (especially to doormen), reorganised the notice board, which had originally read 'Union Hotel', so that it now read 'Le Onion Hut'. Not very big or clever, but it made me laugh – every time. Bit sad.

Then, beyond the doxology of the blessing, we heard music. We followed the sound. Tina Turner's 'Nutbush City Limits' was rocking and rolling from the Hotel Xanadu just up the road! We were on the move like bushmen following the track, through the brightly lit foyer (Chris mute but doing a very good impression of brooding macho menace). Filled with expectation, we swept through the wooden door into the noisy, warm, high-pitched, blinding dark. A small round woman who was built like a marble said, 'You can't come in. It's hen night!' At least it was something like that. So, deflated, with tails between our legs, we walked back into the foyer and went and sat at the bar.

Then the world changed. The marble rolled up to the bar and said, 'Are you with the Lions?' We were dressed in our blazers. (Mine was later to be swapped for a zebra skin and then a stuffed booted owl.) Well, blow me if Chris didn't speak for the first time in living memory and said, 'Yes.' A huge conversation for him.

We were swept back into the centre of the universe. A small dim light shone upon the marble, who made introductions. 'Girls, two Lions for you!' It was like a bizarre reversal of throwing the Christians into the arena. We were immediately surrounded by acres of heaving, excited women. It was awful! For the first time in my life I had an inkling of what it must be like to be a woman going into a room of drunken, leering men.

I haven't really got the words, but in a repressive society women in particular become scary beyond the boundaries of scarydom when those repressions are momentarily dumped. Normally repressed, momentarily abandoned, wanton, inhibitionless women cloaked by darkness en masse can do dangerous things. Chris and I wimped out to the safety of the now distant bar.

Suddenly, we were saved! Eric the Viking entered (he was the official stripper booked for the hen night). We were totally forgotten and dismissed to the irrelevance of a far distant table, and that's where we stayed . . . cos that's where we met the two Afrikaner twins, neither of whom could speak English. Obviously, this was just perfect for Chris, because, as far as I knew, neither could he.

A race of robust young men with active habits and manly sympathies? Reverend, you would have been proud of us.

BY HIS WORD

STEWART McKINNEY

The tour was over, and as we relaxed on the plane home we reflected on aspects of it. Ian McLauchlan, small in stature, made of granite and huge in strength, was a remarkable player. He was a terrier, as hard as nails, and a man for whom I have the greatest affection and respect. We sat quaffing champagne, smug and self-satisfied, when he asked me what would happen next year. 'What do you mean?' I asked him.

'Next year, when we face each other in the Home Nations? If you make selection, of course,' he added. 'If you're killing the ball, as you always do, I can't make any allowances, you know, Stewartie. I'll just have to give you the slipper.'

'I'd expect no less, Ian. That's the way it is,' I replied.

The matter settled, we continued the flight in companionable camaraderie, relived some of the glorious tour moments and wondered what the future held for us.

I kept my place in the Ireland team and the following year had occasion to meet Ian when we faced Scotland at Murrayfield. The hard wee bastard wellied Dick Milliken. Of course, I sought retribution and, recalling the conversation on the flight home, gave him a good right hook. Ian went down, and while he was on the floor I lowered to one knee, ostensibly to re-tie a bootlace. As I leaned over him, I whispered, 'Remember that wee talk we had on the plane, Ian?'

BEST ROOMIE ON TOUR

ROGER UTTLEY
LOCK/NUMBER 8/FLANKER Gosforth
ENGLAND 1973–80, 23 caps
LIONS TOUR '74, 4 Test matches

The 1974 British Lions tour to South Africa. It was the midpoint of the 22-match itinerary. The Lions had won the first two Tests and were big news wherever they went. I was just pleased to be there. Aged twenty-four, I'd just completed my first season for England and had four caps to my credit. Life was good.

The Lions had just moved back to Johannesburg after some R & R in the Kruger National Park! We were booked into the President Hotel, which the team were not particularly happy with. I didn't mind because I was to share a room with Gareth Edwards of Wales. Already recognised as one of the greatest players of his generation by friend and foe alike, I really looked forward, with a touch of hero worship, to the experience.

Johnny Moloney, the Ireland scrum-half, was injured, which meant Gareth had played eight or nine games on the bounce. That's midweek *and* Saturday matches, so he needed a rest and was not chosen for the next game against Transvaal, but I was.

As soon as we got to our room the phone started ringing. 'Hello, is Gar there? I need to speak to him. I come from Cardiff/Swansea/Llanelli, etc., etc., and I want him to come out and have a drink, *braai* [barbecue], meet the wife, etc., etc.'

Gareth, being the nice chap he is, found it very difficult to disappoint people or have them take issue or offence, so quickly asked me if I could answer the phone to avoid this. 'An honour, Gar,' I said. 'It will be a pleasure!' With unfettered enthusiasm, I quickly slotted into the role of PA for the great man.

On the day before the match, Gareth, Broon from Troon and Mike Gibson were all invited out for a round of golf (senior-pro privilege and keen golfers) with Gary Player ('The harder I practise, the luckier I get!') after training. Gareth's parting words as he left were, 'Don't worry, roomie, I'll be back late, but I won't make a noise, as I know you're playing tomorrow.'

'Thanks, Gar!' I thought. 'What a considerate, top man!'

Having dealt with his phone calls, taken messages, put the laundry out and read a few pages of my first Wilbur Smith novel (banned at the time), I fell asleep dreaming of the great game I was going to play the next day. (Modern coaches would probably call this visualisation and mental rehearsal. I was just dreaming.)

My slumber was disturbed when I awoke in the early hours to the sound of a feeble clawing noise on the door and some miserable groaning emanating from the corridor. I rose to investigate and on opening the door discovered a dishevelled Edwards, who promptly fell into my arms slurring with his lovely Welsh lilt, ''Ello, roomie. Sorry, but I think I'm a bit pissed. BURP! And I'm not feelin' too great. I'm really sorry, 'cause I know you have to play tomorrow. Sorry, Butt!'

This edifying little speech formed a loop in Gareth's head, and he droned on endlessly about how sorry he was as I led him backwards and forwards to the bathroom and eventually to bed alongside the compulsory bucket. Unsurprisingly, he then fell into a deep sleep and proceeded to snore, as only drunks can, with resonance and a decibel level that defied the laws of science and nature. The night wore on with the sound of Gareth snoring loudly and relentlessly despite my best attempts to stop him. When I whacked him with a pillow, he just mumbled, 'Sorry, Rog,' and started snoring again.

The following morning found us both rather red-eyed but for different reasons. Gareth was extremely remorseful and grateful for the care and attention I had rendered in the early hours. 'Rog,' he said, 'you are the best roomie I've ever had – honest.'

'Gar,' I said, 'coming from you I consider that a huge honour!'

Needless to say, the Lions went out that afternoon and won. We were good at that. Unsurprisingly, however, the young 24 year old did not have one of his better games, but, then again, he was the best roomie Gareth Edwards had ever had!

BATTLE, BACK-UP AND BOBBY'S BIG MOUTH

IAN McLAUCHLAN
PROP Jordanhill
SCOTLAND 1969–79, 43 caps
LIONS TOURS '71, '74, 8 Test matches

In 1974, prior to the tour to South Africa, the Lions were sworn to keep our London hotel meeting place secret due to fears of demonstration, disruption and protests from the hugely vocal and well-organised anti-apartheid supporters in the UK. Each player arrived to find that only two people constituted the full 'mob': Peter Hain and his sister, who were eventually invited in to meet the players and join them for a cup of tea. Despite their strong opinions on the politics of South Africa, they were very reasonable people and fully respected our rights as young sportsmen to tour the country. We had occasion to meet again with Peter's sister when on our victorious return from the tour we were greeted by the leader of the Opposition, Edward Heath, who was hit by a flour bomb ... allegedly thrown by the same Miss Hain! Perhaps it was the elation and celebration of the moment or perhaps it was his politician's polished facade, but Mr Heath continued to smile benignly whilst brushing the flour from his suit. Three months of touring provided many memories from both on and off the pitch, and here are a few that still sit at the front of my brain with ready recollection.

Eastern Province was a team with a hard reputation and an ambition to soften up the Lions. Unsurprisingly, their main target was the stupendously swift and talented Gareth Edwards. Rugby is known for its physical intensity, and often the confrontations appear worse than they are, but as long as the assaults steer clear of between the legs or between the eyelids, anything pretty much goes as far as contact is concerned. On this occasion, a particularly unsavoury incident followed a lineout. Gareth was poked in the eye, dangerous and debilitating in any sport, and while our attention was diverted as a groggy Gareth left the field for attention Stewart McKinney felled the culprit with a marvellously agricultural 'haymaker'. (Often screened on TV as an example of violence in sport, Stewartie's actions are viewed out of context as an apparently unprovoked, random and thuggish act. Now you know the real story!) The restart lineout began with our South African rubs man, Dave Goddess, in scrum-half position, complete with water pail and magic sponge, until the cries for him to get off were finally heeded.

One of the R & R highlights for the squad was a tour on the Zambezi River. Everyone was spread out on the deck to take in the sights and maybe spot some of the larger game and river wildlife. However, rather than expounding the virtues of a balanced ecosystem, the beauty of the scene or indeed the destruction caused by illegal poaching, the guide chose to educate his captivated audience with tales of terrorist activity on the far bank, where only the previous week a tourist had been shot! Ulstermen Dick Milliken and Stewart McKinney both dashed below deck, reckoning it would be just their luck to cop a bullet in a foreign land having successfully survived the indiscriminate flak of 1970s Northern Ireland.

Back on the field and back in the battle, we resumed our purpose now that the rest was over. The South African players were hard, tough, gnarly, mean and unforgiving. Physical blows were given out and taken back without complaint. Each match was fully fought for on both sides, regardless of its Test stature. Pride, ego, kudos and reputation are all positive motives for success. Neither fear nor fatigue would stop our concentrated efforts. The competition struck up a notch with each meeting.

Transvaal fielded a team of giants against us, man-mountains each one of them. Their tight-head prop was Johan Strauss, not a musical man as far as I know and probably ticked off with the constant leg-pulling about his famous namesake. The atmosphere in the stadium was gladiatorial and partisan, heightened by the decision that both teams should come out together. Bobby Windsor, our hooker, spotted Johan in the tunnel and couldn't resist the quip, 'Hey, Johan, the mouse is going to tune your piano for you today!' Thanks, Bobby, for that one!!

BLESS HIS COTTON SOCKS

JOHNNY ROBBIE
SCRUM-HALF Trinity, Cambridge University, Greystones
IRELAND 1976–81, 9 caps
LIONS TOUR '80, 1 Test match

It's so hard to believe that our era is now the dim and distant past. We used to meet guys from the 1955 or 1962 Lions and think of them as curiosities. Now we are the same, curiosities from the old amateur days of rugby. Mind you, things happened then that couldn't happen in these hard-nosed days of the professional game . . . such as Tony Ward and his boots.

I sneaked onto the 1980 Lions as an early replacement for the injured superstar Terry Holmes. Despite the controversy of the trip in those far-off days, it was a happy tour, and the series, although lost, was close. At 2–0 down, the third Test in Port Elizabeth was the clincher. If the Boks won, they took the series; if it went to us, it was 2–1 with all to play for in Pretoria. The All Blacks and Aussies weren't especially strong at the time, so the game in Port Elizabeth was in effect the deciding Test of the World Series. It was that important.

The day was a shocker. It rained, hailed and sleeted so badly that as the Lions drove to the game, crowds leaving the old open stadium for the warmth of the hotels down the hill delayed us. We were thus late getting to the ground and had to change in a hurry. Nerves were taut to say the least. I was reserve scrum-half to Colin Patterson, and as was the norm in those days the replacements got changed and out of the way quickly so the starting XV could have their final, emotional build-up in private.

With five minutes to go Tony Ward, reserve fly-half and goalkicker, tapped me on the shoulder. He was ashen-faced and in a hushed, terrified whisper confided that he had just discovered that he had forgotten his boots. There was no chance of getting them from the hotel because of the chaos on the road, and as he has tiny feet little chance of getting a replacement pair from anyone else. There would be holy war if the captain and coach found out. As subs in those days only got on in the case of injury, I told him to say nothing. No matter what, say nothing.

The crowd had backed tight into the grandstand to avoid the rain, and we couldn't get from the changing-rooms to our allotted place in the stadium. The door was jammed tight by the weight of bodies.

As a result we were taken down in the lift to the car park and had to walk around behind the terrace, climb it, force our way through the crowd and make our way to the front of the grandstand. As all this took time, we heard the roar as the teams ran on and then the whistle to start the vital Test. To this day, in my mind's eye I can still see Wardy's stockinged feet sloshing through the gravel and water that had gathered on the ground. He cut a sad figure in front of me as we headed for the fray.

As we finally emerged we could see through the Stygian gloom that there was a stoppage in play. To our horror we realised that Ollie Campbell, the Lion's fly-half, was lying injured on the ground with blood pumping from a nasty head cut. Suddenly, coach Noel Murphy was present and looking our way. In that high-pitched Cork accent of his, he shouted, 'Warm up, Wardie, you're on.' Tony looked at his stockinged feet and then at me and I remember then got quite cross . . . with me! He asked what he should do, and I told him to pray. That was all that was left.

I know there is a God because Ollie recovered and lasted the match. To this day, I don't know if Noel Murphy, Billy Beaumont and Syd Millar know how close they were to watching their reserve fly-half and ace goalkicker taking the field for the world-decider rugby Test in his stockinged feet. Somehow I can't imagine it happening today.

A FIVE-STAR MEAL

STEWART McKINNEY

I sat down for breakfast in the Landrost Hotel, Johannesburg, a five-star establishment. Bobby Windsor joined me and I was glad of the company. When the waiter arrived to take our order, I asked for kidneys, bacon and scrambled eggs. Bobby, after a little thought, ordered cold sausages, greasy bacon, rubbery eggs and burnt toast.

'We don't serve food like that *here*,' the waiter sneered indignantly.

'That's bastard funny,' retorted Bobby. 'That's what I got yesterday bastard morning!'

THE NEW RULES WOULD HAVE SUITED ME FINE

JOHN O'SHEA
PROP Cardiff
WALES 1967–8, 5 caps
LIONS TOUR '68, 1 Test match

Saturday, 29 June 1968 – a day that is written in rugby history, sadly for all the wrong reasons, for it was the day that I became the first and thus far only British Lion to be sent from the field and remain there.

I had been picked to play at tight-head prop for the match on the Highveld against Eastern Transvaal in a town called Springs. The portents were not good: a year earlier on the same ground France had played Eastern Transvaal in a brutal match that had required the referee to blow early to avoid further bloodshed. In the wake of that match, one of the Eastern Transvaal players – if my memory serves me correctly, a flanker named Britz – had been suspended *sine die* (a little-known Welsh phrase meaning 'not likely to play again'). However, with the Lions in town, he was granted a permit to play, and a party of white hunters was sent into the bush to capture the flanker and bring him back to Springs.

As expected, the match proved a bad-tempered affair, punctuated by skirmishes that forced the referee, Mr Bert Woolley, to issue a general warning to the forwards against foul play, stating that the next man to offend would get his marching orders. Early in the second period, our half-back Roger Young followed his opposite number around a scrum. As he did so, Britz attacked him, and as I was on the tight-head it happened right in front of me. I took exception and immediately intervened on Roger's behalf. This was a big mistake, because whilst I was avenging this despicable act Eastern Transvaal scored their only try.

I found myself engaged with a number of the opposition in what appeared to be some sort of fisticuffs, although I might add that I was guaranteed to come second in any two-man boxing match. Mr Woolley, who had been temporarily distracted by the act of awarding a try, was presented with this scenario and made a summary decision.

'Number 3 off! Number 3 OFF!'

It seemed to echo around the stadium as the referee called out. Naturally, being a prop forward I wasn't sure what number I was wearing. I asked one of the wingers (they always carry a programme), and he confirmed I was wearing number 3.

Desperation was now setting in, to such an extent that I turned to

Delme Thomas, one of our second-rowers. He asked me where I was going, and I said I was going off.

'Why? Are you tired?' he asked.

'No!' I said. 'The ref's sent me off.'

I was now in panic mode, and so was Delme. He suspected that if I went off he'd be moved up to tight-head. He suggested that I go behind the posts with him for the conversion, hoping that because the opposition had just scored a try the referee might forget my misdemeanour. Now, front-rowers don't put much store in a lot of what second-rowers tell them; for example, 'I promise I'll push in the next scrum.' But this seemed like a good plan at the time. Sadly, Mr Woolley proved to have a remarkable memory for a referee and once again delivered his sentence: 'Number 3 OFF!'

Delme's last words to me as I headed off were, 'I think you're right, Tess! I'll see you after the game.'

This was the beginning of the end. As I approached the touchline, the crowd erupted and started throwing a variety of objects at me, including seat covers and large oranges with knobs on, which I believe are called *naartjies*. Throughout the tour we had noticed these oranges on sale outside the grounds, but we had never actually seen anyone eating them. It occurred to me that people might have been waiting for a British Lion to be sent off so they could throw them at him, and I can understand why South Africa produces so many good extra-cover fielders, because most of the naartjies hit me.

There was more to come! As I was about to leave the field a well-dressed gentleman came through the gate and approached me with his hand out. I thought he wanted to shake my hand in consolation, but instead he closed his fist and struck me on the jaw. Fortunately for me, Ronnie Dawson, our assistant manager, Tony Horton, Haydn Morgan, a '62 Lion now living in South Africa, and a number of South African police escorted me to safety. Unfortunately for my assailant, Willie John McBride jumped over the fence, took him in a head-lock and battered him in no uncertain terms, an act for which I'll be eternally grateful.

The Lions won the game with fourteen men, thirty-seven points to nine, which probably meant that they had played a lot better without O'Shea than they would have with him. The South African police charged my assailant with assault. I was told that he stated in his defence that the reason he hit me was that it was a very hot day and the toilet facilities at Springs were very poor. I am still not sure who he thought I was. He received a 200-rand fine.

They say that out of adversity great things can be achieved. That was certainly the case on this occasion. After my departure from the field, the management sent a message to me in the dressing-rooms via Keith Jarrett: 'Get dressed as quickly as possible, take your place in the grandstand next to the management and hold your head up.'

On arrival at the after-match reception, my teammates told me to lead them into the room, showing that I had their support. Although the judicial hearing had not been held at that stage, the management selected me for the next game against Northern Transvaal, a selection that should have gone to Tony Horton. This decision also indicated the management's support.

Because of the stand taken by the management, the crowd behaviour, the assailant and a favourable report from the referee, I only received a severe reprimand and took my place in the team as selected. J.B.G. Thomas, the leading sports writer of the *Western Mail,* took me aside at the team reception and introduced me to Bert Woolley, whom he had met previously when Woolley had brought a South African schoolboy cricket team to Wales. I offered my apologies and said that I understood his decision to send me off. We kept in touch and even exchanged Christmas cards for a while; in fact, 11 years later Woolley stated in an interview with a South African newspaper that under the current laws involving touch judges he 'would not have sent O'Shea off' on that fateful day in Springs – just a bit late!

The game has moved on, as have we all. Rules have changed; for example, in our day lifting was an illegal art form, now it's compulsory. In 1968 I was awarded the honour of being a member of a British Lions side, a side that included players who would go on to become legends of the game of rugby. However, 40 years later, at a reunion for the '68 Lions in London, to be with the lads again proved that long after the games had been forgotten, the special spirit and friendship we'd forged was stronger than ever. Rugby union and my fellow team members have given me a gift that is priceless. For this I will be eternally grateful.

PULLING TOGETHER, PULLED APART

PHIL BENNETT
FLY-HALF Llanelli
WALES 1968–78, 29 caps
LIONS TOURS '74, '77, 7 Test matches

The '74 Lions tour to South Africa will live in my memory for three reasons: the brilliant rugby played throughout the trip; the unbreakable bonds of friendship and loyalty between us; and the wonderful humour we enjoyed being among mates.

Willie John commanded so much respect and set the tone early on. We were not going to be bullied or intimidated, and our strength lay in our unity. Willie's motto was 'All for one and one for all!' We played together, fought together and drank together, and nothing could pull us apart. At least that's what I thought.

During the second Test against the Springboks in Pretoria, I ran through to score a try after sidestepping inside their full-back. But he caught me with his studs on my instep, and it felt like I'd been cut by a razor. As I limped back after scoring, the blood was pumping out over my boot, and Gareth Edwards came running across. His first words were, 'Don't worry, I'll take the conversion.'

At least I'd get more sympathy, I thought, when we had our break at the game reserve in Kruger National Park. Willie John had promised to look after me. To be fair, he carried me on his back from one hut to another. There were parties in every one, and the beer and wine were flowing. J.P.R. and Mervyn Davies seemed to be in all of them – still standing – but poor old Billy Steele was flat out on a pile of empty beer cans.

It wasn't long before it was getting very dark, and the only way Willie, still carrying me, could determine which was my hut was to feel the outline of the numbers on the doors. There were background roars and grunts and screeches from the animals nearby, and they seemed to be getting closer as Willie wobbled along the track with me hanging off his back.

Suddenly, I felt something crack me on the head as we tried to dip under the branch of a tree, and I fell on the floor in a heap. The blood was streaming from a cut on my head. There were louder grunts and roars, and in a flash Willie was off and running. 'Hey, what about all for one and one for all?' I shouted after him.

'Not now,' he said. 'It's every man for himself!'

FLOWER OF SCOTLAND

BILLY STEELE
WING Langholm, Bedford, RAF, London Scottish
SCOTLAND 1968–77, 23 caps
LIONS TOUR '74, 2 Test matches

The 1974 tour had its fair share of characters, all of whom played their part in ensuring that just as much fun was had off the pitch as on it! In keeping with the long-standing tradition of rugby touring sides, these recreational hours were often filled with a sing-song. As a Scot, I felt it my duty to contribute, my chosen number being the now famous 'Flower of Scotland'. Despite our large repertoire of Irish songs and the number of players heralding from the 'land of song', I was the only member fortunate enough to know the words. This stirring ballad soon emerged as *the* song of the tour, culminating in the team performing a live rendition at the BBC Sports Personality of the Year presentations the following December.

During the first few weeks of the tour, whilst rooming with the 'Duke', Bobby Windsor, I recall being woken up on more than one occasion to confirm the words. Inevitably, this resulted in the pair of us completing numerous full renditions before eventually dropping off to sleep.

On match days, in order to calm the nerves and tune in to the battle ahead, it became customary to sing on the journey to the ground, always culminating with a stirring performance of 'Flower of Scotland'. In fact, one of my most poignant memories is of one such occasion. As our coach pulled into the ground for the second Test in Pretoria, a vast crowd had assembled, waiting for our arrival. Unfortunately, we had only just completed the first verse of this rousing tune. Despite the best efforts of some disgruntled South African officials, we could not be persuaded to disembark. Not one of our party moved until we had finished the song in its entirety. To quote Willie John McBride on his thoughts during our procession from the coach to the dressing-room, 'There was no way the Lions were going to lose that day!' The rest, as they say, is history.

On the 25th anniversary of the '74 British Lions, celebrations were held in the capital city of each of the home nations. After enjoying the festivities that Edinburgh had to offer, the team set off on its leg to Dublin. A dinner had kindly been arranged at the Burlington Hotel, just outside the city centre. During the journey to the evening's entertainment, I had the pleasure of accompanying the always jovial Stewart McKinney at the front of the coach. Stewart has always been regarded as a bit of a Jack the Lad, but on this occasion he seemed unusually quiet and subdued. I enquired as to what was wrong, half expecting an account of the previous night's excesses. However, a hangover was the least of Stewart's worries as he informed me that he was in fact barred from the very hotel we were to visit. I immediately consoled him, simply explaining that any misdemeanours carried out 25 years ago would have been long forgotten. During the ensuing conversation, it emerged that Mr McKinney's violation had actually occurred no more than three weeks previously, after the England–Ireland Six Nations match!

On our arrival, I felt it my duty to have a quiet word with a senior waiter and explain the predicament – requesting that he perhaps approach Stewart and abruptly ask for his name. Sadly, the waiter's knowledge of British Lions tourists circa 1974 must have been hazy, as ten minutes later he stormed to the table and accusingly pointed his finger at an innocent-looking Sandy Carmichael, demanding if he was a Mr S. McKinney? Carmichael's retort was instant. 'No, but he is . . .' gesturing towards a now red-faced Stewart McKinney. I never did find out the reason why Stewart was not welcome, but the look on his face confirmed that he hadn't been joking!

MENDING RELATIONS AND DEFENDING REPUTATIONS

ALAN MORLEY
WING Bristol
ENGLAND 1972–5, 7 caps
LIONS TOUR '74

In 1972 I made my England debut against South Africa in Johannesburg. At that time we had the ignominy of being the Five Nations wooden spoon holders. Despite facing the unofficial world champions and expecting a heavy defeat, we won, and I scored the only try. Then, in 1974, I was called up as a replacement for Clive Rees during the victorious Lions Tour. My parents were on holiday in Europe, and I had no way of notifying them.

Ten days into the tour I turned right coming out of the tunnel of the East London Rugby ground and bumped into my parents . . . word travels. The Lions management had known of their presence, and the result was a unique tour, both for them and for me.

One incident, which sticks in my mind to this day, was the evening following the victory over Northern Transvaal, which many considered the fifth Test. Celebrations were in full swing at the hotel, and the forwards were 'thoroughly enjoying themselves' whilst we backs were quietly sat in the lounge! The hotel manager, having earlier that evening voiced his concern, felt that things had gone far enough (perhaps too far) and was threatening to call the police if the roistering didn't desist. Our captain appeared in the lounge in an attempt to calm the manager, who was having none of it. 'Even though you are the British Lions . . .'

Finally, after negotiations had failed and the manager was about to carry out his threat, Willie John removed his jacket and began rolling up his shirtsleeves. 'How many will be coming?' he asked the manager, laughing. The manager, unaware of Willie John's sense of humour, imagined all sorts of potential damage to the hotel, including its reputation if it was associated with a fracas involving the all-conquering British Lions. Reluctantly, in a damage-limitation decision, he pleaded with Willie John with as much dignity as he could retrieve from the impossible situation, 'Look, Mr McBride, this has to be the last time.'

'Oh, don't worry yourself. The boys are only having a little fun.'

Crisis averted, relations restored.

WATER

STEWART McKINNEY

Willie John had an aversion to water – the drinking kind, that is. I don't know what advice his witch doctor gave him up in Moneyglass, his townland, but it was against all the theories of dehydration. There were no people running onto the pitch in 1974 to relieve the ravages of thirst. 'If I catch any of you swallowing water, you'll answer to me!' he'd threaten. 'Just rinse and spit it out!' You might get the odd wee sneaky in and take a little swallow as you were rinsing, but such was McBride's power that you didn't risk a full mouthful.

The result was, in my case, weight loss of up to 7 lb during a game. In the dressing-rooms after the match it was the same. 'Don't drink water. Have a Castle Lager.' The dehydration mixed with the altitude and the beer used to cause me to hallucinate at about eight o'clock on a Saturday night, and anything after that – fire hoses, guns, etc. – was not my fault but down to Willie John's policy on water intake.

Well, blow me! Didn't he give the 1976 Ireland team going to New Zealand the same advice? The Irish Rugby Football Union had taken counsel, and, in their wisdom, thought it better to break up the journey to Auckland by stopping in Hong Kong, as this considered step would decrease the effects of jet lag. Although Willie had retired, he came to the Shelbourne to advise us on the forthcoming tour. He was inspirational, but when asked about Hong Kong he had the likes of Willie Duggan, Moss Keane, Pat Whelan and me licking our lips in anticipation. 'The Irish team that went to Australia in 1967 stopped in Hong Kong. Half the side went down with gastroenteritis and couldn't play in the first three games in Aussie. Whatever you do, don't drink water or take ice in your drinks. Please believe me. Drink beer.'

And we did! We should have flown directly to New Zealand. The stop cut down jet lag, right enough, but we had terrible hangovers when we arrived in Auckland.

GARETH – GRIM AND GRITTY DETERMINATION

DICK MILLIKEN
CENTRE Bangor, Ulster
IRELAND 1972–5, 14 caps
LIONS TOUR '74, 4 Test matches

The first Test was played at Newlands on a very heavy, muddy pitch on a rainy day reminiscent of the usual conditions back in Ireland. One of the crucial scores that victorious day was a dropped goal by Gareth Edwards. He broke down the narrow side from a ruck, and I anticipated a pass would come to me. There was nothing on, no real danger to South Africa and we were running on a particularly heavy part of the pitch. The 'Genius' stopped, looked up and dropped one of the most magnificent goals I have ever witnessed. It wasn't a beautiful or typically classical dropped goal that flew high through the posts but remarkable because I am convinced that when he dropped the ball to execute the kick he was momentarily stuck in the mud. Only his immense strength, grit and grim determination overcame the laws of gravity, and the ball, heavily suspended in time, managed to clear the bar.

It wasn't the prettiest or the subtlest skill I saw on the rugby pitch in South Africa, but, in its own way, it was an act of pure genius. I remember running back wondering how on earth he had managed to drop that goal. Even now I can still hear the great thud that converted a no-danger situation into a significant three points. I suspect, given the same conditions, I should spend the rest of my days in emulation of such a feat without success.

Genius is often the simple things done well. This incident, one of many on a great tour, was one of those moments of pure genius. It was great to have witnessed so many.

OPEN-DOOR POLICY

TONY HORTON
PROP Blackheath
ENGLAND 1965–7, 7 caps
LIONS TOUR '68

1968 Lions Tour, Salisbury, Rhodesia

Though we were not encouraged by the Labour government of the time to visit Rhodesia, the Lions had made a commitment to play and were made most welcome. Rhodesia had an open door to any visiting team who braved the politics of their country to visit them. The match was played on a Bank Holiday Monday, with a tremendous reception being given to the Lions on their arrival at the Police Ground.

Later that evening the hospitality continued, and the Lions were invited to a superb party. So relaxing and enjoyable was the party, with plenty of refreshments, that things got out of hand and a door was damaged in the process. Perhaps it was symbolic, perhaps an ironic protest – who knows? Regardless of the reason, the hotel manager was none too happy and informed the Lions management that the police had been called. Now, some observers might think that Willie John asking the manager *just* how many police would be coming was intimidating, but really it was only that dry Ulster humour of his, evidenced by the following whip-round that had the damaged door replaced in time for breakfast!

A LITTLE LOCAL DIFFICULTY

BOBBY WINDSOR

I'm from an ordinary working background, and I never knew – I don't boast about it – about this discrimination and what this racial thing was all about. I never gave it a thought. I played down in the Valleys with black blokes, and I never even gave it a thought. But when I arrived in London at the hotel there were all these people with bloody placards around the car, shouting about apartheid and all that.

Phil got out of the car and said, 'What's all this about? What's this "apartheid" on the placards?'

I thought they were Wales supporters giving us a send-off. I said, 'I dunno. It must be Welsh for "All the best"!'

I'd never heard the word before in my life.

DISPARATE AND INDELIBLE

IAN McGEECHAN
CENTRE Headingly
SCOTLAND 1972–9, 32 caps
LIONS TOURS '74, '77, 8 Test matches

Many memories are as clear as if they happened yesterday, simply because they were very special. I remember meeting up in London and taking in the fact that I was going to play in the same team as Gareth, Willie John and J.P.R.

Disparate memories, such as when Bobby Windsor asked what type of omelette he would like and replied, 'A bloody egg one, of course!' or sitting down with Dick Milliken after the first Test win in Cape Town and seeing the reaction on the faces of Syd Millar and Willie John. (They'd had many disappointments in South Africa.) Dick and I looked at one another – we'd never expected a Lions side to lose! With all those great players, it wasn't something that could be contemplated.

Other memories: flying in Dakotas to the Kruger National Park and the stewardess locking herself in the cockpit with the captain! Or landing in a field in George on the way to Cape Town to deliver the mail and then flying out through a pass between the mountains! Stewart McKinney's furniture appearing on a hotel canopy, 'Pickfords' having been at work again, or the hosepipe appearing at an after-match reception in Port Elizabeth. Some very expensive dresses and suits got 'damp' that evening.

Andy Ripley appearing at a De Beers reception in Kimberley with his bow tie round his neck and a T-shirt with the words 'I'm so perfect, it even scares me' on it. (But he had obliged – he had worn his bow tie!)

But most of all the silence in Pretoria as we mounted a record score and, in particular, the tries of J.J. Williams and Phil Bennett, and the enjoyment of a partnership in the centre with Dick Milliken that produced a very special friendship.

AND THE MORAL OF THE STORY

MERVYN DAVIES
NUMBER 8 London Welsh, Swansea
WALES 1968–76, 38 caps
LIONS TOURS '71, '74, 8 Test matches

If you don't like flying, then a rugby tour to South Africa is not really for you! Several of our party were distinctly nervous of being airborne. This was not aided by the fact that we flew twice a week for three months, all over the country. I doubt our choice of songs for the flight did much to assuage any doubts or worries held by the nervous, the anxious or the fearful.

Take-off song: 'We're leaving, on a jet plane . . . Don't know when I'll be back again.'

Landing song: 'Oh, this could be the last time, this could be the last time, maybe the last time . . . I don't know.'

It is difficult, I imagine, for those reading this to appreciate the abject panic that took place on one particular 'little hop'. However, picture the scene, if you will: a short three-quarters of an hour flight to East London airport in the Eastern Cape. Unbeknown to a number of our party, a bird had been sucked into one of the engines on take-off. Despite this bird strike, the engine was still operational, but for safety purposes we flew around for a while to lose some fuel before making a perfect landing – back where we had started.

Several others and I had not heard the captain explaining any of this over the tannoy, and it came as something of a surprise to find ourselves not in East London airport but back where we'd begun. However, a

Wales player had, and I heard a rather distressed and agitated Gwent accent saying, 'Didn't you hear what the fucking captain said? A fucking big albatross deliberately flew into the fucking engine and tried to kill us! These fucking South Africans will do anything to stop us fucking winning! That's it. I'm never flying a-fucking-gain!' (Fear and paranoia nearly always lead to speculation of conspiracy theories.)

Well, he and a couple of others (scared witless) didn't fly again ... well, not until the following week. They went by car to East London, a journey of nearly ten hours' duration. The rest of us waited for a replacement aircraft and were safely tucked up in our bunks while the grounded Lions still had a further five hours of bumpy, dusty driving to do.

If there is a moral to this true story, it could be: 'It took a little bird to bring the victorious Lions down to earth with a bump, something the might of the Springboks could not do.'

Another theory often quoted is that attack is the best form of defence. As amateur players we only had a small allowance on tour, a paltry sum, so it was a bonus to be allowed to make a phone call home. This perk was restricted to one call in three months, which was not to exceed £1 – anything more, you paid for yourself!

Halfway through the tour we were gathered on a coach for a trip to the Kruger National Park for some 'rest and recuperation'. However, the manager, Mr Alan Thomas, was not in a good mood. He stood up and addressed us all. In his sternest voice he announced, 'Someone has been telephoning home from my room! I've checked, it's been going on for over two months and the bill amounts to nearly 2,000 rand! I'd like that person to own up – if he would kindly do so now, nothing more will be said on the matter.'

Silence. No one moved.

Agitated now, he continued, 'All right. I'll give you a clue.' He paused and looked around in the hope that the culprit would come forward to avoid any further embarrassment.

Silence. No one moved.

'It's a Welshman!'

Still no one moved.

With irritation growing in his voice, he carried on, 'All right, then, I'll give you another clue. The telephone number is Pontypool 234!'

Bobby Windsor, the Test hooker and resident of Pontypool, leaped to his feet and cried indignantly, 'All right, then, which one of you bastards has been phoning my wife?'

As they say, the best form of defence is attack.

SECRET RENDEZVOUS

J.P.R. WILLIAMS
FULL-BACK London Welsh, Bridgend
WALES 1968–81, 55 caps
LIONS TOURS '71, '74, 8 Test matches

Unknown to the other members of the 1974 Lions party, my wife Scilla was in South Africa doing an internship at Addington Hospital for the duration of the tour. Wives on tour (in those days) was definitely not the done thing! However, it had been my wife's ambition to do some medical work in South Africa, and so it came to pass.

I arranged, clandestinely, to take her out for a meal in one of the most fashionable restaurants in Durban. Scilla knew I was paranoid about the other members of the party seeing me with my wife, so, in true cloak-and-dagger style, she colluded with me and disguised herself with a wig.

I was happy, she was happy and all was going well until after we were led to our table, where, to my horror and surprise, the diners opposite us were Willie John and Syd! I don't know who was more embarrassed. They thought I had taken some other woman out for a meal. (Shame on you that it should cross your minds!) It was only then that Scilla, to protect my reputation and diffuse any possible rumours, revealed her true identity.

All was explained, and with great relief I realised that the management thought the situation was perfectly acceptable. We proceeded to have a wonderful meal and an entertaining evening. I returned Scilla to her quarters at Addington Hospital, very relieved that the secret was out in the open and there had been no repercussions.

IF THAT'S THE WAY YOU WANT IT!

STEWART McKINNEY

Mike Burton and I were injured and were not considered for the first three games of the '74 tour. Western Transvaal, South West Africa and Boland were hard but fairly clean games. It was with great relish, then, that we looked forward to the encounter with Eastern Province.

Syd Millar was an extremely astute coach and through his underground information network had heard that Eastern Province were going to test our 'manliness', our stomach for the rough stuff. Would we be like previous sides and protest that this wasn't rugby and then turn the other cheek when they dished out the dirt? Syd's fears were confirmed when J.T. Classen, the Springbok coach, was seen entering the Eastern Province dressing-room and not re-emerging for an hour. (I don't know what he said, but I can guess, and if my guess is right, he had made the biggest mistake of his life.)

It was brutal! I was kicked twice in the throat in the first ten minutes. We were down to one scrum-half, as John Moloney was injured, and Gareth Edwards, captain for the day, was their big target. From one lineout – and I must say that our blocking was bad in that particular lineout – a prop came through the gap and smashed Gareth from behind long after the ball had gone – a cowardly act. Gareth was groggy, and when he gathered himself together he said to Hannes Marais, their captain, 'Cut it out, Hannes!' Hannes smiled. 'If that's the way you want it, that's the way you'll have it!' said Gareth.

No '99' was needed.

Burton left a huge gap in the next lineout and one of their props, Rowley Parker, thought all his wishes had come true . . . Gareth was about to receive a second helping. Parker woke up quite a while later – a Burton classic! Like the 'Hounds of Hell', Gareth let us loose, and we savaged them.

Now, Willie John, in his latest autobiography, said that I hit one of their players for no reason at all and that he crumbled like a pack of cards. I'd every reason for hitting him, as he was sticking the boot into Geoff Evans, and he was the one I suspected of kicking me in the throat. Edmund Van Esbeck, who was covering the tour for the *Irish Times*, reported it this way:

> Eventually Eastern Province realised that it would pay no dividend and Stewart McKinney, twice the recipient of a well directed boot, had the final say with as neat a left hook as I have ever seen delivered. It was a well-aimed and well-timed punch to the chin of flanker Van Eyk, and thereafter the match became a test of rugby skill. That ends the battle report.

The problem was that the punch was shown on a programme called *Violence in Sport*, and my mother saw it and wouldn't speak to me for months. She was ashamed, as she hadn't brought me up that way.

After the game, Gareth reiterated that if that was the way the South African teams wanted it, that was the way they would have it. The

South African press made a meal of it. There was uproar. However, when asked again on the Monday, Gareth said he'd had a slight concussion after the game and couldn't remember what he'd said. But he'd gotten the message across!

By the way, Willie John was a very caring captain and came out of the stand just before the final whistle to walk beside me as I came off the pitch in case any spectators attacked me for my punch on Mr Kerrie van Eyk.

RUNNING MAN

J.J. WILLIAMS
WING Bridgend, Llanelli
WALES 1972–9, 30 caps
LIONS TOURS '74, '77, 7 Test matches

They say that the modern rugby player is a fitter and faster animal than any rugby player in the history of the game. The class of '74 would easily challenge that statement. The running sessions on that tour would have tested any top athlete from any sport. I can always remember the so-called warm-up jog. It always took place on a huge expanse of field, with the squad starting off at a gentle pace. However, due to the competitive element within the team – especially Messrs Ripley and Moloney – it ended up more like a flat-out finish of a 400-metre race.

After this 'gentle' warm-up, Syd Millar always wanted to see his squad engage in murderous sprint sessions. As I had been an international athlete, a certain Fergus Slattery would test my reputation on every run. This smooth flanker would always stand next to me, and I found out that if I coasted on any run he would beat me and would remind me of it time and time again.

The only good thing about these killer sessions was that however ill you felt, you only had to glance backwards and see Tommy David with vomit hanging all over his hairy moustache to know that you weren't feeling quite as bad as someone else.

HEALTHY COMPETITION

BOBBY WINDSOR

Well, me and the boys always trained very hard. I mean, when we went on tours we only went drinking on a Saturday after the game – when we'd get a bit baldy – and we trained twice a day. And fitness was good, cos the training Syd put us through was the hardest, and that's why we got such good results. Without doubt, everybody, *everybody*, on that squad, even though we were all together and all best of mates, was fighting for a Test place, so when you did have your scrummaging practice or your practice game or whatever there was a lot of bumping and blood about, you know. But after the game, after the training and all that, everybody was together again. Everybody was focused on what they had to do.

However, Syd made a mistake when he said that if we won the third Test and won the series, we could all bugger off to the jungle. Well, we took him at his word, so we all went a bit AWOL after that! It must've shown in the fourth Test, cos we only drew!

ALTITUDE TRAINING

GEOFF EVANS
CENTRE Coventry
ENGLAND 1972–4, 9 caps
LIONS TOUR '74

As one of the junior members of the party that toured South Africa in 1974, the thing that made the greatest impression on me was the fantastic team spirit, both on and off the field. Most vivid, perhaps, is the memory of Andy Ripley and Mike Burton leading the dirt trackers in singing 'Keep Right on to the End of the Road' to welcome the Test side onto the bus before every Test. Bizarre and random and such unexpected levity prior to an international contest!

Humour permeated the tour. One of the most amusing off-the-pitch incidents occurred when we were on 'holiday' at the game reserve. The first night there saw us all relax and possibly have one or two too many drinks. Strange things happen when you're in a strange country, and we were out of our usual environment. Some players adapt quickly to new surroundings; others take a little longer. For some, it offers an opportunity for reflection on performance, improvements that might be applied. However, in the darkness of the African night a man's mind can become disturbed. There are wild animals that prowl through the jungle. Survival of the fittest – or the smartest – is uppermost in men's minds.

Whether it was an alcohol-assisted prank, an attempt to provide extra protection for a fellow player or an experiment in altitude training, I don't know, but when one player returned to his rondavel to sleep he could not find his bed. The look on his face the next morning when he discovered it 20 feet up in a tree was priceless!

JOURNALIST AND PURVEYOR OF FINE SAUSAGES

BILL O'HAGAN

> Bill O'Hagan, the man who brought the South African boerewors to the palates of England, writes about his father, flanker Ebbo Bastard, who played for South Africa six times between 1937 and 1938.

William Eberhardt (Ebbo) Bastard was born on 10 February 1911 in Kokstad in South Africa and died on 14 February 1949 after a domestic incident at his Franklin farm in Marshmead. He was the eldest child of Hector and Dorothy and became famous when he played rugby for the South African Springboks in 1937 and 1938. His involvement was a great cause for concern, as he was not invited by the South African Rugby Football Union to attend the trials at Newlands in Cape Town. So convinced that he should be there, the Natal Rugby Football Union sponsored their flanker and sent the uninvited Ebbo to the trials, where he was promptly selected for the tour to Australia and New Zealand.

He played, at the age of 25, in his first Test match on 26 June 1937, against the Wallabies, and he played his last Test match, against the British Lions, on 10 September 1938. From 1937 to 1938 he competed in six Test matches.

In 1937, the Springboks first visited Australia and beat the Wallabies 2–0. They then visited New Zealand, where they won their three-match series with the All Blacks 2–1. The All Blacks won the first Test but bowed at the next two. The 1937 Springboks are sometimes described as the best team to have ever played in New Zealand. Ebbo played in two Tests.

While in Sydney, two of the team's players were out on the town. They were Ebbo Bastard and Syd van der Fyver. After several 'tinnies', they attempted to climb a lamp post. A policeman confronted them and after telling them to behave asked them for their names. Ebbo answered 'Bastard', spelling it out, and Syd said 'van der Fyver'.

'No bastard is going to get a fiver out of me,' replied the astonished policeman.

Ebbo was the only Springbok ever to come out of Kokstad. But the club has produced many great characters and personalities besides the legendary Ebbo. In 1990 the Kokstad Rugby Football Club, affectionately known as the 'Blacks', celebrated their centenary, and what a memorable occasion it was, complete with commemorative centenary booklet outlining their splendid history, compiled and edited with the help of their elder statesmen John Vos, Gordon Dick and Gordon Eagle.

There can be no doubt whatsoever that the Kokstad club was founded in 1890, as the occasion is reported in the *Kokstad Advertiser* and *Transkei Gazette* on 2 May 1891. The club accepted its first black player in 1979 and has always been renowned for its exceptional hospitality, dating back to when it was founded. A report published in the 135-year-old *Advertiser* in 1891 says:

> After a game between Town and Country, the losers dined with the winners at the Royal Hotel. Mr G. Fowles featured on the piano while Mr R.T.S. Baker was the right man in the right place as chairman, although it was feared his many toasts were accountable for the numerous headaches the next day.

Needless to say, nothing much has changed since then, and the many clubs that travel to play at Elliott Park still experience that old-fashioned country hospitality.

Elliott Park, complete with the 116-year-old original clubhouse, was established in about 1932, and the first game ever recorded on the grounds was played in 1933. The ground was named after J.F.D. Elliott, a well-known personality in the area whose contribution to game and club was immense. His grandson Barry continued serving the club years later, while his sons Bryn, Kevin and Rex, all products of Maritzburg College, all played the game with distinction.

The club has produced a number of great players, including their only Springbok Ebbo, whose brother Cedric represented Natal. Many people believed that he too should have played for South Africa. Great Natal players such as Hannes Viljoen, Rex Greyling and Tiny Walker hail from the area, while legends such as Jimmy Wardlaw, Gus Brown, Roy Pringle, Eric Groom, and Graham and Billy King all contributed to the game with distinction in the district. It is also reported that former Natal-playing brothers Jules and Paul Langenburg originate from the area.

Ebbo went to Hilton College. A total of ten Old Hiltonians have represented their countries at the highest level. Of these Keith McMillan (Scotland) and Michael de Jongh (USA) turned out for countries other than South Africa. The Old Hiltonian Springboks are Ebbo, Paul Johnstone, Clive Ulyate, Brian Pfaff, Gary Teichmann, Bob Skinstad, Wayne Fyvie and Hentie Maartens. (Roddy Grant has also recently been selected to play sevens rugby for Scotland.)

When Ebbo left Hilton, he farmed for his father for a while before taking over Summerhill Farm near Cedarville and marrying Una O'Hagan, a Grey's Hospital-trained nurse and daughter of Kokstad's mayor, William O'Neill O'Hagan.

They later moved to Marshmead, from where Ebbo played whatever sport he could. He was an accomplished trout fisherman, hunter, cricketer, polo and tennis player, swimmer, bowler and, of course, rugby fiend.

BOBBY AND DICK TRAVEL IN STYLE
AND BURTON'S BUM MOVE

STEWART McKINNEY

Gordon Brown, the legend of Scottish rugby who won thirty caps between 1969 and 1976 and played eight Test matches for the Lions, touring in 1971, '74 and '77, was a fabulous guy, and his memory still lives on in the many stories he told and the ones he was part of. He was a great raconteur, and this book wouldn't be complete without some of his tales. These are the two of his that I love the most, and I'm sure Dick, Bobby and Burton would not be offended at their inclusion.

Bobby and Dick Travel in Style

Following a victorious Lions fixture in what used to be Rhodesia – now Zimbabwe, of course – a black-tie function was held at the prestigious Rhodesian Police Club. The evening progressed nicely, and it got to the point when the prime minister of the day, Ian Smith, rose to make an address. As with all the functions we had attended on tour, the hospitality that night had been fantastic, and sensing the speech had indicated an end to the occasion Dick Milliken and likely lad Bobby Windsor decided to return to the hotel.

Waiting in the reserved space at the club entrance was a beautiful Cadillac with black-tinted windows. Just ever so slightly influenced by the high spirits and the excellent hospitality of the evening (and very probably imagining their status elevated), they seized the opportunity to avail of the considerate transport arrangements provided – it would be rude not to accept a ride in this beautiful vehicle that had been laid on for the Lions – they slipped into the front seats and found the driver's keys waiting. They were tremendously impressed with the opulence of the Rhodesian VIP taxi fleet . . . It simply had to be taken for a test drive!

Five or ten minutes of joyous 'testing' later, to their surprise the partition separating the front seats from the back slid open! It revealed none other than the prime minister himself, who smiled calmly and said, 'Are you gentlemen looking for a job, because I'm advertising for a chauffeur?'

Burton's Bum Move

Our match against Border XV in East London turned out to be a pretty boring event and was without doubt no contest for Willie John's Lions. Thank God for stupidity and petty amusement! Mike Burton, our English prop forward, provided the only moment worthy of mention, but what a moment it was.

Mike's shorts had been ripped off him, thus requiring a replacement pair. Nothing funny in that ordinarily – it happens quite often in games. Mike ran over towards the main stand from the far side of the pitch, where the Lions baggage man managed to haul out a few pairs of new shorts. Mike, being a well-built man, found it a wee bit tricky to find a pair that fitted. The only pair that he managed to heave over his thighs and backside were so tight that there was no room for tucking in his jersey. His top, hanging outside his skin-tight shorts, was so long that he looked like he hadn't bothered with a replacement pair of shorts at all.

Mike made his return across the pitch to rejoin play, jersey flapping wildly around his legs, until he reached the halfway line and abruptly stopped, turned and glanced backward at the stand. Perhaps just a wee bit of a hint of the devil danced in his eyes. Slowly and teasingly, he lifted his shirt tail, eventually flipping it up in a flourish to reveal his hairy bare arse – the shorts had obviously been incapable of containing the expanse involved! After a couple of crowd-pleasing, tantalising bum wiggles for the stand's benefit, he eventually hoisted up his shorts (which were there) and managed to squeeze his bum tightly into them before running across to rejoin the match. Delighted with the hilarious diversion, the whole stand cheered in riotous uproar.

The tour manager, Alan Thomas, stared in disbelief, his face flushed red with shame, hoping that the match might continue without further episode or embarrassment. However, fate can often be fickle – and at times downright wicked – and barely ten minutes on Mike Burton was again detached from his breeches. Again he went to the stand for kit rummaging, and again he was poured into a pair of shorts that were far too tight for him, his jersey once more trailing over hips and thighs. This time the stand buzzed expectantly for a replay of the earlier burlesque. Mike, with his sense of humour, comic timing and showman's sense of occasion, rushed to the halfway line, came to an abrupt halt as before, once more gave a teasing glance over his shoulder towards the main stand and again reached for the lower hem of the jersey. The multitude gasped. Mike waited. They moaned their disappointment in unison. Mike Burton's rump *was* displayed but this time modestly clad in his replacement shorts. He turned toward us and wagged a finger reproachfully, giving a mischievous little grin.

TALES FROM THE FREE STATE

HAROLD VERSTER
FLANKER Shimlas, Orange Free State

I am Harold Verster, currently the president and managing director of Free State Rugby. I had the privilege of playing for Free State against the British and Irish Lions, captained by Willie John McBride, in 1974. My two counterparts who played against me that day were Fergus Slattery and Stewart McKinney.

We were leading 9–7 until the dying moments of the match when J.J. Williams scored in the corner. The Lions won 11–9. We lost one of our locks at the last scrum due to injury, and the replacement was not allowed onto the pitch before the scrum took place. The Lions hooked a tight-head against the Free State, and Gareth Edwards slipped the blindside and flipped the ball back to J.J. Williams, who scored in the corner. The touring side of '74 acknowledged the Free State to be one of the toughest teams they played against on that tour.

I was really surprised to bump into Stewart McKinney 35 years later, during this year's 2009 Lions tour. We were both at the pre-match function before the game in Bloemfontein, which was held at the rugby museum of the late Choet Visser, the liaison manager for the Lions in '74 and a very popular man.

Stewart and I had a lovely chat, and then he mentioned that he was soon to publish a book of rugby stories. It is indeed my privilege to put forward these tales for your consideration.

A Good Laugh with the Referee: Free State v. Bulls

When the Free State plays against Northern Transvaal (currently named the Bulls), it is usually a very tough and physical encounter. When Naka Drotske, the current coach of the Free State, and his team played against the Bulls in Pretoria one particular Saturday afternoon, it was the same old story.

Tappa Henning (a very well-known referee in South Africa) was officiating on the day, and he tried hard to keep the game clean and focused on rugby – but it was the same old story. Not long into the match, the players started to goad each other, push their opponents around and throw a few punches. Tappa immediately stopped the match, called the players together and indicated that he would not tolerate any negative play.

For a minute or two, everything was OK, but the dirty tactics started again, so Tappa called them back. He then instructed the two captains to talk to their teams and tell them to calm down. Once again, for a minute or two things improved, but then things got really out of hand.

Tappa stopped the game in its tracks, called all of the players together and said, 'I have had enough! There are about 12 referees on this pitch today, and it is unacceptable!'

Willie Meyerthe, tight-head prop and a man full of humour, immediately replied, 'Tappa, you are right. There are about 12 referees – and you are by far the worst of all . . .'

In the laughter that followed, Tappa could not help but end up with a smile across his face – and restart the match there and then. Free State won.

Stoffies' Big Plan

My lock-forward friend Stoffel Botha (known as 'Stoffies') played with me against the Lions in '74. He and Johan de Bruyn of the Free State formed a formidable and frightening pair for any opponent.

Earlier in the season, before the Lions match, we played against the Eastern Free State at Globe Park in a town called Bethlehem, right in the middle of the Eastern Free State. Stoffel Botha was born in Senekal, not far from Bethlehem, and he played his school rugby in the Bethlehem/Senekal district.

In those days, farmers would drive right into the stadium and park their *bakkies* (pick-up trucks) and cars on the eastern side of the stand so that they could sit in them and watch the match. This meant that you would hear the vehicles' horns being sounded by the farmers when they were enjoying the game or if they had a problem with the referee or whatever.

The Free State were struggling that day and just couldn't get enough points on the board. As it approached half-time, we were leading 6–3, but everybody expected us to win by a large margin, which was not happening. Then, close to the end of the first half, Free State got a penalty on the 22, right in front of our opponents' poles. Everybody turned around to call on our fly-half Jackie Snyman, who played for South Africa against the '74 Lions and who was a very accurate kicker, to take the penalty.

However, to our surprise, Stoffies decided to take the penalty himself and go for the line. As he picked up the ball and charged over towards our opponents, he saw to his surprise that the forwards were right there, waiting to tackle him. He changed his plan and tried to run around them, but they chased after him like a pack of wolves. He could sense humiliation so decided to go for the corner flag, but the pack got hold of him and drove him over the touchline at their ten-metre line. He had lost us about 12 metres! The farmers were all tooting their horns and laughing.

When Stoffel got up, he was red in the face, and he just stared at us all. No one dared to say a word. However, as he joined the lineout, Kleintjie Grobler, who also played for South Africa and the Free State against the '74 Lions, remarked, 'Stoffies, next time you try this kind of move, just ask us all for directions, please!'

Both teams could not help but enjoy the joke, and Stoffel had to take it and calm down. A good game was played, and, thankfully, we went on to win by a good margin.

Leon Schuster – The Comedian

Leon Schuster played hooker for Free State in 1974. He wasn't big, but he was quick and had a quick foot, surprising opponents from time to time with a tight-head hook here and there.

On one occasion, we played against a touring university side from Paris, and their number 8 was none other than Benoît Dauga. One of their centres that day was Jo Maso, who is currently manager of France. He was up against the well-known Joggie Jansen, the man who had tackled the '72 All Blacks almost out of the picture.

Schuster became famous for the movies that he produced later in his life, films such as *There's a Zulu on My Stoep*. He also composed numerous rugby songs and stories. One of his most famous songs was released before the 1995 World Cup and was called 'Heir Kom Die Bokke' (Here Come the Boks).

It was a tough match against the Paris university side, and the Free State pitch was a bit wet. At one point, Dauga got the ball in hand on our 22 and started to run like a runaway train towards the try-line. Leon Schuster chased after him and jumped onto his back like a cowboy. Whilst doing so, he even shouted, 'Yee haw,' but it did nothing to halt Dauga's stampede. It took two prop forwards to bring the number 8 down – about two metres before the line.

To this day, I can still remember the smile on Dauga's face when he got up and looked at Schuster – the man who had tried to tackle him!

Free State British

As you might have detected, we in the Free State struggle with the English language. We speak a strange kind of 'Free State British'!

On tour, when asked to tell stories about themselves in English, Free State players will often react with the very short and brief remark, 'No English!' This is because they are afraid to make mistakes.

Once on tour, when the lady at the shop counter of a chemists asked a Springbok player who was trying to buy some soap if he wanted it scented or not, his reply was, 'No, I don't want it sented. I'll take it to the hotel myself.'

COACHING
AND SELECTION

COACHING AND SELECTION PREFACE

Willie John often says that when he began to play international rugby the coach was the vehicle that took him to the ground! Today there are so many coaches, you'd almost need a coach to take *them* to the ground.

This section is related to coaching (and its close cousin, selection). I owe a great debt to my coaches, as they helped me so much – Ronnie Dawson, Syd Millar, Roly Meates, Noel Murphy, George Spotswood, Ken Armstrong and, of course, Jos Lapsley. When Stranmillis College ceased to function as a PE college in Belfast, Ulster rugby suffered terribly, as every year Jos Lapsley had sent his graduates to practise his principles throughout the schools and colleges of Northern Ireland.

Coaches inspire and motivate their players and form close relationships with them in order to see what makes them tick so that they can get the optimum performance from the team selected. Selection for a team is the first thing a player wants, followed by putting in an impressive performance to secure further selection. Being chosen or being dropped stirs strong emotions in players, and sometimes it is a player's endeavour to return to a side that shows his true mettle.

Stewart McKinney

THE WEIGHT OF SELECTION – A BURDEN UPON US

KEVIN FLYNN
CENTRE Wanderers, Leinster
IRELAND 1958–73, 22 caps

Having left school in 1957, I joined Terenure College RFC. I enjoyed an excellent season with the club, which was well coached and advised by the late Hugh Church and Michael Pender. Keen and ambitious, I decided to leave Terenure, as it was a junior club, and join Wanderers FC in 1958 to see if I could make my mark. Wanderers were captained by the late Boldy O'Neill, who was a very positive and enlightened player, and, again, I was lucky enough to be encouraged, coached and protected by a good team.

Good fortune smiled on me, and I met Ronnie Kavanagh, who in my opinion was pound for pound the best forward I ever saw or played with. He was years ahead of his time, visionary in that he promoted an all-round game with a carefully practised and well-executed repertoire of skills – that is, that passing, tackling, sidestepping and swerving were essential for each and every player regardless of his position. Of course, certain position-specific skills did need to be practised – for hookers and scrum-halfs, for example – but in general the squad needed to be prepared for every eventuality, including manoeuvres, and Ronnie helped me improve all aspects of my game.

I received some good press notices at that time; however, one well-meaning journalist (aren't they all?) suggested I was perhaps too light to play interprovincial rugby. Brian, my very clever brother, found a solution to the problem of my lack of bulk. He fashioned a seven-pound lead weight with a waist string that slipped into my jocks! The late Judge Conroy, a serious UCD Leinster and Irish committee man of some gravitas, was to weigh us in at one particular trial – in only our underwear! I'm a modest man, and I couldn't see how the seven-pound weight could be discreetly hidden in a pair of underpants. Concealment would be difficult if not impossible and discovery would be embarrassing and potentially career destroying. My mind was running away with itself as I panicked to conjure up a satisfying solution to the problem that confronted me. It turned out that I worried needlessly. My fellow players were a bunch of conservative and modest men, so the judge was shouted down on the grounds of decency, and we were allowed to wear our shorts, which convincingly disguised the bulge of the weight. (To my knowledge, eight players put the weight to good use.) I weighed in at 11 st. 3 lb, which apparently dispelled the press concerns about me being a 'lightweight'.

For at least two or three more years at Leinster and Ireland weigh-ins, the lead weight made an appearance, so to speak. Mind you, I most certainly would not have enjoyed playing with it in place!

I was off the international scene from 1966 to 1972, initially because of injury, and then due to other reasons that are no longer important. In 1971, Roly Meates, the Leinster coach, asked me if I was interested in trying out again for the province and hopefully starting a comeback to international rugby, which I did.

In 1972, I regained my place in the Ireland team thanks to the encouragement and support of Ronnie Dawson, the 1959 Lions captain. He was a good friend who helped me enormously and was captain of Ireland on the occasion of my first cap. Subsequently, he was a great administrator in rugby worldwide and Ireland in particular after a serious ankle injury had ended his playing career in the early 1960s.

To all who helped me in my rugby career, I give thanks ... especially to my clever brother Brian and the lead weight that gave me the start.

VICTORIOUS
The British Lions, led by captain Willie John McBride, arrive back in
London to the cheers of the waiting crowd (© Press Association)

THE LAST MIDWEEK MATCH
Eastern Transvaal: (from left) Tommy David, Gareth Edwards, Andy Ripley (back),
Stewart McKinney, Mike Burton and Chris Ralston (© Colorsport)

HOLDING THE BABY
Nico du Plessis Jr with Ken
Kennedy (courtesy of the Choet
Visser Rugby Museum)

I TOLD YOU TO HIT HIM THIS WAY
Stewart McKinney and Ian McLauchlan
with a stuffed British Lion (© Colorsport)

GET AWAY, BURTON, IT'S MY BALL!
McKinney and Burton work the ball back as Carmichael blocks,
Eastern Transvaal, 1974 (© Colorsport)

THANK YOU, SUBS AND DIRT TRACKERS
Victory after the third Test, Port Elizabeth:
Willie John McBride, Fran Cotton and Gordon Brown (© Colorsport)

THE DEADLY DUO
Ian McGeechan (left)
and Dick Milliken
(© Colorsport)

FREE STATE, THE BRAVEST TEAM
After the battle, the team are bruised and battered
(courtesy of the Choet Visser Rugby Museum)

THE GODFATHER WITH NELIE SMITH
Choet Visser (right) with Nelie Smith
(courtesy of the Choet Visser Rugby Museum)

THE LAST TEST
IN JOHANNESBURG
Hannes Marais,
Springbok captain
(© Colorsport)

Rapport
DIE HELE
VERHAAL
AN NELIE
N CHOET

DO AS YOU ARE TOLD!
Syd Millar coaching
(© Colorsport)

THE '99' CALL
Third Test, Port
Elizabeth, 1974
Lions tour
(© Colorsport)

BROONIE SCORES AGAIN
Bobby Windsor jumping for joy with Fran Cotton,
as Gordon Brown scores a try in the third Test (© Colorsport)

THE NURSERY
SLOPES OF A BIG
CELEBRATION
Tommy David, Bobby
Windsor (back), Gordon
Brown, Mervyn Davies
and Ian McGeechan
celebrating after
the third Test
(© Colorsport)

WE PLAYED
SOCCER, TOO
After winning
the third Test:
Tony Neary,
Ian McLauchlan,
Stewart McKinney's
back, Fergus Slattery,
Andy Irvine and
Irish Times reporter
Ned Van Esbeck
(© Colorsport)

THEY WERE
BOTH VERY
PRETTY
Stewart McKinney
with dolphin and
dolphin handler
in Port Elizabeth
(© Colorsport)

DOWN THE ZAMBEZI
J.P.R. Williams and Gareth Edwards (front), with Clive Rees and the rest of the gang, prior to the Rhodesia tour, 1974 (courtesy of the Choet Visser Rugby Museum)

ALAN THOMAS DIDN'T THINK SO
Andy Ripley wearing that T-shirt while relaxing in the Kruger National Park (courtesy of the Choet Visser Rugby Museum)

THE MAFIA
Fergus Slattery and Syd Millar (back row, left to right),Ian McLauchlan, Choet Visser and Willie John McBride after the last game of the fourth Test in Johannesburg, 1974 (courtesy of the Choet Visser Rugby Museum)

A FAMOUS FOUR BALL
Mike Gibson, Gary Player, Gordon Brown and Gareth Edwards during a game of golf, 1974 (courtesy of the Choet Visser Rugby Museum)

THE GREATEST RUGBY PLAYER OF ALL TIME
Gareth Edwards feeds his backs during the 1970 Five Nations Wales v. Scotland match (© Press Association)

HE COULD KICK AS WELL AS DANCE
British Lion Phil Bennett (© Press Association)

MY FAVOURITE IRISH BACK ROW
McKinney, Duggan and Slattery (© Press Association)

FOLLOW THE INSTRUCTIONS

STEVE SMITH
SCRUM-HALF Sale
ENGLAND 1973–83, 28 caps
LIONS TOURS '80 and '83

I arrived late for the 1980 Lions Tour in South Africa. In fact, late is an understatement! I arrived on the Tuesday of the last week to sit on the bench for the Saturday Test match!

On arrival on the Tuesday night I headed straight to the room of Bill Beaumont, one of my best mates and tour captain, and asked him a few questions. Bill said, 'Wait for the training session – you'll piss yourself!'

All was revealed on the Wednesday morning when Noel instructed the squad during the warm-up to 'pair off in threes'. I looked at Bill and tried not to laugh too much. However, I couldn't contain myself when only a few moments later we were told 'spread out in a bunch'! Bill then completely finished me off when he told me that at the start of the tour when the English, Welsh and Scots lads were looking completely confused, the Irish lads knew exactly what to do!

Noel Murphy was a lovely man, and at the end of the session he thanked me for coming all that way for just a few days and informed me that if the Lions were winning with two minutes to go, he'd get me on the pitch – we were 3–0 down in the series at the time, so I thought that this was highly unlikely. I then told Noel I'd rather stay on the bench to retain the unique position of being the only Lion in history never to have played a game on tour. Noel was true to his word: the Lions won the Test, and I became a quiz question and had a brilliant week!

THE KING

MICK HIPWELL
NUMBER 8 Terenure, Old Shootershillians, Leinster
IRELAND 1961–72, 12 caps
LIONS TOUR '71

Carwyn James utilised those members of the 1971 Lions squad who were not on the pitch by allotting them activities relating to match analysis. Apart from anything else, it made you feel useful and actively involved, and that you were making a valuable contribution to the overall strategy and game plan.

For one particular game, my brief was to gather statistical data regarding crossing the gain line. At the next team meeting, Ray McLoughlin, armed with my data, was having the better of an animated discussion with Barry John about the back line not crossing the gain line. Ray was a master of logic, and Barry was losing the argument. Frustrated and exasperated by the facts and figures, he finally blurted out with complete conviction, 'To hell with the gain line! Give me three quick balls tomorrow, and I'll score in the left-hand corner, score in the right-hand corner and then drop a goal!'

End of discussion.

A PENALTY KICK

STEWART McKINNEY

Today there seem to be coaches and specialists for every situation in rugby: attack, defence, lineouts, scrums, diet, liquid intake and kicking.

Ireland played Scotland in 1974 at Lansdowne Road, a game that was to win us our first championship since 1949. Now, I had kicked regularly for Dungannon at club level, but that was about it, apart from the very, very rare attempt for Ulster . . . and I certainly never had a kicking coach.

Dungannon had played NIFC the week before the Scotland game, and I had kicked four penalties, all from the left-hand touchline, and all from about 40 yards out. Mike Gibson was playing for NIFC, and he must have taken note. The Scotland game was only ten minutes old when Ireland were awarded a penalty . . . yes, on the left-hand touchline, 40 yards out. Gibson tossed the ball to me. 'It's yours,' he said, and I saw Willie John giving him a very dirty look.

Richard Harris gave me the video of the match some 22 years later, and I saw it for the first time with Bill McLaren's commentary. 'And it's a penalty for Ireland . . . and it's . . . well, believe it or not, it's Stewart McKinney from the Dungannon Club taking this one. I can see Willie John McBride telling the rest of the pack to chase it up [he was obviously not very confident of my ability as a place kicker].' There was a moment of silence . . . 'And it's over! They'll be celebrating this one back in the Dungannon clubhouse!'

Had Gibson told me the night before, I wouldn't have slept a wink. I never took another penalty kick for Ireland; in fact, I was never offered one. Still, I retain a 100 per cent record! Who needs a kicking coach?

JIMMY D. – LOST FOR WORDS

IAN BROWN
FLY-HALF King's Scholars, Malone, Ulster

My early connection with Jimmy D. began when he was coaching Queen's and I was playing for Malone. At that particular time, the early '80s, tradition was that Queen's were a young student XV who loved to keep the ball on the move. In contrast, Malone XV were regarded as very much a forward-orientated team, with backs who complemented this style. Therefore, when Queen's played Malone, it was very much a case of 'last man standing' to dictate the outcome of the game. But, as Jimmy D. and I later discussed, things were changing with regards to Malone's back play, whilst they still retained the philosophy of being a forward-orientated team. And so, as history has shown, Jimmy D. became the coach of Ulster, and I was to wear the number 10 during that era.

Jimmy D., being a man of vision and a brilliant strategist, started preparing Ulster for games in a way that many players had never experienced: increased training sessions, edited-video seminars and coach-player interaction, all geared towards ensuring good team organisation and understanding between players – in essence, the creation of 'Team Ulster'. And Jimmy D. always had the right words for the right occasion. It was almost as though, overnight, Jimmy D. had created a team that did not know the meaning of defeat.

One particular match sticks in my memory. Ulster were on the verge of becoming the team to beat in the Interprovincial Championship, and Munster, at home at Musgrove Park, were faced with the prospect of losing their crown in their own backyard. Friday night saw the Ulster squad, under the guidance of Jimmy D., arrive at Ginger McLoughlin's bar for the team's 'pint' before returning to the hotel and preparing for the match the next day. Saturday morning arrived, Jimmy D. talked to us for the last time before we left for the ground, departed the team room and left it to Willie Anderson and David Irwin to muster their troops for the battle ahead.

Historic victory was assured, and Jimmy D., as controlled (and analytical) as ever, asked me how I was feeling after such a marvellous win. I replied that it would be a bonus if we both woke up the next morning! A memorable night followed.

On the coach back to Belfast, a journey of some six or seven hours, the moment when Jimmy D. was lost for words arrived. As described, Jimmy D. had created a sense of Team Ulster. All the players momentarily suspended partisan club loyalties, camaraderie bonding everyone together into a single unit. A tradition on such a journey was to bag items of clothing and draw items from the pile to wear on the coach. As a consequence, sartorial elegance, even a good fit, wasn't guaranteed, depending on what you pulled from the lucky-dip bag.

Jimmy D., the consummate professional, kept the media and management entertained whilst his players enjoyed their little game. However, being very much a player's man (and having a wicked sense of humour) he had contributed his teeth to the bag. After all, what could happen to them?

Time moved on, the game ended, everyone got back into their own clothing once again and normality was restored. But what of Jimmy D.'s teeth? It probably occurred to him that delivering lectures at the university would be compromised by a speech impediment if he was minus his gnashers. How long would it take to get a replacement set made up and fitted? For the first time ever, we had Jimmy D. at our control. Being somewhat the elder statesman of the players, I had kept a constant vigil on his teeth and had instructed a fellow teammate to keep them safely until the appropriate moment arrived. Meanwhile, Jimmy D. contemplated the fate of his teeth, lobbed out the window or 'eaten' by someone – or perhaps worse! As to where they had been safely hidden, Jimmy D. never knew, and I never had the nerve to tell him.

As was a feature of the man, he was extremely respectful of the players he coached, but never again did he let his teeth out of his sight.

RUCK IT

ALAN McCLEAN
FLANKER Rainey Old Boys, Ballymena, Ulster
IRELAND B 1977 and 1979

During the 1970s Ballymena had a good all-round rugby side. Training was hard, but the Thursday-night sessions that took place out at the club grounds in Eaton Park in preparation for Saturday's match were slightly less severe, and there was usually more unopposed play. Keeping players motivated and maintaining fitness levels as well as practising skill drills and set-pieces was all part and parcel of the work the players and coach undertook in training. Thursdays were 'lighter' to avoid injury and to give the players an edge for the competitive fixture at the weekend. There was no excuse for not giving your best during the match – no gurning, no griping, just 100 per cent effort by an efficient team keen for victory and points on the scoreboard.

Our coach Maurice Crabbe always wanted the forwards to be involved as much as possible and would continually shout, 'Set up a ruck!' during these sessions and thus destroy the flow. Eventually, one of the characters of the side, Ed Curry, got so exasperated when he heard the shout 'Set up a ruck!' that he kicked the ball up in the air and shouted back, 'For fuck's sake. There's enough rucks in a game without setting them up!'

STEWART DID KEEP HIS PROMISE

ROLY MEATES
COACH/SELECTOR Dublin University, Wanderers, Leinster

In 1976, when preparing the Ireland squad for the forthcoming tour of New Zealand – Ireland's first overseas tour in almost a decade and one on which we came perilously close to winning a Test – I was conscious, being the coach, of the need to create every possible competitive advantage. While always focusing on the technical and tactical aspects of the build-up, I was determined that we would not be exposed in terms of physical fitness so enlisted the help of some well-known athletics coaches. This initiative must have had an impact, because, after one session, Phil O'Callaghan volunteered the quip, 'Roly, I think we'll be all right on the track, but I'm very worried about the field events!'

On reflection, Stewart McKinney might have been secretly honing his skills in the high hurdles or the steeplechase – given the dexterity with which he negotiated a challenge that I later presented to him in Wellington. Although the figures involved were almost laughably small, Stewart was the man in charge of what was then known as the 'players' pool'. This was the pocket-money fund conveniently topped up by revenue from the dispersal of match tickets allocated to members of the tour party. With demand for Test tickets so strong, I was concerned about one possibility and stated unequivocally, 'I don't want to hear about any of those tickets being sold above face value.'

Without hesitation, Stewart's equally unequivocal reply was, 'Never mind, Roly. You won't hear.' And, true to his promise, I never did.

WITHOUT GUIDANCE BUT WITH GREAT HELP

STEWART McKINNEY

Jos Lapsley started it all off. At the end of my last season at college he called me aside one day. 'Mr McKinney, I must tell you that at this stage of your career you'd be on a par with Ronnie Lamont if you could improve your tackling a little.' Now, Jos was a clever man and practised wonderful psychology on his students. He knew I revered Ronnie Lamont. I was also very proud of my tackling, so he'd sort of hit me with a low blow. He also knew that if he had told me to dedicate myself to the game and train every day that I would only laugh and say bollocks! He knew I had to set my own goals. I lay in bed that night and decided that I was going to dedicate five years of my life to chasing the dream of playing for Ireland. I would train every day, sometimes twice a day.

Today, someone of my age and of a similar ability would be in an academy with professionals advising him on diet and nutrition, skills, conditioning, strength, and what and what not to drink – and when. Today's players seem to live on pasta. I was in my last term at college, broke and starting off on my crusade. There was a big bag of Kerr's Pinks potatoes in the corner of the flat, and my mother would buy trays of two and a half dozen cheap hair-cracked eggs from Moy Park Chickens. That was my staple diet – never worry about cholesterol.

With all the training I was doing, this diet needed supplementing. On a Saturday night I would set off for a party – not to pursue the pastimes of the previous three years but to steal food that would be quickly hidden in the grip bag I always took with me. After a few weeks my colleagues got wise to the takeaway tactics. One Saturday night at a party in University Street the food was all set out in the living room, but a tray of salmon sandwiches had seemingly been overlooked and left in the kitchen. It was a smooth transition from tray to grip bag, and I made a swift exit, mission accomplished.

The salmon sandwiches supplemented the Kerr's Pinks and eggs up to the Tuesday of the following week. In the common room of the student union my great friend Mervyn Elder asked me if I'd nicked a load of salmon sandwiches the previous Saturday night. I nodded, and he creased up giggling and began to mew like a cat. 'We left you a loaf of Kitekat sandwiches, you eejit!' he finally managed to rasp out between bouts of laughter.

I have never seen at first hand the fitness programme of modern players. I'm sure it's very scientific and designed specifically for the individual. There was no such thing for me. I went to the library and read books on conditioning by Paavo Nurmi, the great Finnish Olympic distance runner, and on how the All Blacks got themselves fit. I wrote to Bill Shankly, and he wrote back, stressing the importance of Liverpool FC's pre-season conditioning work. So, it seemed that this conditioning thing was pretty important, and I started to run on the first of June every year, six miles a day for six weeks. I sought out my hero, Ronnie Lamont, and he preached the virtues of interval training. After the first six weeks, in mid-July, I'd start the interval work, cutting the long runs to one a week. I was lucky to be putting the shot for Northern Ireland at this time, and my club, Shorts, was also attended by the dedicated band of Beattie brothers, who let me join them in their sessions. Shorts Athletics Club also boasted Don McBride, a Northern Ireland sprinter, who worked with me on sprinting and bounding (plyometrics) as we got into August.

The best bit of luck, though, in this entire muddled training programme, was to start lifting weights with Michael Bull, who was lecturing at the Jordanstown Polytechnic. Michael was Great Britain's first world-class pole-vaulter and later became the Commonwealth Games decathlon champion in Christchurch, New Zealand. He worked the Buster McShane methods and theories that had helped Mary Peters run to gold in Munich.

My strength increased tremendously working with Mike Bull, but, funnily enough, even with all the Kerr's Pinks and Kitekat sandwiches, I stayed the same weight, 15 st., throughout my rugby career. At a body weight of 95 kg, I managed to dead lift 250 kg.

In a way I envy the young players of today, but I had great fun training, probably all the wrong way, and in my seven seasons playing for Ireland I was never once not available through injury. I must have been doing something right.

GREAT OAKS FROM LITTLE ACORNS GROW

JOS LAPSLEY
SCRUM-HALF King's Scholars, Loughborough,
Collegians, Ulster

Stewart McKinney enrolled at Stranmillis College to study to become a teacher, and that is where I first met him. He turned up at the college playing fields for the first 'fresher' trials and was prepared to play in any position just to get a game. I was impressed. His older brother Joe had played for the college first XV and was widely respected as a promising scrum-half. Stewart let it be known that he could also play scrum-half, but with his good physique and aggressive approach it was inevitable that he would find a place in the back row. He had an ambition to emulate the achievements of Ronnie Lamont, a former King's Scholar captain who had gone on to play for Ulster, Ireland and the British and Irish Lions. Stewart's adventurous journey from junior rugby was about to begin.

Some years before Stewart enrolled as a student, I was appointed to the staff of Stranmillis College as a lecturer in physical education. One of my responsibilities was to help students in the teaching and coaching of rugby football in schools. In a short time I became involved in coaching the first XV. This provided me with a unique opportunity to experiment with coaching and fitness practices. However, there was a minor problem. At my first coaching session, only six players turned up. No one had remembered to bring a ball, and those who had turned up were preparing to go home. I quickly realised that urgent action was required and asked them to get changed. Using a stuffed rucksack as a ball for some crude handling practices, we had a most strenuous session followed by hot showers and a visit to a local hostelry.

From that low point, King's Scholars RFC went from strength to strength, and ten years later the club received an invitation to go on tour to Canada to play seven matches, visiting Calgary, Vancouver Island and finally Vancouver. This tour was an outstanding success and a milestone in the history of the club. It was during this tour that I fully appreciated the immense potential of Stewart McKinney as a player and also as a leader. As one of the senior members of the squad, he played a vital role in both playing and training. Robin Godfrey, who had played as an outside-centre for Ireland and who was our medical officer on tour, agreed with me that if Stewart continued to apply himself to his future training and playing with the same dedication as he did on tour, he would play for Ireland in the years ahead. What we did not foresee was that he would achieve an even higher distinction, that of being chosen to go on tour with the British and Irish Lions to South Africa.

I was fortunate to be involved with student rugby for almost 20 years, and during that time I came to realise that rugby players aged between 18 and 22 need the opportunity to develop and add to their basic skills before being exposed to the rigours of first-class senior rugby. Those players with natural ability who are encouraged to work on the skills required for their position will have more resources to call on when they are eventually chosen to play at higher levels. To illustrate this point, King's Scholars, who were classified as a junior club, can proudly name a considerable number of former members who played international rugby: George Ross, Jim Stevenson, Ken Armstrong, Ronnie Lamont, Stewart McKinney, Ian McIlrath, Roger Clegg and Ronnie Hakin. Scott Kelso, who captained the King's Scholars touring team to Canada in 1969, played for the American Eagles. These players, when they were students at Stranmillis, had both the time and opportunity to prepare themselves from both a skills and a physical perspective in order to progress from senior-club to interprovincial and, when ready, international level.

Each year after the Schools Cup competition, people often ask why so few members of the successful cup-winning sides go on to play international rugby. I believe that this is a question that should be addressed by those who are involved and concerned with the future of rugby in Ulster.

As part of my studies in physical education, I was made aware that a teacher must take into account the stage of maturation that his pupils have reached as he plans his teaching/training programme for their physical and sporting development. This is vital in the teaching of rugby football. The following points are worthy of note:

- Children who have not reached the age of puberty will quickly and easily pick up physical skills that require dexterity and good balance. Many of the handling and running skills required to play rugby can be learned and improved at this stage. Those elements of the game that require good physique, strength and aggression are better left to a later stage of the child's development. Well-meaning parents should be given a cup of tea and hidden away in the pavilion!

- Having entered puberty, children will compete naturally and enjoy competitive games based on running and handling. The kicking of a rugby ball is a skill in itself and time should be devoted to teaching and practising punting, drop-kicking and place-kicking. Controlled tactical kicking should be allowed. The major emphasis during passing practices with this age group should be on good positioning to give and receive passes. Good technique and speed of passing will improve with practice. Confidence in their ability to pass the ball accurately will grow, and the players who have good running skills will make a major impact in games. Tackling should be taught in a controlled environment, and the children should be made aware of good and safe tackling technique. Non-competitive scrums and competitive lineouts should be introduced as a means of restarting the game after a stoppage.

- During puberty, aggression is natural, and boys will want to compete. This should be encouraged in all aspects of play. At this stage of development, controlled competitive games will be welcomed by the players, with the teacher encouraging improvements in all aspects of play, concentrating especially on individual skills. It is worth noting that at this age fitness comes naturally during a well-structured practice or competitive game. Fitness training as such is not required and indeed can detract from the main aim of the development of skill. Boys at this stage of development are rarely bored with repetitive skill practices, as they anticipate using them in competitive games.

- In late puberty and early adulthood, young men are eager to compete, and the more physical aspects of rugby can therefore be encouraged. Time devoted to tackling practice, again with the emphasis on correct technique, is time well spent, as safety and efficiency in this aspect of the game go hand in hand. Forwards must be made aware of the importance of set-pieces, with considerable time being spent on scrums, lineouts and loose play. It is important to note that there is a positive correlation between the safety of the players and an awareness of good technique in scrums, lineouts, rucks and mauls. This attention to detail applies to all aspects of forward play.

- Rugby is a running game! Possession of the ball allows a team to dictate the patterns of play. Whilst the forwards engage their opposite numbers, backs can use their speed to probe open spaces. To do this effectively, time must be devoted to the improvement of passing, to the positioning of the receivers and the angles of their running. These are not easy skills to master. It takes time to perfect them so that they can be carried out under pressure. Without them, however, players are unable to use and exploit the open spaces available to them and usually resort to repeated and aimless kicking.

- If players have been fortunate enough to have experienced this graded development of their rugby football skills, they will be better equipped to progress to their optimum levels within the game. Individual players mature at different rates, and some will get to the top of the rugby ladder earlier than others, as much depends on individual ability and physique. Good coaching should include motivation of the individual, and all the players should be encouraged to be ambitious. The one common factor that all successful sportsmen and sportswomen share is self-belief. Good coaching will help develop this.

I followed Stewart McKinney's rugby career with great interest from school through college and then into the senior ranks. He achieved all his aims not by accident or luck, but because of a single-minded dedication to all aspects of his game. Some critics bemoaned the fact that he lacked the speed of Fergus Slattery or the Gallic flair of Jean-Pierre Rives, but no one could question his positive attitude to training and playing. If he lacked sprinting speed, he made up for it with an intelligent appreciation of the flow of play and an uncanny positional sense. Selectors built the back row around him, and he rarely let them down. From those early days at Dungannon Royal, where he was content to play in any position, his rugby career progressed through his student days at Stranmillis College, where his dedication to the game set an example to fellow team members, to playing senior club rugby for Dungannon to interprovincial rugby with Ulster then representing Ireland with distinction and finally the ultimate accolade of touring with the British and Irish Lions. Stewart achieved success by steadfastly pursuing his dream.

POOLA, POOLA, POOLA

BOBBY WINDSOR

Well, we were very successful at Pontypool in the 1970s and '80s cos we had a very good team and Ray Prosser had us all fit. Swansea and all them wanted to cancel fixtures with us, you know, cos they were all gentlemen and what have you and said we were too rough. The press loved it, saying we were a lot of dirty bastards and all that sort of thing. I s'pose half the time they were right, but then again Pontypool had five forwards in the Wales pack at a time when the Wales team was successful, so whatever Ray Prosser was doing forward-wise he was doing right, hey. He was my idol when I joined Pontypool, because he was very famous in the Valleys, you know, and a proper donkey, but a great coach and a great man, a great man, one of the best men I ever met in the game.

PROBABLY, POSSIBLY, DEFINITELY, MAYBE

BILLY BROWN
WING Malone, Ulster
IRELAND 1969–70, 4 caps

It seems like only yesterday, but it was over 40 years ago this December in 1968. This was the height of the amateur era when selectors were chosen from each province to religiously attend each of the autumn interprovincial matches and at the end of the series select two teams to play in an international trial at Lansdowne Road. This prize at the end of the interpros always added increased significance to the games.

The teams were imaginatively named the 'Probables' and the 'Possibles' (perhaps not the most motivational of titles, but at least there was a chance to impress once on the pitch) and they both stayed the night before the game in the Shelbourne Hotel. I had a reasonably good series of games for Ulster and found myself selected for the Possibles, along with the great Noel Murphy from Munster, who was to captain the side.

Now, I had admired Noel's exploits for both Ireland and the Lions while I was still at school and was in awe of playing alongside him, hoping that his captaincy, knowledge and experience would add substantially to my very limited understanding of the game at this level. On the Friday night Noel made a point of seeing each of his players in the hotel, and his message was very simple and to the point. 'Team talk in my room at eleven o'clock in the morning. Don't be late.'

After a very restless night, brought about through a combination of nerves and an exceptionally warm room (to cater for the rich American tourists), I picked over my breakfast, waiting until time came to go to Noel's room. What was I going to hear? How was the team going to gel? I felt both real tension and excitement.

The rooms given to the rugby party were neither the most luxurious nor spacious, and the sight of 20-odd mostly large bodies in such surroundings really was a sight to behold. Noel called the team to order, and I thought to myself, 'Here it comes. A speech from a legend.'

He spoke quietly in that engaging west Cork lilt of his and said, 'This is a great opportunity and chance for you all, and they say that if the Possibles play as a team, they will beat the Probables. That may be so. The team talk for today is, *it's every man for himself*. Now let's go.'

That was it, and as everybody filed quietly from the room I was in a daze.

The game was played in a great spirit, and the time flew by. The Possibles did beat the Probables, Noel made the team and on that occasion I made the Enterprise train back to Belfast and had to wait until the 1969–70 season before being selected.

NEW ZEALAND

NEW ZEALAND PREFACE

Dungannon, my home town, has two very close links to New Zealand. The Earl of Ranfurly of Dungannon was appointed Governor General of New Zealand from 1897 to 1904. He was also president of Dungannon Rugby Club. In New Zealand he had an avid interest in the game and sent to England for a shield in 1902 that was to be a challenge trophy open to the unions affiliated to the New Zealand Rugby Union, and James Dilworth, a pupil at the Royal School Dungannon, was instrumental in the establishment of the Dilworth School in Auckland in 1906.

Ireland toured New Zealand and Fiji in 1976. At the end of the previous season many of Ireland's great forwards had retired: Ray McLoughlin, Ken Kennedy, Sean Lynch and Willie John himself. Dick Milliken's career had been tragically cut short by injury. Slats was unavailable for the tour, and the press gave us no chance; in fact, some cruelly forecast that we wouldn't win a game. We did a lot better than expected and won the second half of the Test 3–0; unfortunately, the All Blacks won the first half 11–0. But most importantly, under the leadership of Tom Grace, the tour was a huge social success and the happiest month of my life. I will bear the fond memories and the scars of the Canterbury game to my grave, but I regard those scars as battle honours earned in the toughest rugby environment of them all.

Stewart McKinney

COMMITTED? (P'R'APS HE SHOULD BE!)

IAN McILRATH
CENTRE King's Scholars, Ballymena, Ulster
IRELAND 1975–7, 5 caps

I had the privilege of touring New Zealand with the Ireland team in 1976. Every touring team of that era produced its fair share of characters, and this Ireland team did not disappoint. More stories, most of them untrue, have been told about Moss Keane than about any other player. I add to the list.

The Ireland coach on that tour, Roly Meates, was exhorting us to greater things during the course of a pre-match talk prior to our midweek game against North Auckland. Hamish MacDonald, a brute of a man and an All Black, was in direct opposition to our dear Moss on this occasion.

The ever-optimistic Roly had been cheered by our encouraging if somewhat unexpected early successes on the tour. He maintained that Moss would play a crucial role in the encounter and goaded him thus: 'Moss, you are playing great. We can win this, but we need you to win your battle. Can you take this man MacDonald out of the game?'

The silence was deafening. The response, when it eventually came, was typical: 'Roly, is that just for today or permanently?'

End of team talk.

P.S. We won!

THE BATTLE OF AUCKLAND – JULY 1966

RONNIE LAMONT
FLANKER King's Scholars, Instonians, Ulster
IRELAND 1964–70, 12 caps
LIONS TOUR '66, 4 Test matches

The 1966 Lions Tour in New Zealand was not going well. We were frustrated with ourselves, New Zealand rugby in general and New Zealand referees in particular. Since the beginning of July, the tour party had been on the back foot. It didn't help that we had lost to Otago and Wellington, and many people on the tour had come to the conclusion that if we were playing 'Cowboys and Indians' every match, the Lions were never going to be the cowboys.

I had been injured in the Otago match, paying the penalty of staying on the pitch when anyone with any sense would have come off. I had come back for the first Test at Dunedin, and we were hammered 20–3. By that time I had come to the conclusion that to survive New Zealand rugby, you hit first and asked questions afterwards. Our next Saturday match after the first Test was against Canterbury, who were desperate to beat us. It was a horrible match, which was won by a whisker. Jim Telfer, our captain for the day, in his after-match speech summed it up by saying, 'I did not think today's match dirty, considering that all rugby in New Zealand is dirty!' That went down well.

Have I painted you the picture? Here's the scene: 30 July, 55,000 spectators, muddy pitch, Auckland. The Ranfurly Shield holders were waiting for us, and they were going to win by any means. Two minutes into the match, at a lineout, an Auckland flanker kicked Noel Murphy right across the kneecap. Now, the thing I liked about 'Murph' was that he was keen to share his problems. Once the obvious and immediate pain had left him, he sidled up to me and muttered, 'We are going to get him.' We did. That was the start of the inglorious 'Battle of Auckland'.

Terry McClean wrote in his book of the tour that for 60 minutes of the match the temper was evil and for 20 minutes it was foul. By the end of the match, which we managed to win 12–6, I had given and received in about fair measure, and I had managed to score a try – an obvious highlight.

Mr Taylor's final whistle was a relief all round, and as we trooped off the field a spectator suddenly assaulted me. She was at least 5 ft nothing, 80 years old, rotund and the spitting-image of the famous Granny from the *Sunday Express* cartoon. Whilst she berated me, punctuating her dismay with violent strokes of her umbrella, she used a lot of expletives that grannies would not be expected to use! The situation didn't allow me the time to explain that really I had strong pacifist tendencies and that I was sorry to have annoyed her. How the mighty are fallen!

Directly behind me, bloodied but unbowed, was McBride. His ability to read the situation was classic. 'Do you always need to be looked after?' he growled, snatching the umbrella from supergran before breaking it in two and handing it back to her then shoving me through the crowd to safety.

It took a lot to live down the incident . . . as the only Lion to be beaten up by a granny. Naturally, I appeared before the tour court and pleaded guilty to damaging the image of the British Lions. It cost me a crate of beer.

SWITCHING CODES

JOHNNY GALLAGHER
FULL-BACK Askeans, Wellington; Leeds and London Broncos
(both rugby league)
NEW ZEALAND 1987–9, 23 caps

I have been teaching now for the last 14 years, and my pupils ask me a number of questions. One of the most popular is, 'Sir, you were so good at rugby union but so rubbish at rugby league. Do you regret switching codes?'

In 1990 I was quite big news in the rugby world. I had just been named World Rugby Player of the Year by *Rugby World & Post*. At the same time the Leeds rugby league club had approached me and offered me a five-year deal worth £300,000, a world-record fee at the time – and it was a part-time contract!

A number of factors conspired in me switching codes. They included the money (mortgage rates were running 21 per cent in New Zealand, and I always seemed to be in debt), family (all of my family were still in England, and after nearly seven years away I was feeling a little homesick) and the chance of a fresh challenge (I thought that league could offer me that).

My first big match was in the Yorkshire Cup quarter-final against Bradford Northern at Headingley, Leeds. Looking back now, it sort of set the tone for my time at Leeds. It was a Sunday afternoon in late August, and it was warm. Headingley had about 16,000 crammed in, with about half of the spectators hoping that I'd get off to a good start and the rest hoping for the worst.

It was roughly midway through the second half, and we had just hit the lead for the first time. Moments later I found myself with ball in hand, running down the right flank in front of the North Stand, soon to be hit high and low. Still managing to hold onto the ball, I slowly got to my feet to play-the-ball. I then found that I was standing opposite the Bradford and Great Britain winger Henderson Gill. Henderson was not a tall man – the top of his head came just below my chin. As I crouched to play-the-ball through my legs, he body checked me before the ball had touched the ground; in fact, it was at least two feet away from the playing surface.

Now, I would never claim to be completely knowledgeable about all the nuances of rugby league, but I did know that the opposition player had to stand a metre away and could not compete for the ball until it had hit the floor. Henderson Gill and the referee seemed blissfully unaware of this basic rule, and I found myself resetting the play-the-ball, only for Henderson to body check me again, this time catching me under my chin with his head. The Headingley faithful in the North Stand had seen enough already and were hurling all sorts of abuse in the direction of the Bradford player and the referee. I glanced over to the referee, hoping that he'd intervene and award us the deserved penalty. He returned my glance with the words, 'Bloody get on with it!'

Again I tried to play-the-ball, again I was checked, but this time I managed to hold Henderson off with one hand and roll the ball with the other. The ball was finally back in play. I then felt the dull thud of Mr Gill's head as it caught me on the chin again. I pushed him back, this time glaring at the referee. At last, he blew his whistle. Sarcastic cheers echoed around the North Stand, everyone waiting for the obvious penalty decision in favour of my team. But the man in the middle had different ideas. He penalised me for retaliation, and when I quizzed him on his decision he said in a thick Yorkshire drawl, 'Welcome to rugby league!'

The next three years at Leeds were not much different, although there were a few good points (squeezed in between the late hits, high tackles, cheap shots and usual verbal abuse) before I signed for the London Broncos and had a very enjoyable and eventful couple of seasons with them.

DEAR OH, DEERO

STEWART McKINNEY

Seamus Deering (Deero) was a gem of a man, and I loved him . . . as a person and as a rugby player. Shay was Ireland's pack leader in New Zealand in 1976 until his tour finished in Auckland, the result of a cheap shot. Well, it didn't finish his participation completely, as he immersed himself in the day-to-day running of an international tour. He asked to be permanent duty boy and threw himself with great vigour into looking after our needs.

I think he must have felt that I needed a drinking partner the next Saturday night after we had played Canterbury in Christchurch and pursued that cause with so much fervour and enthusiasm that we didn't return to the hotel until seven o'clock the next morning, still in our number-one tour uniforms, with the intention of grabbing breakfast and a few hours' sleep before moving off to Invercargill and Southland.

Now, Ned Van Esbeck was the rugby scribe for the *Irish Times*, and a very good writer he was too. We became friends over the years, and as a devout Catholic he always said that he would one day get me to accompany him to Mass – me being a Protestant from Ulster.

When Deero and I were just about to enter the dining room, Ned emerged from the lift. He looked at the pair of us. 'Some things never change,' he said. 'Seamus up early for Mass and McKinney just back from a night on the tiles.'

'As usual, you're totally right,' said Deero, and off they went to worship.

For once I was too gobsmacked to say a word.

THANK FOG!

BRYAN WILLIAMS
WING Auckland
NEW ZEALAND 1970–8, 38 caps

My story relates to a couple of my old All Black teammates, Jon McLachlan and Andy Haden. Auckland had played a game against Canterbury at Lancaster Park and had lost badly, 42–3. Fergie McCormick, the All Black full-back, had passed 2,000 first-class points on the same day, and some people felt he was well on his way to the next 1,000 – a reasonable excuse for celebration by anybody's standards. The Auckland coach, Eric Boggs (himself an ex-All Black), was, however, annoyed at his team's performance so imposed a curfew after the game. Everyone was to be in bed by 10 p.m. (Not likely!)

Anyway, the party (it was going to happen regardless) was in full swing at about 2 a.m. in one of the rooms. Andy Haden, always a practical joker, decided to play a prank on his mate, Jon McLachlan. He picked up the phone and dialled a number. Jon's wife, Linda, had gone to Pakatoa Island, a resort near Auckland, for the weekend. 'Jon,' he called, 'I've got Linda on the phone for you.'

Jon grabbed the phone. 'Is that you, darling?'

The voice on the other end of the phone said, 'No, it's Eric Boggs here.'

Jon immediately responded with, 'What are *you* doing in Pakatoa, Eric?'

Tee-hee, tee-hee, snigger, snigger, came the sounds from the various party animals present in the room. The next minute, however, all the players fled as the irate coach burst out of his room in search of the perpetrators. Bodies leapt into cupboards, under beds, wherever they could find cover and concealment.

Boggs wasn't a pretty sight when he was displeased – a somewhat 'clouded' All Black – and his mood had been foul after the loss of the match. He burst into the party room to find a very bewildered Jon staring at the phone in complete puzzlement.

Jon had to face the music the next day: the enquiry about the party, the breaking of curfew and the phone-call accusation. The only thing that prevented him from being sent home was that the airport was closed by fog.

RUGBY SUCKS!

WAKA NATHAN
FLANKER Auckland
NEW ZEALAND 1962–7, 14 caps

My rugby had been going well. I had been lucky enough at the age of 19 to be a member of the Auckland side that had enjoyed a good run in the Ranfurly Shield, I'd toured the Pacific Islands with the New Zealand Maori team and in 1962, when I was 22, I'd made my debut for the All Blacks when they'd toured Australia. Good health and good fortune also meant that I'd been selected for the 1963–64 five-month tour of the British Isles, France and Canada that was to take in thirty-six matches, a match every three to four days.

Things were looking good until I turned out at Llanelli in December – New Year's Eve, in fact. We had expected a hard game. Our matches in Wales had shown the closest scorelines, and our only defeat to date had been against Newport in the third match of the tour. At half-time Llanelli were leading the All Blacks 8–3. During the second half, I made a break and had only their full-back to beat. I crashed over the line for a try but was tackled from in front and ran into the opposition player's elbow. I'd scored, but I'd also broken my jaw, although I played the full game.

A day later the team was announced to play England at Twickenham. My jaw was killing me – I couldn't chew porridge! However, I went out on a training run, and it was clear as the pain shot through my jaw with each step that something was wrong. This could be a major problem, so, of my own volition, I went to see a doctor, and the X-ray confirmed that my jaw had been broken in two places, resulting in it being wired. I was told that I'd be out for eight weeks, which would have meant no further participation in the tour – the last match was against Vancouver on 24 February. I missed the Twickenham game, and that sucked!

A couple of weeks later saw the All Blacks touring Ireland, north and south. I went to see another doctor and told him I'd already been wired for four weeks (what's a fortnight between friends?), and when we reached France at the beginning of February I called in with another medic – a lady – who believed me when I told her I'd already been wired for seven weeks – time has a way of flying when you're enjoying yourself! She had a look, gave me the all clear, cut the wires and said I was OK to play.

I turned out against France B (four weeks after the break) and thoroughly enjoyed the win. I got back into the Test side against France, another match that the All Blacks won.

So, there you have it, I lied, but not playing rugby sucks even more than eating eggs through a straw. Little did I know that I'd learned valuable lessons on how to cope with a broken jaw that would serve me well when it happened a second time, in 1967 . . . but that's another story.

TRYING CIRCUMSTANCES

IAN KIRKPATRICK
FLANKER Canterbury, Poverty Bay
NEW ZEALAND 1966–77, 39 caps

One game on the All Blacks thirty-match tour to Great Britain, Ireland and France in the 1972–73 season caused more controversy than any other – the game against Ulster at Ravenhill in Belfast. We were aware that Scotland and Wales had not fulfilled their international-championship fixtures eight months previously. The All Blacks are made of sterner stuff and were determined to play at Ravenhill, come what may, even though the situation in the North of Ireland had worsened. George Ace of *The Newsletter*, having spent some time with us in Dublin prior to the Leinster game, wrote, 'This All Black team would have played in the Bogside.'

What we weren't prepared for was the amount of security we would be afforded. Our hotel, the Dunadry Inn just outside Belfast in Templepatrick, was like a fort – there were soldiers everywhere. We selected a very strong side for the game, as the Ulster pack, led by an old adversary, the great Willie John McBride, contained three other current internationals in Jimmy Davidson, Ken Kennedy and Stewart McKinney, and the other four were later to be capped: Paddy Agnew, Roger Clegg, Charlie Murtagh and Harry Steele. We were disappointed but slightly relieved that Mike Gibson was unable to play because of injury.

The All Black side that historic day was Joe Karam, B.G. Williams,

Mark Sayers, Duncan Hales, Grant Batty, R.F. Burgess, S.M. Going, Jeff Matheson, Ron Urlich, Keith Murdoch, Andy Haden, Hamish MacDonald, Alex Wyllie and Ken Stewart, and I was captain.

Bizarrely, on arrival at the ground there were no cars parked in the vicinity, and to add to the eeriness armoured cars were stationed outside the changing-rooms, with police and soldiers swamping the place. When we ran onto the pitch, the roaring ovation from the 25,000 crowd was fantastic. The Ulster fans made us realise how much they appreciated us and confirmed that we had made the right decision to play.

.The match itself was hard-fought, but we won 19–6. Afterwards, our changing-rooms were not spared the army presence. Soldiers with guns mixed with us, and I'm sure they would have been in the showers, too, if they hadn't been concerned about getting their ammo wet! It was then that one young British soldier came out with a classic that broke the tension. He announced, 'You know, these Ulster people are an odd lot. One of them told me, in no uncertain terms, that if the All Blacks got close to forty points, I was to shoot the bloody ball!'

R & R

STEWART McKINNEY

I damaged my right collarbone very badly against North Auckland – sprung it from the sternum. It was two and a half weeks from the Test match, and the immediate prognosis was not good – six weeks out. The liaison officer from the New Zealand Rugby Football Union said he might be able to help but the union mustn't find out. (I knew I was on an Ireland tour, but this was more *Irish* than the Irish!) He would send me to a physiotherapist called Graham Hayhow on the Khyber Pass Road in Auckland, and the physio would recommend me to a specialist sports doctor. I knew I was seeing a first-class physio when I met Brian Williams, an All Black legend, in the waiting room.

Graham Hayhow treated me, reiterated the initial diagnosis and prognosis but reckoned I could play in ten days if I went to see Lloyd Drake, the best sports doctor in New Zealand . . . but, again, the New Zealand Rugby Football Union must never find out! In order to avoid dropping everyone in it by submitting taxi bills to and from Lloyd Drake's practice, a huge Olympic discus thrower called Robin Tate was press-ganged into ferrying me around Auckland in this clandestine operation. After a thorough examination, Dr Drake ascertained that I could play against Canterbury in nine days' time but that he would have to inject me with cortisone. I'd heard a lot about adverse side effects from this treatment, but after only a few seconds' thought I asked him to do it. I wanted to play.

I was sent back to the Khyber Pass Road physio after the jab, and thanks to the attentions of Messrs Drake and Hayhow I was able to rejoin the team in Christchurch the Thursday before Canterbury. (I've never had another day's trouble with that shoulder since.)

When I was receiving treatment in Auckland, Derek McKeen, the Dungannon number 8 who'd joined the police there, said he'd arrange for a few of the lads to train with me. He picked me up from my hotel, and when I arrived at Mount Eden waiting for me were John Walker, mile world-record holder, Dick Quax, who in the next few weeks would break the 5,000-metre world record, and . . . press photographers. As soon as we rounded the first clump of trees I decided we would go our separate ways at different paces, as by then we'd left the cameras behind.

Incidentally, Tom Grace demanded a final fitness test before the Canterbury game. He insisted I tackle him six times with the bad (right) shoulder. Remember the Irish element of this story? Though I knew perfectly well which shoulder he wanted to test, I had rationalised that me poor auld left shoulder was probably now the weak one – after all, it hadn't had the benefits of the jab or the physio. So, I hit him hard five times with the good (left) one, and Tom said that five would do, as that doctor back in Auckland had fixed me too well.

ALWAYS MAKE A GOOD AND LASTING IMPRESSION

MARK HUDSON
NUMBER 8/FLANKER Otago, Wellington, Canterbury, New Zealand Maoris, Vale of Lune, Askeans, Richmond

I left Dunedin in October 1983 with nervous excitement, after a so-so season with both Otago and Zingari-Richmond, to accept an offer as the overseas guest player with the Vale of Lune Rugby Club in the north-west of England in Lancaster. When I say 'so-so', it was Laurie Mains's first year as coach of Otago, and I found myself in and out of the first XV. Getting hammered by Wellington and having to be awoken a couple of times in order to catch the team bus didn't help . . . but, then again, I did come away as the rugby sprint champion at Forbury Park, where players represented their clubs by pulling a trotting sulky with a fellow player in it. In this case it was the smallest player in our team, the scrum-half Gary Watson, mate of the legendary (maybe not in Wales!) Keith Murdoch.

I should have played the previous season after the English cricket commentator Don Mosey had teamed up with his Kiwi friend and fellow cricket commentator Iain Galloway to find a young loose forward to play for Don's local team. Unfortunately, I had been involved in a car accident, fracturing two vertebrae, in August of 1982 – which also put paid to a potential trip to Wales with New Zealand Maoris. Apparently, the Maoris wanted me to go on tour – well, that's what Mattie Blackburn told me! At the last minute Iain had to get a replacement for Don and ended up getting some bloke called Jock Hobbs from Canterbury.

And that's why I was nervous! Jock came back from his stint at the Vale and slotted straight into the All Blacks. Mate, that's pressure! I knew I had to perform, because Jock's boots were going to be hard to fill.

I should have known that I'd be in for some banter on my arrival at Heathrow, with members of the club there to meet me. Banter and pranks are part and parcel of team life. David Bennett quipped that I might want to change my white shoes before the boys from the team saw them – no need to add fuel to the fire or fan the flames.

On arrival in Morecambe, where I was sharing a flat with the team captain Jimmy Ashworth ('Ashpit', as he is affectionately – or not – known, is now biding his time in Cambridge coaching a women's team), the hospitality was great. After a reasonable debut I was looking forward to the team party, when I would experience the legendary Vale shenanigans for the first time.

Trevor Glover, the fly-half and double Oxford Blue (rugby and cricket), was hosting the party. There was a good turnout of players, wives, girlfriends and even a few single ladies, some of whom I was introduced to by Brian Bonny's wife.

It was about midway through the evening, and I was drinking in the party atmosphere, as well as a couple of beers, and enjoying the party games. I'd noticed a group of players who were obviously up to something, and their number was growing and growing as the night wore on. Curiosity got the better of me, and I asked what was going on. 'Spoons!' I was told.

Spoons? The rules were explained to me, and I listened incredulously as my teammate described the scene. 'Two players sit facing one another in chairs and take turns to hit the head of their opponent with a spoon, which they hold in their mouths.'

'Ridiculous,' I thought but edged closer to get a better view. Sure enough, the game was exactly as it had been described to me. I had always thought Poms were a bit different, but this was silly. Despite looking like very soft impacts, contestants were retiring hurt to sympathetic oohs and aahs from the spectators as they imagined for themselves the amount of pain inflicted. Challengers came and went, but one character (Phil Sutcliffe, I think) reigned supreme. I was intrigued, and my competitive nature told me that I could beat him. 'The others must have soft heads,' I thought. To me, in my inebriated state, it looked fairly harmless.

Soon the chant 'Kiwi! Kiwi!' resonated around the room; even the women joined in, encouraging me to take on the champion. 'Yes!' I thought, my ego now charged, 'I could become the spoons champ and gain a little kudos and notoriety amongst my peers, make a good impression . . . and I've only been here a week! Game on!'

I swaggered confidently to the chair and eyeballed the champion. He looked scared. This, I was sure, gave me a psychological advantage. Sutcliffe was doubting his abilities, obviously afraid of the unknown, and, by God, I was going to ruthlessly make purchase of this. As I took my seat, I pondered the options: should I put him down with one crucial blow with all the strength my neck and mandibles could muster or should I test the water and save the best for last? I chose the latter.

A hush descended upon the room, and the music was turned down. In the silence I could feel the crowd contemplating their new champion – a confident Kiwi. This was serious stuff to them, and it would be a classic showdown. I lowered my head, but thanks to my tremendous peripheral vision I could still see Sutcliffe's head rise and come down. I tensed and grimaced in anticipation of the blow, but, to my surprise, the contact was faint and puny. Glory to the world. It wasn't as painful or fearsome as I had expected. 'I'm going to screw this bloke!' I thought. The crowd oohed and winced, but I let them know it was nothing, a painless glance.

Now it was my turn with the spoon. I popped it in my mouth, and in keeping with my game plan I brought it down with a moderate clunk. Well, he lurched back in agony, much to the crowd's sympathy, and I was convinced that the contest was going to be over sooner than I'd thought. I'd made a good impression, it seemed, and had declared my intentions. A couple more exchanges took place, but, to my surprise, the dude hung on in there – the poor bloke!

Then the strangest thing happened. Suddenly, there was a remarkable comeback. He must have dug deep into his reserves. As I put my head down, I could see the movement of his downward strike, and there was most definitely an improvement in the strength of impact. The crowd could sense that their man was rallying, whilst I felt I was losing momentum and the game plan was not working. Like All Black teams to come, there was no plan B.

Bang! I felt a bruise rising. Pandemonium broke out in the crowd as I tried to regain the upper hand, but my assaults to his head were making no impact. Bang! 'Shit, this guy is good!' I now had a bruise upon my bruise. Then . . . the killer blow! It felt like a sledgehammer. I was impressed, literally! I was stunned, not quite poleaxed, but any harder and I would have been unconscious. Alcohol-assisted or not, I had to give in. I'd been stuffed. I noticed, despite my battered head, that the crowd's mood had changed and some of them had tears in their eyes. Pain? Sympathy? Laughter? I turned round to the horrible realisation that the person who had been hitting me was not in fact the champion but another who had been standing behind me whacking me with a soup ladle! Well and truly stitched!

Nobody was laughing more than the group of women I'd been introduced to earlier in the evening by Bonny's wife. When she asked me, 'Which of these lovely ladies would you like?' I replied, 'I'd rather have a wank!'

Sore head, sore loser, sour grapes . . . silly boy!

AULD ENEMIES AND GOOD FRIENDS

COLIN FISHER
HOOKER Waterloo
SCOTLAND 1975–6, 5 caps

I was born to rugby – it was in my blood. My father, Alastair Fisher, played hooker for Scotland in 1947, the same position I was to play in the blue shirt of my country in the 1970s. I gained my first cap against the All Blacks on our tour of New Zealand in the summer of 1975, and like all young players about to make their debut I was excited, nervous and keen to give my best both on and off the pitch.

VOICES FROM THE BACK OF THE BUS

On the journey to New Zealand I was taken under the wing of Sandy Carmichael, by then a seasoned international and well versed in all the etiquette and protocols that are observed 'on tour'. As we checked in our baggage I noticed he had two very large suitcases and remarked on them, asking if he'd brought his kilt for the dress dinners to be attended whilst we were away – there's always something to be learned from the players who have been around for a while. 'No,' he said. 'That one there's empty.' My confused expression and bewilderment at bringing an empty suitcase must have been obvious, as he went on to explain, 'That one's for the freebies we'll gather up during the next four weeks!' He continued, matter-of-factly, 'And that one is full of the last three weeks' dirty washing.' By this time I must have looked dumbfounded and awestruck, as he further explained, 'The first hotel we get to will have that sorted for me.' I let this sink in for a moment, quickly recovered from my mute state and thought of what else I needed to ask him.

At last I came up with a pertinent question. 'How much money have you brought with you?'

He put his hand in one of his very deep pockets and produced a handful of coins. 'Six and eightpence,' he said. 'You don't need money, you don't need clothes, you just need an empty suitcase to bring back all the freebies.' This all sounded very good, and I boarded the plane – none the wiser, really – with great expectations of the delights that awaited us in the 'Land of the Long White Cloud'.

Playing rugby requires great self-sacrifice, and the Scotland team made every effort to return the hospitality we were shown off the pitch. When we arrived at our first destination, Nelson Bays at the north end of South Island, we were staying in a brand-new hotel, the Rutherford. Making sure that all the players felt involved, we were allocated different jobs. 'Big Al' McHarg had been 'appointed' as the squad's 'entertainment officer'. We'd arrived on the Monday, and Al had decided that once the boys had recovered from jet lag it would be good to throw a party on the Wednesday evening to get the tour off to a good start. I asked him if I could do anything to help, because time was tight, but he just said, 'No, thanks. Don't worry. Everything's under control.'

Anyway, I was lying in bed recovering from jet lag on the Tuesday, and the hotel radio was playing a local pop station, which interrupted its programme every ten minutes with the following announcement: 'There now follows a message for all eligible females in the City of Nelson between the ages of 16 and 55: please come down to the Rutherford hotel at 8.30 on Wednesday evening and enjoy some traditional Scottish hospitality from the Scotland rugby team, who have just landed in town.' I quickly realised the meaning of 'everything's under control'! About 1,500 people turned up, and the party was fantastic! I liked this world, and I was learning more each day.

The long white cloud must have had a subtropical surfeit for when we came to play the Test match at Eden Park, infamously known as the 'Water Polo Game' at 'Lake Eden', heavy rainfall had pounded the pitch beyond saturation. It was completely flooded at either end, and much of the rest of the pitch was underwater; in fact, it was unplayable. However, despite the dangerous conditions (danger of drowning – I joke not) the match was played because our captain, 'Mighty Mouse' Ian McLauchlan, was never going to accept a cancellation of the only Test match, his threefold rationale being that Sandy Carmichael was not going to miss the chance of equalling the then record for the highest number of caps held by a prop (this would be his forty-first, equalling the record held jointly by Hughie McLeod and Dave Rollo), there were three new caps waiting to making their debut (I was one of them) and there were 55,000 screaming fans in the stadium (all of whom had paid good money for their tickets) who might turn nasty if the game was called off. Scotland's men were going to play. If the referee chose to abandon the game after one minute, that would be fine by the Mouse, but Scotland were going to start!

In 1976, while playing for Waterloo and Lancashire (ever the exile), I was still donning the blue shirt, and when the Calcutta Cup match was played at Murrayfield that year, the first time Her Majesty had visited the ground, I found myself up against several of my Lancashire teammates. (During the 1970s, county rugby was especially strong in England and very often the stepping-stone for players to achieve international selection. In our Lancashire team there were thirteen players who were full internationals – ten English, two Irish and one Scot, me – and the other two were England Under-23 caps.) England had brought a very powerful team to Murrayfield, and on the day we were seriously under pressure in the scrums. Ian McLauchlan, Sandy Carmichael, Al McHarg, Gordon Brown and I faced Fran Cotton, Peter Wheeler, Mike Burton, Chris Ralston and Billy Beaumont, and in one particular scrummage we were pushed back about ten yards – at a rate of knots! The Scotland scrum finally disintegrated, and as I lay on the ground waiting for Billy Beaumont's size-14 boot to crush my chest he stared down at me, momentarily hesitated and then blurted out, 'Oh fuck – county final next week!' before stepping over me. Now this wasn't the act of a gentleman as such, nor was it that Bill had suddenly taken a pledge of non-violence – it was the sudden presence of mind to realise that I'd be needed by Lancashire the following week when we would be playing together in the County Championship final against Gloucestershire. Auld enemies can indeed make good friends!

Footnote: I'd like to thank Stewart McKinney for my introduction to Sunday drinking (Sunday opening hadn't been legalised in Northern Ireland in those days) in the York Hotel in Belfast . . . but that's another story!

I BARED MY 'S'OLE

BRENT POPE
FLANKER Canterbury, Otago, South Island, St Mary's, Dublin

> *Brent Pope was an All Black trialist and is now a rugby pundit for RTE and sports journalist in Ireland.*

There are lots of embarrassing and humorous moments that stand out from my rugby career, and I certainly had a penchant for putting my foot in it at the wrong time. While I was playing for Otago during the 1980s, I loved being a practical joker. When a young player made the team, I would call him using a fake journalist's name and ask him to tell me his life story. That interview would be secretly taped and played back at a kangaroo court, much to the player's embarrassment. Quite often the interviews were cringe-worthy, as players often went on at length about how good they were. I would also do it while on tour, with the other players listening in around the phone. I would often ask the recipient about certain characters in the team, who were listening in, of course, and hope the player being interviewed would say something embarrassing – which they quite often did.

But I was guilty of making a fool of myself on a few occasions. In the early 1980s I was playing rugby for the Otago University first XV, alongside the likes of Mike Brewer and David Kirk, and trying to make it all the way into the All Blacks. At that time, Brian Lochore, the great All Black number 8, was the convener of the New Zealand selectors, and I vividly remember discussing with a number of other players at the Southern Rugby Club in Dunedin that Lochore had got his selections terribly wrong. Under the lubricating influence of Speight's Ale, I was quite forthright with my opinions. Upon hearing my views, a woman in a nearby group commented, 'Is that so?' Slurring through my argument, I soon realised that this woman certainly had a good grasp of the selections. In the end we finally agreed to disagree, and the lovely woman moved off to another area of the bar.

About an hour later, a friend reintroduced us. 'Brent, this is Mrs Lochore, Brian's wife.' Of all the bars in all the towns . . . I could not believe it. Apparently, the Lochores' son was studying in Dunedin, and she just happened to be at the clubhouse – Murphy's law. Still hoping to become an All Black, I made my feeble excuses but realised the damage had already been done. Luckily, she was a great lady and saw the funny side of it. And she couldn't have relayed the message too well, because about a year later Lochore gave me an All Black trial.

Incident number two was more sensitive, and to this day I'm sure I remain the only aspiring player to bare his buttocks to a future All Black coach. Laurie Mains was my coach at Otago for about ten years, and when you got to know Laurie he was a funny, good-humoured guy. However, he was nicknamed 'Funeral Face' or 'Lemons' by young Otago players, because you dared not approach him, such was his steely, unfriendly stare. You most certainly did not fool around the night before or on the day of a game. Players had to wear the face of a focused individual, thinking of nothing else but the match. For me that was always difficult. The night before a game, Laurie even checked what you ate, walking army-fashion behind the dinner tables, looking at the composition of your plate. Still hungry but afraid to eat what they wanted from the menu, players would sneak in Mars bars or Kit Kats from the local shop like they were smuggling contraband into prison. One year three hungry props huddled together and boiled sausages in a kettle on the end of a coat hanger while another took the lookout spot down the corridor, but that's another story.

Otago were playing an important National Championship game against Waikato in Hamilton. I was rooming with my good mate Arran Pene, soon to be an All Black number 8, and next door sleeping, as he did 23 hours a day, was Paul 'Ginge' Henderson, a player also destined for greatness. The two rooms had an adjoining door, and I was often in and out of Ginge's room, enjoying the company.

After dinner, all the players were sent to their rooms. Some played cards and others watched movies, but I always had to go and have my hamstrings rubbed by Donny Cameron, our popular team masseur. My hamstrings were so tight that my nickname was 'Ping Pope', as they would tear if I moved too quickly without warming up. They were so bad that if a truck was coming as I crossed the road, I would struggle to get out of its way.

I had my ritual rub down and then went back to the room, where Arran was lying on the bed watching television. Because my legs were still covered in massage oil, I decided to take a hot bath, which had the dual purpose of removing the liniment and also relaxing the leg muscles. It was my usual routine the night before a game.

I stripped down to a towel, and as I passed the adjoining door I banged loudly on it, yelling for Ginge to get up and come to the door urgently. With no response, I banged again, and as the door swung open I dropped the towel, turned around, slapped my bare buttocks and said, 'Well, what do you think of that?' – or words to that effect, although probably not quite so polite. There was no reaction, which was unlike Paul. I was expecting the flick of a towel at least. When I peered up between my legs, I saw Funeral Face himself, angrily glaring at me with his arms crossed. Without even a smirk, Mains slammed the door – and I mean he slammed it.

At that stage, Arran was rolling around in stitches. He was the reserve number 8 and probably thought that that was the end of me – he would get a game instead. Mortified, I went and lay on the bed with a pillow over my head. I couldn't even bring myself to offer any sort of pathetic apology or excuse; after all, I had just bared my naked rear to my provincial coach. What could I possibly say?

Unbeknown to me, Mains had swapped rooms with Paul earlier in the evening, because my teammate could not sleep with all the noise, but nobody had informed me of this – least of all Ginge.

Next day, fearing for my rugby life, I played a stormer and was named player of the match. Nothing was said about the incident until about five years later when Mains finally admitted that he went back into his room after the show and cracked up.

Laurie Mains deservedly went on to become a well-respected and successful All Black coach and was desperately unlucky to lose the World Cup final in 1995. However, I bet I'm the only player he ever coached who showed him so much flair and panache the night before a big game.

A FINE SPREAD

STEWART McKINNEY

A Friday afternoon light run-out at the Honourable Artillery Company's ground in the heart of the City of London; a nice cup of tea and back to the Kensington Close Hotel to relax and prepare for the approaching battle – no such luck! Off we went to either the Northern Ireland Office or Irish Embassy (depending what year it was, as they alternated venues). In Paris it would be the Irish Embassy or in Dublin the French Embassy – canapés and champagne-cocktail receptions, just the thing to finish off the preparations, except that there was no way the Ireland players could drink, as the selectors were ever-vigilant.

As you wandered around an already inebriated company, the committees having arrived much earlier to mix with the dignitaries and invited guests, you tried your best not to make eye contact with the opposition, who were also compelled to attend these functions. It was no time to have a tête-à-tête with Jean-Pierre Rives or, even worse, that beast Alain Esteve.

Invariably, some upper-class woman, slightly the worse for wear, would lurch up to you and ask in plummy tones if you really were a rugger bugger, dahling. Of course, you would politely reply in the affirmative, secretly entertaining the thought that if this was the following evening after a dozen pints of Guinness, the answer might be slightly different. God, those receptions were a bore, but what wonderful social occasions for the committees.

Wellington, New Zealand, 1976, the eve of the Test with the All Blacks – a reception at the residence of the governor of New Zealand. This was much better than making strained, polite conversation with the rugger-bugger women. Many famous All Blacks were in attendance – great retired players such as Brian Lochore, Colin Meads, Waka Nathan, Wilson Whineray and Ken Gray – and the 1976 Irish tourists were wonderful mixers and singers, although this wasn't the time or the place for 'Dicey Reilly'. It was magnificent to meet such All Black legends, who really seemed to enjoy each other's company.

There's only a certain amount of mixing you can do, so gradually the two Test sides began to take their own company to different parts of the reception. A cursory nod of acknowledgement was given to the likes of Ken Stewart or Billy Bush, but this was not the time to socialise with them. There would be plenty of that after three o'clock the next day at Athletic Park.

A harassed butler made his way through our group with a plump little Jack Russell on a leash. It looked as if it'd snaffled too many crumbs from under his master's table and more than likely retrieved any fallen cocktail sausages from the floor. The butler appealed to us. 'I'm very busy,' he announced. 'Would you be so kind and look after the dog for a short while?' We nodded. The dog would be a welcome diversion during the time we had to kill. 'And, oh,' the butler continued as he left our company, 'mind you don't give him any food. He's way overweight and on a diet.'

'No trouble,' said Shay Deering, a vet, to the departing figure. However, I could see a glint in Moss Keane's eye, and I read his mind immediately. We ignored the protests of Deero. 'Jaysus, no, lads. It will be very bad for him.

We quickly formed a book. The spread betting was of a slightly different kind – those little two-inch by two-inch crustless sandwiches that are served at a canapé function. Jack had a voracious appetite, and by the time the butler returned the greedy little bugger had devoured 48 and was looking for more. None of our bets were remotely close to the result. Needless to say, the butler was none too pleased, but we were happy to have had our minds taken off the game for a while, and it was better craic than talking dead sober to a drunken rugger-bugger woman.

THE POWER OF THE ALL BLACK JERSEY AND BLOOD IS THICKER THAN THE JERSEY!

GREG COOPER
FULL-BACK Otago, Askeans
NEW ZEALAND 1986–92, 7 caps

The Power of the All Black Jersey

Reflecting on twenty-five years' involvement with first-class rugby, both in New Zealand and overseas, there is one highlight that stands out amongst many fond memories. It was gaining my first All Black jersey and playing in my first Test, against France in 1986, a few days after my twenty-first birthday. For those fortunate enough to have been selected for the All Blacks, it is probably the exact same memory that is to the forefront of their minds. For my family and me, however, it was the end of a difficult and uncertain five-year journey.

In February 1981 we were told that I had developed the disease Ewing sarcoma (bone cancer). The survival rate in those days was extremely low. Success sometimes meant the amputation of a limb to remove the primary site of the cancer. In my case the bone cancer had attacked my first rib and was complicated by that area containing significant nerve structure. The projected outlook over the next six months was indeed very bleak.

The hospital beds all around me continued to be occupied by new faces. Most of those with whom I shared the room did not survive. I had a 15-year-old sick body with a mind rapidly understanding the realities of life.

Why was I one of the lucky ones?

I believe there were many reasons why I was one of the lucky ones. The treatment: the two years of chemotherapy were gruelling, but that coupled with the radiotherapy was critical. My family: I received incredible support, care and love, which provided strength when I needed it. My religion: my Catholic upbringing was a great source of comfort – when I was at the lowest of lows, I knew I had someone to turn to for help. Me: for all the other areas of support to work, I had to play my part. From the day of diagnosis it was not a matter of 'if' I will get well, but 'how long' it will take.

I never had a goal to live, because I never thought I was going to die. I did, however, have a burning desire to be an All Black. To be an All Black was for me a payback to those who had done so much for me and an outward sign to everyone that I was no longer sick. I had personalised my battle with cancer, and I believed that to be selected for the All Blacks was to win my own personal battle. There were many times when I had finished a bout of chemotherapy and I had gained enough energy to train when I would give all I had to beat the cancer during that training session. It was personal.

There were many, many difficult times from diagnosis in February 1981 until All Black selection in June 1986, but in amongst the many support systems I relied on was the 'Power of the All Black Jersey'.

Blood Is Thicker than the Jersey!

My brother Matthew and I share something that not many brothers have shared in the history of international rugby. You're possibly thinking, 'Did they both represent their country?' Yes, if you thought that, you're correct. We are both fortunate enough to have played Test rugby for the All Blacks, and, yes, that is a reasonably rare occurrence. However, what I am alluding to is slightly more rare than that. After the first Test, Matthew replaced me as full-back for the second Test against Ireland in 1992 in Wellington!

As brothers we grew up competing against each other in everything we did, from cricket to tennis to racing each other to the dinner table. Of course, there was always rugby. Because I was one year older than Matthew, he had the perfect plan laid out for him: watch what I did and then set about repeating the process. So it went like this: I was picked for the New Zealand schoolboys rugby team; Matthew was selected the following year. I was picked for the New Zealand Under-21 team; Matthew was selected the following year. I was picked for the All Blacks; yes, you guessed it, Matthew was selected the following year!

The process took a little twist when Matthew decided he wanted a taste of Test rugby. But instead of showing respect towards his older brother, he broke the one-year time sequence and changed it to one week! I was dropped after the first Test against Ireland . . . and in to take the number 15 jersey was M.J.A. Cooper of Waikato!

I had mixed emotions. I was disappointed to be dropped, but I was not playing at my best, and I understood that. However, I was so pleased for Matthew, because we were and have always been great mates, and I had played seven Tests and he was yet to be capped. I was the first to ring and congratulate him, and I knew his feelings were a little mixed, too: delighted for himself, but disappointed for me. Then there was the rest of the family . . . exactly the same emotions.

During the week, I was constantly on the phone providing advice, trying to help him where I thought I could. I was confident that he would do well, because he was in good form and we had not played well in the first Test. I expected an All Black backlash.

Matthew had an outstanding game. In fact, he got a world-record points haul on debut of 23 points! (This record has subsequently been broken.) I think I was the first to ring again, this time to say well done, but also to remind him of his position in the family – a world record on debut after replacing his older brother was not demonstrating respect!

It was a proud day for the Cooper family, and I was as pleased as anyone. I'd had my turn, and now it was Matthew's.

FOR THE RECORD

STEWART McKINNEY

The English rugby team that came to Lansdowne Road in 1973 and received a wonderfully appreciative reception probably saved the Five Nations Championship, and for that Irish rugby will be forever grateful. Thank you.

The seventh All Blacks visit to the province, four months previously, received every bit as grand an ovation from 25,000 Ulster supporters who had missed out when the Springboks fixture had been cancelled in 1969. It was to have been my first big game, and I still remember the disappointment.

At the Dunadry Inn after we had played the All Blacks, I was seated between two props – one had the biggest thighs I'd ever seen, Kent King Lambert from Manawatu, and the other, Keith Murdoch from Otago, had the biggest chest I'd ever seen. Kent was a bit full of himself, which was only natural, as he was only 19, but Keith was quiet and seemed to be in a reflective, somewhat pensive mood. After the speeches, the dance was due to begin. The giant-chested man didn't look as if he was in the mood for a bit of a boogie, so I asked him if he would like a drink. He refused, saying he was on his way with a couple of crates of beer to drink with the soldiers who had guarded him and his teammates over the previous few days – they must be cold out there. It was the action of a thoughtful person.

I was deeply saddened when he was sent home after New Zealand played Wales. He had blotted his copybook somehow, and the team management felt this was a justifiable course of action. I didn't know the full circumstances, but I and hundreds of other rugby players have raided hotel kitchens in the wee small hours. It was a rugby tradition bordering on the compulsory, a sort of rite of passage. Was a fracas involved? I don't know and therefore can't vindicate his actions, but, for the record, I will always remember Keith Murdoch as the caring man of Dunadry Inn.

SWEET GUINNESS

STEWART McKINNEY

The Springboks are coming! Great excitement and preparations busy the rugby aficionados of Brighton, Bournemouth, Cambourne, Belfast, Pontypool and Gosforth. The gospel of rugby will be spread to the far outposts this 1960–61 season.

I watched along with 25,000 others at Ravenhill those huge South Africans, and like many who were there to witness the spectacle I can still remember their names: Johan Classens, Avril Malan, Franny Kuhn, Pieter Du-toit, Frik du Preez and a one-eyed flanker called Martin Pelser.

The next touring side after the 1960–61 Springboks were the 1963–64 All Blacks, and my hero was on that tour: Waka Nathan! In my opinion, he was the best openside in the world at that time, and he made a lasting impression on me.

The professional game has necessitated that the All Blacks, Springboks and Wallabies fly in, play a Test and depart. I find this very sad, as it really was a big, big day when a touring side came to town, especially for a kid like me. Imagine my delight when years later my heroes, the All Blacks, had Sunday lunch at our clubhouse, the Ranfurly Shield having originated from Dungannon. We still talk about them and the friendships that were made that day in our small town.

When Ireland toured New Zealand in 1976, everywhere we went there was bottled Guinness in our hotel rooms. We hadn't a clue where it came from, but it certainly was unusual to find such an anonymously donated cache. The Guinness itself was strange – it wasn't like our stout. It was a very strong 8 per cent and disgustingly sweet to boot. Obviously, this Guinness was valued by the locals, so instead of ditching it we gave it to the maids at the hotels, who were most grateful for the delicious brew.

On the Thursday afternoon before the Test in Wellington I was invited along with some others to the New Zealand Barbarians club. Some All Black legends were there: Colin Meads, Wilson Whineray and my schoolboy hero Waka Nathan. I met him in the flesh, and I wasn't disappointed. He was wonderful company. He told me that on one tour he had broken his jaw and had to have it wired, but he loved the Irish because they'd unwired it on Saturday nights so that he could drink Guinness and eat steak, rewiring him on the Monday mornings.

The Irish were so kind to him, and now that he worked for Dominion Breweries he had repaid the hospitality by sending Guinness to our hotels. He asked if we were receiving it all right. 'Jaysus, Waka, the boys can't get enough of it,' I lied. 'They're lapping it up!'

He had mighty big hands, and I wasn't going to upset him!

HOARY TALES FROM AROUND THE WORLD

HOARY TALES FROM AROUND THE WORLD PREFACE

Such is the diversity of the memories and recollections brought to mind because of rugby that the contributions in this section vary widely in content, and it was impossible to categorise them. Many of them are the sort of yarns shared over a pint when talk turns to, 'D'you remember the time when . . .' Others are accounts of individuals' rugby *raison d'être*: how and why they became involved in the game; whom they admired and when they felt they had 'made it'; what they did in the company of their teammates on the bus, in the hotels, on the pitch, or wherever events and destiny had placed them. There's no 'kiss and tell' or salacious sensationalism, but there are stories here that are thought-provoking, romantic in their recollection and often amusing in their telling.

Not all international rugby players spent their time hanging out with other rugby players. As amateurs, they had jobs in offices, schools, building sites and steelworks, and they mixed with the general public in their places of work, in the pub and in the clubhouse, pleased to be recognised after a good game and willing to take the flak if they had put in a bad performance. These are tales with rugby as their common thread – no divas or prima donnas allowed.

Stewart McKinney

MUTUAL UNDERSTANDING

JIM RENWICK
CENTRE Hawick
SCOTLAND 1972–84, 52 caps
LIONS TOUR '80, 1 Test match

Being born and bred in Hawick was fantastic, for it was a great town in which to learn the game of rugby football. It has a strong tradition and a strong, unique dialect, which is great when playing for Hawick, where everyone understands each other. Unfortunately, playing for invitation and district teams wasn't quite so straightforward. Even worse were international games, when immediate communication is vital and you have to shout at the top of your voice to pass moves along the back line.

My first international was at Murrayfield in 1972 against France, and one of the things I couldn't fail to notice was the resounding noise the crowd made when Scotland got into an attacking position. It reverberated around the ground at a decibel level that must surely have been outlawed by the health-and-safety officers. It was marvellous!

I remember calling the move to my outside centre, John Frame, and although we were in the heat of battle he came right up to me and shouted, 'Jim, you'll need to speak fucking English!' It wasn't really so important – we only had two moves in those days, so he had a 50–50 chance of getting it right anyway.

France have always been one of my favourite teams to play against and also to watch. There's something unique about the way they play, with their inimitable Gallic flair. The French say, 'To win without style is to triumph without glory!' I was fortunate to play against France 11 times in the Five Nations Championship between 1972 and 1983. I lined up against a hard French centre in Roland Bertranne eight times in all, and in all the times I played against him I never spoke to him – not even once. He couldn't speak any English and neither could I! What chance did we have? We just used to wink at one another before the game and shake hands after it. I've not seen him since I've managed to learn a bit of English . . . I wonder if he has?

Ian Barnes (Scotland and Hawick second row) and I were invited to play at Ballymena in the Willie John McBride v. Syd Millar match in the 1970s. Barney has a really broad dialect and was even harder to understand than me. (He also has a speech impediment – he can't say 'no'.) Barney and Moss Keane (from Kerry, with an equally strong accent) packed down in the second row, and throughout the match they were gibbering away to each other. It was only in the last few minutes of the game that they finally realised what they were trying to say. They wanted to swap sides in the scrum!

There's no doubt that the modern game demands effective communication. It is vital to any successful team, but sometimes in rugby it's what you see and what you do, no' wha' comes out of your mouth, that is important.

A LION IN THE MAKING (OR, SCHOOLBOY RAY GRAVELL TAKES OUT BRIAN THOMAS)

JOHN EVANS, RAY GRAVELL'S FORM MASTER

Ray Gravell, a centre three-quarter who won twenty-three caps for Wales and played in four Lions Test matches in 1980, was a hard centre with a soft heart. He was one of the first people to ring me

when I had to go into hospital for a heart operation. He was full
of life and lifted my spirits; the call was very much appreciated.
Sadly, three weeks later, Ray was dead. One of his former teachers
has written a piece in his memory.

Stewart McKinney

In 1967 Ray Gravell was a student at Queen Elizabeth Grammar School, Carmarthen. He already possessed an excellent physique and, as a 16 year old, was first XV scrum-half. I was Ray's form master, a role that was essentially administrative but one that offered pastoral opportunities. I coached rugby at the school, which yielded four of the three-quarters for a Wales international match against Ireland in 1974, Ray being one of them.

One morning at registration young Ray asked me if my wife and I would like to see a rugby match the following Sunday morning. It was to celebrate the opening of a new clubhouse for his club, Cydweli, and was to be against a Rhys Williams Invitation XV. Ray would be playing in his then position of scrum-half. We went.

Playing for the visitors was Brian Thomas, at that time a veteran and former Neath and Wales player. Big man. Bigger reputation! Thomas was one of the early examples of a player whose 'fame' attracted placard carrying by spectators and fans for his club and country. I recollect TV cameras catching notices that read 'Tomo bites yer leg' and 'B.B.T.', which apparently meant 'Bitten by Thomas'.

In this match Brian Thomas stood head and shoulders above everyone else in the lineouts – there was no lifting in those days – and received regularly on the visitors' throw. On one such occasion, close to the host team's try-line, and near to where I watched from the touchline, Thomas caught the ball, stormed through the defence forwards and ran straight at the young scrum-half.

I winced at the prospect of what might happen next. Fortunately, I did not close my eyes and so witnessed a young 'David' confronting an apparently unstoppable 'Goliath'. As Thomas came at him, the schoolboy leant forward, driving his head into the big man's midriff. The forward momentum carried Brian Thomas over Ray Gravell, but to the ground. Try saved – for the time being. Damage done? Ray was on his feet instantly and got what I prefer to think was an appreciative comment from the ex-international.

The form master's period the next morning was much less boring than usual. I knew then and still know now that I could not have made that tackle myself. It is only with the benefit of hindsight that I realise I was witnessing a Lion in the making.

Note: Ray went on to play centre for his club, Llanelli RFC, between 1970 and 1985, making 485 appearances. At the time of his death in 2007, he was the club's (now 'The Scarlets') president. Between 1975 and 1982, Ray gained 23 caps at centre for Wales.

During the Lions' tour of South Africa in 1980, Ray played in all four Tests.

PEEL'S PIQUANT PLACEBO

PHIL BENNETT

Good humour was also never far from the surface when I played for Llanelli, especially when Ray Gravell was about – even if it was at Grav's own expense. I remember one match in the 1970s when Grav very nearly didn't make it onto the pitch, even though he was in the dressing-room.

We were at home to Cardiff – a massive game – and there were so many Scarlets fans trying to get into Stradey Park that afternoon that all the roads around were blocked. I only lived a couple of miles from the ground, but I'd left too late and got stuck in traffic. Luckily, I knew the back roads, but even then I was late arriving, and our captain, Delme Thomas, wasn't too pleased.

It seemed that not only was I running late, but Grav was also refusing to play on account of some terrible headache. I tried to persuade him by telling him how great he was and how disappointed the crowd would be if he didn't go on. That failed, so I tried provoking him instead, insisting he was soft. That didn't work either, so the masterstroke was to offer him a miracle cure.

Grav loved his pills and potions for all his aches and pains, so I told him Brendan Foster had given me a 'wonder tablet' that was imported from America and cured everything. Bert Peel was our physio at the time, a lovely guy who is the grandfather of Dwayne, the Wales scrum-half. Bert could see where I was going with the plan and pulled out a small orange pill, which he popped into Grav's mouth. Within two minutes, Grav was telling everyone how the Yanks knew everything. They even had magic pills to instantly cure blinding headaches. He played, of course, and never found out that he'd been miraculously cured by an orange Tic Tac!

THE EASTER EGG

STEWART McKINNEY

Moss Keane was a mighty man and immensely strong, although he was often unaware of quite how much strength he possessed, especially when he was fortified with a few pints of Guinness. A hug of endearment, a friendly slap on the back or an amicable punch on the arm could be quite an ordeal for the recipient. You didn't mess with Moss, and you didn't unduly upset him.

In 1977 the Lions, including Moss, were in New Zealand, and there was a radio link-up from four locations in Great Britain and Ireland, coordinated by the wonderful Cliff Morgan. Willie John had arranged for late food in a Chinese restaurant in Ballymena, which served well as ballast/blotting paper for the following six hours of hospitality at Eaton Park. During this time, Willie John and Syd Millar had been called by Cliff to give their views on the forthcoming game, and I continued with my libation and relaxation in the company of my great friend Ian McIlrath.

Half an hour before the kick-off, Cliff Morgan asked if I was in the clubhouse. When they put me in the chair, he asked if I was still eating daffodils. I informed him that I was, and as we were on the subject of eating decided to tell a story about Moss, knowing that he wouldn't hear it as he was 10,000 miles away, preparing to run onto the pitch. I felt safe.

I began the story and described how Moss had come onto the scene in 1974 at a time when Ireland had introduced the odd extra squad session on a Sunday. We'd train in the morning and then have a set lunch – no pasta in those days – in the best roast-beef restaurant I have ever eaten in: the Saddle Room in the Shelbourne Hotel. Each week there was exquisite roast beef, a seasonal-vegetable selection and a baked potato done in tinfoil. Everyone had the same. Barry McGann, who had an inkling of Moss's likely reaction to the sophistication of the Saddle Room, had us all primed to wait until Moss began his meal before we started eating ourselves. We engaged in small talk and animatedly discussed the morning's moves. With such conversation and activity, none of us were able to take a bite from the food before us.

Moss was a big fella, hungry and impatient to get the victuals into him, but he was perplexed by the tinfoil. In fact, had no idea what it was! He gave it a flick with his knife to turn it over, but wasn't it the same on the other side? Moss looked around for a clue from the other diners, but nobody had attacked their plate yet. With no clue, he lifted the object off his plate to inspect it closer and conduct a little investigation under the table. He still had no idea, so he announced to all and sundry, 'Bollocks to this! Where I come from in Castleisland in Kerry we don't eat Easter eggs with roast beef!' and threw it over his shoulder, much to the astonishment of the Dublin aristocracy and nobility, who were out for Sunday lunch in the Shelbourne. We all cracked up. Moss had arrived and was much loved around the world for many years.

Great story, huh? Good craic? What a *bon vivant* and brilliant raconteur was I? Well, late on in 1977 I was attending another squad session in Dublin, and after a few pints of the black stuff Moss said that he wanted to have a word with me – a serious word. I thought perhaps it was to do with not lifting him properly in the lineout or something of that matter. I was wrong.

'I heard that story about the Easter egg on the radio,' he said. I protested that he couldn't have, as he'd been about to run out onto the Eden Park pitch when it had been aired. 'I heard it on my car radio last week,' he said menacingly. 'It was replayed!'

He then gave me one of those excruciatingly painful bear hugs of his, and to this day I still don't know if it was one of endearment or if he was trying to kill me.

DOPPELGANGER

MICKEY QUINN
FLY-HALF Lansdowne, Leinster
IRELAND 1972–81, 10 caps

It was 1974, during a season in which Ireland would go on to win the Five Nations for the first time since 1950, and I was feeling awful! I had the flu, and I wondered if I would recover in time for the Wales match. I told no one except my roommate Johnny Moloney, as I was determined to make the park for this fixture. It was Thursday, and we were to play the star-studded Wales team on the Saturday. They had some great players: Phil Bennett, J.P.R. Williams, Gareth Edwards, J.J. Williams, Mervyn Davies, Dai Morris and so on.

I was passed fit and played. All my reserve strength and commitment went into that match, with the passion only a recovering flu victim can imagine. The game was tough and close for the duration, and after a great tussle the final score was a 9–9 draw.

In those days, Johnny Moloney and I were often mistaken for each other, as we sort of looked alike. After the game, both teams retired to the old Lansdowne Tea Rooms, the little building in the corner of Lansdowne Road. As I stood there with my direct opponent, Phil Bennett, a young boy came running up to me brandishing an autograph book and said, 'Johnny, Johnny Moloney! Can I have your autograph?'

I didn't have the heart to say, 'I'm not Johnny Moloney, actually, I'm Mickey Quinn!' So, rather than disappoint the excited young fan, I signed his book: 'To Brian, best wishes, Johnny Moloney'.

Obviously delighted with his autograph from the great Johnny Moloney, the boy looked up from the book and said, with immense gratitude and uncanny insight, 'Gee, Johnny, thanks a million! But tell me, how do you play with yer man Mickey Quinn? He's *shite!*'

OUCH! I BET THAT HURT!

PADDY JOHNS
LOCK Dungannon, Saracens, Ulster
IRELAND 1990–2001, 59 caps

After much thinking, my wife came up with a tale from the back of the bus . . . literally! Having played in Cardiff at an Ireland v. Wales match, the players had been joined by the wives and girlfriends (WAGs) and were travelling back to the team hotel. The subject of past injuries came up, and Morris Field started to talk about all the cuts and stitches he had received playing rugby. Soon, Dennis McBride, Mick Galwey and I joined in, going through our own war wounds, comparing battle scars. Injuries suffered and recovered from were a badge of honour and being rugby players, competitive by nature, we were trying to outdo each other. (It was becoming like the *Monty Python* 'I was so poor' sketch or Peter Cook and Dudley Moore's 'What's the worst job you ever had?')

By this stage the WAGs who were within earshot were getting pretty fed up and objected to this macho whine-fest. From the back of the bus, a WAG put an abrupt end to the conversation by shouting out, 'Lads, sure, that's bloody nothing. Try and beat a couple of kids and ten stitches in yer fanny!'

FIRST CAP

STEWART McKINNEY

When I was awarded my first cap, in 1971, Ireland hadn't won in France since 1951. Stade Colombes, home of the 1924 Olympic Games and setting for the film *Chariots of Fire*, was the venue. Fire and brimstone featured strongly! Ken Kennedy was leading the Ireland pack and had warned us beforehand what to expect from the French. Up to then I had believed rugby to be hard, rough and dirty at times, but Ken had forecast that the next 80 minutes would be outright war and that the first battle would be the first scrum.

With all this talk of carnage, Johnny Moloney, who was also playing his first game for his country, was a trifle nervous. As John was putting the ball into the first scrum, Alain Esteve began his dirty work from the France second row. Kennedy dropped his head and the punch glanced off him. We tore into them. 'Right!' said Mr Lewis, the referee. 'Any more of this and I'll send someone off!'

'Take no notice of him. The next scrum will be worse,' said Willie John. 'Look after Ken.'

Once again a nervous Moloney addressed the scrum, and once again Esteve swung one through. Off we went again. I was loving international rugby. Mr Lewis issued the same warning after things had settled again.

For the third time, Johnny, even more nervously, put the ball into the scrum. A clean strike by Kennedy channelled the ball to Dennis Hickie's feet, and Johnny threw a terrible pass to my favourite rugby person, Barry McGann. Barry was a little stout and didn't like stooping too much; however, he took the ball at ankle height and, with those twinkly feet of his, deftly side-footed the ball into touch. Hands on hips, Barry sidled up to a repentant Johnny. 'I've only one thing to say to you, Moloney. If you want to stay on this Ireland team, I'd like a bit more elevation!'

Johnny obviously listened because he played a blinder, scored a try and was an outstanding scrum-half for many years to come.

THE WALES TEAM AND WILLIE AND MOSS

BOBBY WINDSOR

Well, I was speaking to Mossie recently, asking how he was, and he said about Ireland just winning the Grand Slam, 'When I played in the '70s, we never beat bloody Wales once!' And then he said, 'Wales have only beaten Ireland in the Arms Park, or the Millennium as it is now, once in 25 years . . . that was in '83.' That's an amazing record, that is, but Ireland were always game for it. Playing against the Irish was always the best game, because you knew what was coming, and it was, you know, a punch and a boot for everyone, but after the game it was fabulous, because, well, they were exactly the same when they won as when they lost.

When we were in New Zealand with Mossie and Willie Duggan . . . my God, they were a pair of buggers, they was! Oh, super lads! Sir John Dawes was the coach. Well, for some reason he put me in charge of the pair of them, cos they were out-and-out buggers, they were. Wherever we went, they would somehow find the biggest dive in the worst district to have a couple of pints, you know. And I'd get sent out by the coach. 'You gotta find them,' he'd say. I'd have to search bloody New Zealand looking for them. They'd be in the worst bar in the worst area, and they'd have made friends with everybody, all the worst rogues in bloody New Zealand. Bloody amazing, innit?

The only time I drank shorts that I can remember was when I had the flu in New Zealand, and Mossie and Willie said, 'We'll fix you, Bob.' They came in with a bottle of whiskey, and we drank hot toddies all night. And they said, 'That'll get rid of the flu.' Well, it certainly did. I felt that bad next day I forgot about the flu!

PROUD TO BE AN ENGLISHMAN

DAVID DUCKHAM
WING Coventry
ENGLAND 1969–76, 36 caps
LIONS TOUR '71, 3 Test matches

The record books will show that the 1972 Five Nations was abandoned as a championship when Wales and Scotland declined to play against Ireland in Dublin because of the potential threat of terrorist activity.

A year later, it was England's turn to play over there, and the Rugby Football Union declared that the match would be played. The team was announced, and we were told that we were free to choose not to play, without prejudice. In fact, three players opted out and never played for England again.

Anyway, there was certainly some disquiet amongst the squad when we met for training a couple of weeks before the game, so I offered to ring my good friend Willie John McBride and ask him point-blank what he thought. I did, and W.J.'s reply will be etched in my memory for ever. 'David, you must come. Don't let the terrorists win!' Enough said.

We did all our preparation in England and flew over on the Friday. At the airport we were whisked off the steps of the plane straight into a luxury coach that was surrounded by police outriders on motorbikes carrying some heavy artillery. To make our party even more difficult to spot, a large sign on the windscreen of the coach read 'England Rugby Team'! For the entire journey to the prestigious Shelbourne Hotel on St Stephen's Green, right in the centre of Dublin, Andy Ripley, our number 8, rocked back and forth in his window seat. When he was asked why he was doing this, he replied, 'I'm trying to make it more difficult for the snipers!'

Wearing England blazers and ties and carrying bright-red kit bags emblazoned with the words 'England Rugby Team', we were met on the steps of the hotel by an Ireland official, who was heard to say, 'Welcome to Dublin. Are you here for the game?' It was all quite bizarre.

Ireland were also entrenched at the Shelbourne, and we were all effectively under house arrest – England at one end of the hotel and Ireland at the other. That evening we were quietly watching a feature film in our team room when the door opened behind me and in walked Fergus Slattery, who calmly sat down beside me. Out of mild curiosity, I asked him the inevitable question, to which he replied, 'Our film is fucking shite, so I've come to watch yours!'

We took to the field the next day and received the most ear-splitting reception I can ever recall. There were 50,000 spectators in attendance, every single one of whom was on his feet to welcome fifteen men dressed in white. It was a moment of such high emotion as to be very difficult to put into words. Suffice to say that several of us were reduced to tears, simply overcome by it all. But after the anthems, the referee went and spoiled it by blowing his whistle to start the match, because Ireland then proceeded to kick the shit out of us for 80 minutes and we lost. Somehow, the result didn't seem to matter as much as actually being there. I certainly felt immensely proud to be an Englishman that day.

At the after-match banquet, skipper John Pullin, a man of few words at the best of times, rounded off a short traditional vote of thanks to our opponents with the immortal words, 'We may not be much good, but at least we turn up!'

DAY OF THE LONG STUDS

STEWART McKINNEY

Munster and Ulster were unbeaten, both playing for the Interprovincial Championship at Thomond Park in 1976. I captained the Ulster side and was delighted when John West was appointed as referee for the match. I regarded him as the best in the world for allowing a flowing game, and he had a great sense of humour. It was an extraordinary match – a fluid game, although no tries were scored. Tony Ward kicked seven penalties for Munster and Mike Gibson seven for us. Then Frank Wilson kicked an eighth, and Ulster had won the championship 24–21.

The build-up to the match was even odder. Ireland had toured New Zealand that summer, and I and some others had returned with New Zealand studs – commonplace there but illegal in Britain and Ireland. They were better designed for mountain climbing than rugby! However, a little tickle with those studs discouraged the opposition from killing the ball in rucks.

Mr West duly appeared in the Ulster dressing-room and announced that he knew exactly what the team had been up to: showing referees boots with legal studs and wearing the forbidden ones hidden in their kitbags. He demanded that I line up the Ulster team on the halfway line, where they would kneel and exhibit their studs. I followed his instructions, having warned the lads.

'You first, Stewart,' he said and summoned me forward. As captain, it was no surprise that I had been called first, so, to lead by example, I kneeled down and showed him the soles of my boots. He laughed and said, 'What are you doing?'

'Showing you my studs, of course!' I replied, somewhat confused.

'I don't want to see your studs, you silly bollox. It's just that I've always wanted you on your knees before me, kneeling in front of me with 10,000 people watching!'

I mauled the first ball from the first lineout, headed straight for Mr West, dipped the shoulder and knocked him over. He nearly choked on his whistle as he lay on the ground and tried to halt the game. I stood over him as he got up from his backside and onto his knees, with 10,000 people watching. 'Touché, John!' I said.

We both laugh about it when we meet today for a pint.

RIPOSTE

SYD MILLAR
PROP Ballymena, Ulster
IRELAND 1957–70, 37 caps
LIONS TOURS '59, '62, '68, 9 Test matches; '74 coach;
'80 manager

International rugby is a serious business not to be taken lightly. Teams get hyped up and tensions run high, even in the amateur days. But amusing incidents did occur from time to time. Though they were few, there were a number of characters around who could be depended upon to provide lighter moments in the midst of the intensity that consumed the players and spectators. One such player was Phil O'Callaghan, a Munster and Ireland prop with a quick wit.

I returned to a very good Ireland team, excellently coached by Ronnie Dawson and captained by Tom Kiernan, in 1968 after being out of the picture for a few years, coming back to what was a changed situation. In particular, preparations had changed. The team now met for various sessions prior to the match instead of just the day before the game. As a result, more time was available to determine game plans, strategies and tactics and to identify areas in which we could optimise our strengths to pressurise and dominate the opposition and, equally, those areas in which they might try to pressurise us.

One such occasion was the Ireland v. Scotland match in 1970 and as a prop forward and one of the experienced players I was asked my opinion. I suggested that as Sandy Carmichael, normally the Scotland tight-head, had been selected at loose-head, there was a potential opportunity to spoil the opposition's play. Sandy was an excellent scrummaging tight-head and a very good all-round forward, but there is a considerable difference between one side of the scrum and the other, and Sandy had very little experience on the loose-head side. We decided that we could put pressure on the Scotland scrum by taking advantage of this inexperience, and Phil O'Callaghan was given the task.

After a few scrums, the ref's patience ran out, and he blew a long blast on his whistle and said, 'Penalty to Scotland!' He was obviously exasperated by Phil's scrummaging. Phil, who was well aware why the penalty had been given, looked at the referee with puzzlement and innocence on his face and inquired politely, 'Sir, what was that for?'

'You are boring, O'Callaghan,' replied the referee, meaning he was scrummaging inward at an angle.

'JAYSUS!' said Phil. 'You're not so bloody entertaining yourself, sir!', causing much merriment amongst those within earshot despite the pressures of an international game. Surely one of the best on-field one-liners in rugby history.

MANY A TRUE WORD SPOKEN IN JEST

FRAN COTTON
PROP Sale
ENGLAND 1971–81, 31 caps
LIONS TOURS '74, '77, 7 Test matches

Phil O'Callaghan, the Irish tight-head from the Dolphin Club in Cork, is the front-row forward reputed to have made the quip to the referee who penalised his scrummaging technique (see Syd Millar's 'Riposte'). What he said was true. I myself have first-hand knowledge of the legendary wit and humour of the great man. Moments of levity make for magnificent memories.

Whilst playing a hard-fought match against Ireland at Twickenham, a bit of a fracas broke out following a lineout in front of the West Stand. The referee successfully calmed the situation down and brought an end to the unsavoury spectacle of fisticuffs amongst the players. With order restored and decorum resumed, the referee signalled for play to continue. As the lineout re-formed, O'Callaghan, who was opposite me and had his hands on his knees, looked up and said, 'Cotton, you not only look like a gorilla, you fucking are one!'

Worryingly, it was my England teammates in the lineout who erupted in laughter. Many a true word spoken in jest, as they say! Still, I smiled myself at the time, so I suppose I can't complain now. It certainly diffused a tense moment.

THE GREAT BLACK GLOVES FUSS

LAWRENCE DIAMOND
NUMBER 8/LOCK Rainey FPs, Dungannon
GAELIC FOOTBALL Derry Senior (1963–78), Bellaghy Club,
All-Ireland Championship (1972)

What was it all about? Were people in the early 1960s not ready for the wearing of gloves on the rugby pitch? Having worn gloves while playing Gaelic football on a wet day, it made perfect sense to me that wearing them would be a terrific help when playing rugby on a 'piss' of a day. 'You'll never get away with it, and on your head be it!' my coach told me as I took to the field for the Rainey Endowed School's first-XV match against Campbell College in the semi-final of the Schools Cup in 1963. And to quote a prominent playing member of that Campbell College team, Mr Kelly Wilson, as he watched the Rainey team run out onto the pitch, 'Look at the big girl with the gloves on.'

Having never played Campbell before, they must have thought that this outfit from Magherafelt were there for a spot of morris dancing. But I was happy to burst onto the playing pitch, quite oblivious to the furore my half-crown net gloves, bought in Gerry Donnelly's drapers shop, Bellaghy, would create. The referee, cute as a fox, immediately noticed my unusual attire and summoned me for a consultation. 'You're wearing gloves,' he said.

'Well spotted,' says I.

'Why?' says he.

'Because I have broken bones in both hands,' says I, 'and the gloves are holding them together.'

He immediately rushed over to the touchline and beckoned to Mr Dawson McConkey, our coach. 'Your number 3 is wearing gloves. He tells me he has broken bones in his hands.'

'Well, if he tells you he has broken bones in his hands,' says Dawson, 'then he has broken bones in his hands.'

The referee called me over and said, 'If you have any pain, please inform me.'

I don't think he bought the story, but my gloved hands never dropped a ball, and the bones stayed intact. The morris dancers won 3–0 and went on to play in the cup final, for the first time in the Rainey Endowed School's history, against Belfast Royal Academy – a match which finished in a draw – and the black-net gloves were thrown high in the air on 17 March 1963 on the hallowed turf of Ravenhill.

A trend, first initiated in the early 1960s, has now become the norm for rugby players. Really, a fuss about nothing!

ISN'T IT IRONIC?

MOSS KEANE
LOCK UCC, Lansdowne, Munster
IRELAND 1973–84, 51 caps
LIONS TOUR '77, 1 Test match
GAELIC FOOTBALL Kerry Under-21

The twist of fate that brought me into the rugby fold was, ironically, the 'ban' (or more accurately the removal of same) on Gaelic footballers from engaging in this so-called 'foreign' game.

This lifting of the ban took place on Easter Sunday, 1971. Prior to this any Gaelic games player caught enjoying the likes of rugby, either as a player or as a spectator, was automatically suspended for a period of 12 months. Where I come from in Kerry, no serious rugby was played. Everybody played Gaelic football. The main rugby centres were 60 miles away (a significant distance in those days, nearly 40 years ago) in either Cork or Limerick.

Rugby was, of course, organised at a local level in a few centres such as Castleisland, Tralee, Killarney, Listowel and Killorglin. However, very few people attended these local 'derbies'. The standard was somewhat less than ideal and was compared to watching a pornographic movie – strictly for the enjoyment of the participants and only frustrating the onlookers. The advent of TV in the 1960s brought rugby internationals into our living rooms in Kerry in one fell swoop.

From such a humble background emerged no fewer than six Ireland rugby internationalists in a period of twenty-five years: the Doyle brothers, the Spring brothers, Mick Galwey and me. While both sets of brothers attended rugby-playing secondary schools, Mick Galwey went straight from Castleisland High to Shannon, Munster and Ireland.

However, I had a much more direct route. In 1970 I captained UCC Gaelic senior football team to win the intervarsities Sigerson Cup. The following year I played for the UCC senior rugby side, next year came Munster and in 1973–74 I graduated to the Ireland side. In the professional era that type of progression would be 'off the wall'. However, there was a lot to be said in favour of rugby as a pastime in an era when six-packs were purchased for the train journey home from

Cork, Limerick or Belfast and not used as an expression to describe the condition of your gut.

I found the build-up to my first cap in Paris most intriguing. Thursday – get together for two hours' training at Anglesea Road – feeling bolloxed after it. Fly out that evening after a fair few pints to get courage for the flight. Friday – another short run-out and then on to the Irish Embassy for a reception. One of the props, Sean Lynch, took me on board and advised I drink Tio Pepe – stout would be too obvious, as we would be under the microscope as regards our choice of drink. (Suffice to say that I've never drunk Tio Pepe since.) Saturday – early breakfast and lunch after a shite night's kip. The phone rang a few times in the middle of the night. My roommate, the late great Terry Moore, was not impressed the last time it rang, and I doubt if that particular phone was ever used again! Then there was a team meeting, which lasted about an hour, mainly in a silence that was interrupted only by the sound of our captain, Willie John McBride, lighting up his pipe a few times and the odd fart by the likes of Stewart McKinney. Eventually, we got onto the bus, with a gendarme escort, 100 mph to Parc des Princes.

We were unlucky to lose 9–6, but I must have played OK, as I subsequently made five further appearances for Ireland at the same venue. Happy days.

SATURDAY STEAKS, SUNDAY SIRENS AND THE GARDA SÍOCHÁNA

NIGEL CARR
FLANKER Queen's University, Ards, Ulster
IRELAND 1984–7, 11 caps
LIONS v. REST OF THE WORLD, APRIL 1986

Dublin's historic Shelbourne Hotel was home from home for the Ireland squad. Players from Belfast, Limerick or Galway would trek to Dublin following their Saturday afternoon games ahead of the Sunday training session. Upon arrival, Ulster players of the mid-1980s would seek the strength-sustaining nourishment offered by a prime fillet steak, with prawn cocktail for both starter and dessert (hold the lettuce!).

However, for some Ulster players there was a real and ever-present danger much worse than indigestion. Terrorist atrocities were commonplace, with gruesome acts of violence each stooping to new depths. Ireland players with security-force connections were perceived as high-profile targets, so it was not uncommon for each to be met at the border by the Garda Síochána and accompanied throughout the weekend by armed and plain-clothes officers. One might imagine highly trained, elite personnel whose surveillance skills and precautionary instincts would see them act with military ruthlessness. The truth was that this armed contingent blended in with the team so effectively that by the Saturday night of an international game they were armed and legless!

On one such memorable international weekend Ireland had temporarily relinquished their St Stephen's Green base to encamp in Dún Laoghaire's Royal Marine Hotel. The new setting was far from the hustle and bustle of city-centre Dublin and the invasion of home and away support. However, the solace of the seaside did nothing to dampen the post-match Saturday night/Sunday morning revelry.

It was after such a night that my wife June and I left our Dún Laoghaire hotel to get a connecting train to Dublin. However, a limited Sunday service prompted us to return to the hotel to revise our plans, only to be offered a lift by my Royal Ulster Constabulary international teammate, his wife and their two Garda minders. We piled into their unmarked car, thankful for the offer. Little did we know, however, that the police driver, no doubt trained in the art of high-speed car pursuits and, in normal circumstances, proficient in the skills of advanced and defensive driving, had been up to 5 a.m. in a drunken 'discussion' with the director of rugby development. I should have guessed as he sped around the busy car park unable to find the exit. Things got even worse on the open road as he drove nose to tail in the fast lane of the dual carriageway. His fellow officer in the back seat was coming up with such gems as, 'Change lanes and I'll cover you,' and occasionally urging restraint in a drunken slur that was largely indecipherable, the only positive suggestion to keep death off the roads being to pass the row of stationary cars at the lights by mounting the pavement. Our bumper sticker should have been 'My other car is a patrol car'.

Fortunately, we lived to tell the tale, as we luckily discovered the one thing that radically reduced the chances of us hitting the car in front – June found the switch for the siren. Six variously intoxicated adults (three in the front, three in the back) now effortlessly navigated red lights as if they weren't there and arrived serenely at Dublin Connolly station with lights flashing and siren wailing.

THE RUGBY PSYCHIATRIST

STEWART McKINNEY

Dave McSweeney played for Ireland against Scotland in 1955 and, by his own admission, had such a poor game that the rest of the team wouldn't allow him on the bus after the match . . . so, he had to walk from Murrayfield back to the North British Hotel. John Murphy introduced me to him in 1980 when I first came to London, and apart from being a great character he was a handy man to know if one's mental state was thought to have been a factor in a misdemeanour!

Now, Richard Harris was a rugby aficionado – in fact, he was a rugby nut – and had a huge library of rugby videos. He very kindly brought me some of the Ireland games in which I had featured (and had never seen) when I was landlord of the Turk's Head pub.

Richard owned a house in Child's Walk, Earls Court, that was cared for by his brother Dermot when he was off making films. One Sunday, John Murphy, Dermot, Jimmy 'Muncher' Waldron and Arthur McCoy were sitting around chewing the fat when a little bird flew through the window. Quick as a flash, Arthur McCoy caught the sparrow and detained him under the hat he was wearing. 'Bejaysus!' said Arthur. 'I think I've got a bird on the brain. I keep hearing chirping noises. This could be a case for McSweeney.'

Dave arrived after a call from Dermot, who told him that Arthur was in the bedroom and wasn't in a great state. The good doctor went to Arthur and sympathetically quizzed him about his condition and how he had come to face this predicament. He questioned him about his childhood and tried to pinpoint any crisis that might have triggered this episode. After half an hour of probing and still no diagnosis, McCoy lifted off the hat and up flew the bird. McSweeney wasn't well pleased at the affront to his professional competence but was soon placated when the ploy to get him to come out for a drink with the boys was revealed. They had only wanted him to join them, as he was such great company – neither insult nor offence had been intended.

THE WEST'S AWAKE

**FEIDLIM McLOUGHLIN**
**PROP Northern Connaught**
**IRELAND 1976, 1 cap**

I was born in a little village on the west coast of Ireland called Derrymullen near Ballinasloe, County Galway, and my father and mother were born in an even more countrified village called Killure. I mention this because of the wonderful homeliness to this sort of country life in the 1940s, '50s and '60s, full of helpful, cooperative neighbours, all with farming backgrounds. They were simple times, naive, innocent, gentle, soft, and there was a great sense of community. The kindness of friends was reciprocated, with the exchange of vegetables and so on.

When we got our first black Baby Ford car, some of the villagers, including ladies in their hats, would turn up on a Sunday to go for a spin, which occupied patient, busy Dad (Tadhg) for a whole afternoon. There was equal pleasure when Uncle John turned up with the first 'Little Grey' Ferguson tractor, which seemed so large then, and, again, everybody would gather around to examine it. Incidentally, my brother Colm and I learned to drive at 11 years of age sitting on Dad's knee. Despite this advanced experience, it still took me three test failures before I got my driving licence in the UK.

Great excitements when I was young included preparing the bog banks (referred to as cleaning the bank) in March for the turf cutting and the saving of the turf/hay (wheat and corn later). During the bad weather summers, the _meiteal_ (Gaelic word for a gathering of neighbours) would come into action. Everybody would come together to spend a whole Sunday cutting the turf in one particular neighbour's turf bog bank and the following weekend do the very same thing for the next neighbour. The same applied for the saving of the hay during excessively rainy summers. Another splendid thing was the threshing machine in October. There was great community spirit, and as boys we would have the liberty of raiding the orchards, the owners turning a blind eye. These activities strengthened the bonds between neighbours, essential for village survival.

In my brother Ray's first year at UCD he insisted on cutting the turf in our bank to make himself strong and fit for athletics and rugby. He was known as the 'Slanes Man', someone who never stops throwing up the wet sods, giving the wheelbarrow turf carriers a really rough time. Colm and I were part of the wheelbarrowing team, a chore that also helped to build up our strength, which was very useful in our sporting lives.

VOICES FROM THE BACK OF THE BUS

I refer to this old, rural environment in which our family was reared to give you an idea of the life we led, one which was dominated by Gaelic football, hurling and camogie. My favourite sport at the time was Gaelic handball.

For my, Ray and Colm's birthday parties, my mother would collect the different-coloured tissue papers from oranges and use them as flags to surround our own 'Croke Park', and we would play Gaelic football or hurling with the rest of the village boys. We would all have arguments before the match as to who we were going to be; for example, Christy Ring or Inky Flaherty (famous hurlers), Sean Purcell or Frankie Stockwell (Gaelic football All-Ireland medal winners from Galway).

Our father, an amateur boxer, used to train people in Ballinasloe. My brothers and I would also organise little boxing competitions at our parties, and again we would debate heavily over which famous boxer we were going to be. Ray insisted on being Rocky Marciano, Colm was Joe Louis and I liked John L. Sullivan, the bare-knuckle fighter. We always seemed to beat the local boys, and, sadly, they usually went home crying before the party was finished. This used to infuriate our mother, with all her excellent effort and lavish food wasted as our birthday guests departed. We became accustomed to their mothers turning up afterwards to investigate the scene. Our mother (Mary Ellen) would have little parcels of pacification cakes for visiting mothers to take home to their wounded sons.

Such was the background in which I was brought up, one almost exclusively dominated by Gaelic games. Ray, Colm and I did play rugby at Garbally College, where both Gaelic and rugby were offered. Other Garbally students, beside me, played for Ireland: Dickie Roche, P.J. O'Dwyer, Noel Manion, Dr Mick Molloy, Ciaran Fitzgerald and my brother Ray. Ray also trained in athletics, coached by Father Kevin Ryle, who used to come to our house specifically to train my brother in shot-putting technique. As students, we used to unfairly impersonate Father Ryle from County Kerry (nicknamed 'Puckey the Priest') because his shot-putting coaching consisted of just two words: 'up' and 'out'.

Ray had wooden weightlifting equipment designed for himself in one of the garages attached to the house, and we all copied his weightlifting style – at a lesser weight – which unknowingly helped our stamina and strength for rugby, boxing, Gaelic football, etc.

I didn't really become semi-keen on rugby, in truth, until I was about 17 and as a late developer (I didn't grow until I was 18) played my first senior game for Ballinasloe on the wing. Our home ground was in the local St Bridget's Mental Hospital grounds, and we would change in their dormitories, overseen by the nursing staff. Some of the patients would walk in and out, and we were trained to accept their friendliness and curiosity about what we were preparing for. One of them took my precious boot one day and was trying it on when off he ran with it. It took some very fast men on our team to keep pace with him and eventually coax its return. The reappropriated boot made little difference because I didn't score a try anyway.

When I transferred to Dublin, I played for the Blackrock third and fourth teams, although nobody kept a record of that. I remember turning up in my Sunday suit and hanging it up in a little shed in Kildare, and that was my first feeling that I was playing underfunded rugby just for fun.

I played most of my rugby after that in England. I originally joined Gosforth, where my brother Ray was captain. He had gone across to Newcastle University to study for his PhD in the early 1960s. I had experience in the thirds and fourths, and eventually progressed through the ranks.

From the mid-1960s, I had a number of trials for Connaught before I was chosen to play for them. The culture of the game then was such that nobody would come across to watch the Irish expats play in England – a shortage of funds also contributed to this. Ray was also an unintentional, innocent obstacle at Gosforth, as I was always compared with him. On this basis, I left and went to Northern FC, eventually captaining them from 1974 to 1976. I was finally capped for Ireland while playing for that club in January 1976, for which I had toiled a long time. Incidentally, Stewart McKinney was playing in the back row that day.

County rugby in England was very strong throughout the 1960s and '70s, and our Northumberland team had Colin White (England), Duncan Madson (Scotland) and me in the front row, and Roger Uttley (former England captain) and John Hall in the second row. During that same period, Billy Beaumont, Fran Cotton, Steve Smith and Roger Creed played for Lancashire, and Tony Neary and our own Barry O'Driscoll were in the North West Counties team that beat Ian Kirkpatrick's touring All Blacks (1972–73).

During that same tour, I played with White, Madson, Uttley and Hall at Liddett Green for North Eastern Counties, and Alan Old missed a kick that would have won the game for us that is still talked about today. It was a very dirty game in which, unfortunately, I broke my hand and stupidly stayed on for the duration. I went over to Ireland immediately afterwards for a final trial and decided to do without plaster, with the silly idea of lasting out to the end of selection on Sunday, 10 January 1972. I was rooming with Moss Keane (I think), and I developed a fever during the night, started raving and had to go to hospital to have my hand set. Michael Carroll was then chairman of selectors, and he took me. My plan had backfired, and I had to wait until the following year for another trial, one of many.

The original Gosforth team is sadly no longer around, although they have transferred the honour boards to the new Newcastle Falcons building. It is good to report that Northern FC is still there in its original building and being run as a rugby club.

I travelled year after year to play for Connaught and was dropped five times before I got my feet under the table. They would always start with a home-based team, and when the new team experiment had failed and they were beaten again I would be called up. I used to travel from Newcastle down to Liverpool, get the boat to Dublin and walk up from the docks to where Ray worked to get a lift with him. Dr Mick Molloy, Dr Barry O'Driscoll, Michael Mahony and later Dr John O'Driscoll were also invariably there to get a lift.

During the 1960s, '70s and some of the '80s, the travel expenses were meagre. In an effort to save money, I'd take the ferry rather than fly, and I remember experiencing many rough, seasick crossings between Dublin and Liverpool. On one occasion, having little money, I decided to put in my expenses, which amounted to £5 3s 6d. I courageously approached a non-smiling Bobby Deacy (Connaught's treasurer) and en route decided to change my claim to an even fiver. He asked me aggressively why it was an even fiver – haven't times changed? I also recollect when I was captain of Connaught, with a fair bit of say and temporary influence, I recommended John Hanigan from Liverpool, who was a very prominent full-back (Cheshire). We were waiting for him to arrive on the Friday evening before the game when, eventually, a small bearded individual turned up, came across to me and asked if I could sort the taxi out. Of course, I immediately agreed, assuming it was from Galway Station to the Galwegians clubhouse, and I was dying to get to bed. The taxi man says, 'That will be £56, sir.' John Hanigan had come in from Dublin Airport!

It took immense nerve to tell Bobby Deacy. He came into the bar, pale as a sheet, and had to be resuscitated. John played next day against Ulster and came into the line beautifully, which was his skill. He was never picked for Connaught again. In my opinion, his quality of play had nothing to do with it, but the £56 taxi from Dublin had a major influence on his rugby career in Ireland.

Tony Brown, the former Connaught coach, was a marvellous motivator, and he would always praise me in public, as, indeed, he did all the captains. In particular, he would tell the team about my immense endeavours to get there by boat, horse, donkey, whatever, thumbing a lift through different counties and countries just to get to Connaught. On one occasion, he lavished me with praise as usual and then whispered to me to ask if I minded him giving Ciaran Fitzgerald a crack at the captaincy. I eventually had to give way, and, of course, that was the start of Ciaran's Connaught, Ireland and eventually Lions captaincy.

Ray and I played many times for Connaught and were chosen for one or two final Ireland trials together. At one point, we were tipped to play together in the front row, which would have been an immense honour, and I think it would have been the first time that brothers had played together in the front row for Ireland.

Ray and I were also picked for the Barbarians' Easter tour in 1975, which again would have been the first time that brothers had played together in the front row for the Barbarians. I travelled with my young family into the heavy winter snow from Northumberland to Cardiff, not arriving until after midnight – having meant to be with the team at 7 p.m. on Easter Thursday. Herbert Waddell, the Barbarians president, greeted me and told me that Ray had cried off due to injury. It was frustrating that another chance to make history had passed us by; however, I thoroughly enjoyed the matches, and we won all four, beating Newport, Swansea, Cardiff and Penarth.

I felt I was at my peak (courageous comment – do props ever peak?) from 1971 to 1974 or 1975. I was reserve, on and off, with the Ireland team during that period, and we all remember the drama during the 1971–72 season when Scotland and Wales would not travel to Ireland because of the Troubles. France agreed to play twice that season, and the first game was away on 19 January 1972. I was again reserve. Ronnie Dawson told me I would almost certainly get onto the field for the first time, as both props, Ray and Sean Lynch, had severe back injuries. Ronnie had rehearsed the signal for when I was meant to go on the field, and I duly received it when Sean Lynch had to have treatment for his back. But Sean wouldn't leave the field and, incredibly, Ray, coming to what seemed like the end of his long playing career, scored his first and only international try when he forced his way over the line, to much subsequent publicity. This gave him a new spark. He was chosen again for the home game on 29 April 1972 at Lansdowne Road (Ireland won 24–14) and another season passed.

The political cloud remained the following season, and there was a slight doubt about England travelling to Ireland. They kept their admirable word and travelled. It was unique (from memory) to have both the Ireland and England teams in the same hotel because of high security. Ireland and all the supporters have never forgotten the great gesture of the England team coming to Ireland that season on 10 February 1973. Ireland won 18–9, and the famous words of John Pullin, the England captain, at the after-dinner speech are still much quoted.

In January 1976 I eventually got my long-awaited first cap, against Australia. I think (but am not absolutely sure) that I might have been the oldest player to get a first cap for Ireland. (Davy Tweed beat that record later on when he got his first cap.) I had joined an exclusive group, one which is often referred to in sports quizzes: 'How many brothers have played for Ireland?' (This question has become more difficult to answer as the years have gone by due to the fact that many brothers have achieved that honour since Ray and I.) When I was asked by a BBC reporter how many caps Ray and I had, I was supposed to have said, 'Ray and myself have 41 caps between us. He has one and I have forty, I think.' As our mental state decreases with age, Ray rings me up periodically and says, 'Remind me again, Feidlim, how many caps have I got?'

FIRST CAP AND THAT FIVER

MICK SKINNER
FLANKER Blackheath, Harlequins
ENGLAND 1988–92, 21 caps

Boy, oh boy, do I have a story for you in the Under-11s!

My first cap was away to France at the Parc des Princes. My parents were there, as will yours be on your first tour. I amazingly caught sight of them in the stand as I walked out onto the pitch more than an hour before kick-off. If the same thing happens to you, be careful not to acknowledge them . . . it's not *large*!

They were being looked after by Blackheath mates of mine, and nearby I noticed 'Pretty Boy' Crispin Reed and Tony Crust holding a banner that read 'Mick Skinner ATE my hamster'. I was sure it was a coded message, but to this day I have not been able to work it out . . . any ideas would be welcome.

I played with a heart full of emotion and a stomach full of hamsters. The Frogs did not know what had hit them. My first 'bosh' was on the man-mountain France number 8 Laurel Rodriquez, who wasn't even rocked backwards. He just stood stationary, and I shuddered. I remember striding side by side with him to the next lineout. He didn't know how much that hurt *me* . . . and he never would. I'd tried to *munch* him, but in turn he'd munched me.

It was a fierce game in which we played well but narrowly lost, 11–9. As we had three new caps in the side that day and had made four other changes, we proved our critics wrong. After the game, we went to the dinner with the France team. To my surprise they turned up with their mistresses, which is the norm. They then took us around Paris, and we were given a VIP reception by England and France supporters.

In the morning I was awoken by the telephone. It was Peter Winterbottom, who explained that it was lunchtime and that we'd missed our flight with the team by a good three hours. He suggested a quick livener in the hotel bar. I couldn't detect the littlest bit of panic – he was a seasoned pro. I was then suddenly aware of another body in my bed; it was me that was panicking now. I was pleasantly surprised, as it was a Doris, and an attractive one at that. We got dressed, and I checked my wallet – still had the fiver I'd gone out with. Now that's what I call a good night out.

I couldn't wait to surprise Wints with my new acquaintance. I might have shuddered the day before after my introduction to Rodriquez, but now it was Wints' turn – in disbelief that I had actually pulled.

I strutted into the bar, and it was me who wobbled first, because Wints was also in company, and she was even prettier than mine. I was initially taken aback when both ladies spoke French, but luckily I kept my astonishment to myself, as it eventually dawned on me where we were. How foolish I would have sounded.

Wints and I started doing some serious socialising. We bought drinks in the hotel bar for any supporter we found, dragging them off the street and thinking that we could put it on the Rugby Football Union account. Some four hours later, the spike holding the bar receipts was just about full so we asked for our bill to be put on the Rugby Football Union account. 'Sorry, there is *not* one. It was closed when they departed,' said the barman. There was no way my fiver would cover it.

It was then that the legend who was John Burgess, the president of the Rugby Football Union, walked in with Elvis, his lovely wife. I got the two of them a drink, and when I asked the barman to put it on my tab John went mad. 'No England player, the day after a game, should buy anything. Give me that tab here, barman!' He settled it. Now that's what I call a 'Supatanka'!

John and Elvis couldn't stay and set off for the airport. The phone rang behind the bar, and the barman said it was for me. Now who could that be? It turned out that the two Dorises had left some time earlier and were ringing from a restaurant. Wints and I jumped in a cab and joined them just in time, as the waitress was delivering a bottle of Dom Pérignon vintage champagne – 1982. I explained to the waitress that she had got the wrong table, thinking we were going to get stitched by the girls. But she pointed to a fatboy at another table and said that he'd ordered it. He turned out to be the French owner of the restaurant, and after our meal we joined him for an *digestif* or two. Again, that fiver stayed in my wallet. The owner explained he had enjoyed the game, as we had played so well. 'It is an honour to have you in my restaurant,' he said.

So, the moral of the story is to ignore your parents on the touchline. It will make you play better, and then you'll not have to pay for anything. I have given that fiver to Stewart McKinney, to add to the charity fund.

Skinnerisms

BOSH (noun): the impact or repercussions thereof brought about by a collision or similar between persons in the course of simultaneous perambulation, acceleration or motoring activity.

FATBOY (noun; familiar): a gentleman who, by dint of breeding, body mass or facial disfigurement, may be deemed a forward. Any male who is in the favour of the Munch.

LARGE (adjective): precise etymology not traceable. Suffice to say, the Munch seeks to express the agreeable nature of the experience or recreation being considered or subject described (like 'cool').

MUNCH(ED) (verb; noun): to have the full force of Skinner brought to bear upon you. A distinctly undesirable experience with a detrimental outcome.

PRETTY BOY (noun; familiar): one of the male species who has been blessed with and preserved angelic facial features. Or more specifically one who has not had their head crushed in the pack and is prone to wearing hair gel.

SUPATANKA (noun; familiar): apparently, this is common Geordie parlance intending to convey that the recipient is a cool bloke.

A WELSH HERO

DEREK QUINNELL
NUMBER 8 Llanelli
WALES 1972–80, 23 caps
LIONS TOURS '71, '77, '80, 5 Test matches

After the 1980 Lions tour of South Africa, I was on a short holiday with Madora, my wife, and our two boys, Scott and Craig. Scott was eight years old and Craig was three years younger. We were staying in Aberporth on the Cardiganshire coast, and Madora's brother, Barry John, and his family were on holiday in New Quay a few miles further up the coast, so we made arrangements to meet for a day out at the beach.

After a kickabout with a football (I wanted to be on Barry's side, because he could play a bit, but I had to captain the Quinnell side against the Johns, and I'm afraid it was a bit one-sided), we all went for lunch. A few youngsters came up to our party and asked for my autograph, which was something the boys were used to seeing at Stradey Park. Scott looked surprised when the children asked Barry for his autograph, too, as Barry had retired in 1972, the year that Scott was born, and my eldest son didn't realise that his uncle was a superstar of the rugby world. Scott asked his mother why they were asking for Barry's autograph, and Madora explained that in her view Barry was the best fly-half who had ever played the game. Scott was quick to reply that he couldn't have been better than Benny (Phil Bennett), whom Scott watched every week at Stradey Park. How lucky I was to have played with both players.

A SKINNER'S TALE

PADDY NORTON
FULL-BACK Askeans, Blackheath, Kent

In 1984 Harlequins RFC were invited by Old Belvedere RFC to defend their seven-a-side title in Dublin. However, on that same Sunday in early May the Harlequins' presence was also requested at the Haig Sevens, to be played at Murrayfield. Whether it was due to the lure of the sponsor's product or the chance of a free trip home, the Quins' Scottish contingent chose to attend the Murrayfield event. So, Dick Best – then Harlequins' coach – approached our coach at Blackheath, Des Diamond, about the possibility of a number of Blackheath players representing Harlequins at the tournament in Dublin. It was agreed that seven of our number would team up with a couple of the Quins' own players to make a defence of the Old Belvedere Sevens crown.

After qualifying for the Middlesex Sevens finals at Beckenham on the Saturday afternoon, we seven men of Blackheath, still wearing our playing kit, jumped into a couple of cars and sped across London to Heathrow for an early evening flight to Dublin. Among our number was one Michael Gordon Skinner, later to become better known as Mick 'the Munch' Skinner, a man for whom the publican's cry, 'Time, gentlemen, please!' usually confirmed that once again he had been drinking all evening without ever having reached into his wallet. As the late Chas Chapman of Westcombe Park and Kent once said, 'Mick is well known for his generosity at the bar every 29 February.'

We failed in our defence of the Old Belvedere crown, being beaten by the minnows of Palmerston RFC in the quarter-final. The foundation of the defeat was probably, in some measure, the hospitality availed of in the champagne and Guinness marquee at the hosts' ground the previous evening. Yet there were two benefits of being knocked out of the competition prematurely: a hot shower and an early crack at the Guinness.

We enjoyed the drinking and revelry, so much so that despite the urging and pleading of the alickadoos for us to finish up quickly in order to catch the last London-bound flight, we left our departure from the craic a little too late. On our arrival at Dublin Airport, with only minutes to spare before the scheduled departure, we were informed that two of our seats had been sold to more punctual travellers and the flight was now full.

A consternation circle formed. One of the concerned alickadoos struck a military pose and made a request, Captain Mainwaring style, for two volunteers to stay in Dublin overnight and take the first flight on Monday morning. With only a split second's glance between us, Skins and I registered in unison our willingness to accept the mission. In haste to show his appreciation of our 'sacrifice', another of the alickadoos pulled a wad of £10 notes from his pocket. He made a fan of the money in front of his chest and began to utter, 'Mick, how much do you . . .'

Before he could finish the question or withdraw the notes, Skins had struck like a cobra, removed the money and spat out his response in pure Geordie, 'That'll do mate!' We were in a cab in seconds, booked into a B & B in minutes and back enjoying the hospitality at Old Belvedere within half an hour.

It was this amateur's largest and only pay packet, but I am, of course, still waiting for my share of the balance from the aforementioned 'Canny Lad'.

THE SOUND OF BREAKING GLASS

STEWART McKINNEY

Tom Grace had a wicked sense of humour and was a notorious practical joker. He was also a great strategist and tactician who knew the value of a good plan.

We had a presentation in the team room in the Shelbourne Hotel for the great man, Willie John. I can't remember if it was on the occasion of his 50th cap or because he had become the most-capped Irish player – Willie had broken so many records. I do remember that after the presentation of the beautifully inscribed Waterford Crystal plate, Willie was sitting back contentedly, sucking on his pipe and sipping a well-earned pint. The plate was being passed around the team for admiration, with many an 'ooh' and an 'aah' accompanying its viewing and careful handling by the players . . . until there was a deafening crash followed by non-stop apology from the contrite Gracer.

Willie John was seething. The plate was shattered! (*Apparently*! Nobody in the room had noticed Gracer's earlier sleight of hand.) After five minutes of effusive contrition and repentance, Gracer eventually produced the Waterford Crystal from behind a cabinet.

He had, in fact, dropped some Shelbourne crockery he had hidden before the presentation. I wonder if Bob Fitzgerald sent him a bill for the breakages?

FOOD FOR THOUGHT

HARRY STEELE
LOCK Queen's University, Ballymena
IRELAND 1975–9, 10 caps

I had the pleasure of sharing a room with Moss Keane on the occasion of my first cap for Ireland. I couldn't believe my luck. Sharing with an experienced player was bound to have its advantages, and this helped to alleviate my 'rookie' nerves. Indeed, his wisdom prevailed when he suggested on the Friday that on the morning of the match we should breakfast in our room to avoid the crowds of supporters who would be in the hotel. Obviously avoiding distraction and remaining focused were of paramount importance.

I appreciated the insight, and green as grass and keen as mustard wondered how I might best contribute to the positive well-being the mighty sage was trying to create. We were to play at Twickenham, so I immediately took control and said I would ring room service to order breakfast, smugly thinking that the staff would better understand my dulcet Ulster tones than Moss, who, with his strong Kerry accent, was bound to be misunderstood by the staff. During my conversation with room service, Moss shouted to order some newspapers, so at the end I asked in my best English for a couple to be provided with our breakfast.

Next morning breakfast arrived as ordered, except that instead of a couple of papers there were six plates of kippers! (Hard to explain, hey?) Moss loved my embarrassment and cursed me up and down for being a smart-assed UK citizen. He then laughed and said, 'Sure, it's just as well. We wouldn't have had time to read the papers – but we'll have time to eat the kippers!' And he bloody did – on his own.

After the 1975 Australia v. Ulster match, the reception was held in one of Ulster's finest hotels. Nothing was spared in entertaining the Australians, and a gourmet dinner was part of the celebrations. The waitress for our table was a great 'wee old' Ulster woman, brought in that night to help cater for the many extra guests. She was all business and straight to the point, simple and direct, no dithering in deliberation, a jewel in our crown.

On the menu that night there was a choice of two soups: crème de célerie or consommé Alexandra. When taking the order from our table, she first looked at my opposite number, the Australian number 8 Greg Cornelson, and with great authority and absolutely no sense of occasion said, 'Right, big fella, soup – thick or thin?'

BOXER THE CARTHORSE

CHRIS RALSTON
LOCK Richmond
ENGLAND 1971–5, 22 caps
LIONS TOUR '74, 1 Test match

I left school at the tender age of seventeen with two O levels. (How the kids today manage to get 11 or 12 A★ GCSEs, I don't know! It must be easier now, or perhaps I spent too much time playing sport and smoking Wild Woodbine cigarettes behind the bicycle shed – not exactly a good combination, but it seemed to work at that time.) One of my O levels was English literature, and the book we read and studied was *Animal Farm* by George Orwell. I decided to model my early life on Boxer the carthorse – big, clumsy and simple, but quite nice.

I joined Richmond mid-season, which was just as well, as the then president was a bit of a stickler as to which school one had attended. My school – King William's College on the Isle of Man – did not quite match up to Harrow, Radley, Marlborough, etc., from where most of the schoolboy intake for the club came.

I started my rugby life in the Extra A XV and within a couple of seasons progressed to the Vikings Second XV. However, I was then sent back to the Extra A, at which piqued point I threw a tantrum and left to join Rosslyn Park. However, this move never actually materialised. The first game was an away match against Gosport and Fareham, and when no one turned up to pick me up at Hammersmith Broadway after an hour and a half (already showing commitment and dedication above and beyond the call of duty) I decided I was better off back at Richmond.

After a further season, I was playing in the first XV and for Middlesex. The first game I played for the Richmond firsts I was awarded an honorary

Blue, as I was the only non-Oxbridge member of the team. In those days rugby was very different from today's game, not only on the field but also more especially off it. We trained very hard, but we played very hard as well. The ethos and culture at Richmond was about enjoying life on and off the field. I quickly learned how to drink 15 pints of bitter followed by a curry on a Saturday night. I became quite knowledgeable and discerning about the quality of the brew I was imbibing, whether the landlord kept the lines clean, how the keg had been conditioned, and I always knew if I fancied a korma, pasanda, rogan josh or vindaloo. These were pre-professional days. We were young, fit and strong and could metabolise our carbohydrate/alcohol intake efficiently. We weren't concerned about binge drinking, GI indexes, carb-loading or tissue hydration.

We enjoyed some hilarious Easter tours to the south of France. In fact, I turned down two or three Barbarian tours to Wales in favour of going to France with Richmond. It was really a bit of a no-brainer – enjoying the combined delights of French wine, French cuisine and pretty French girls against getting my head kicked in at Swansea and Cardiff by a lot of hairy, ugly, mental men!

During the swinging 1960s, I was in my early 20s and living in London. Serendipitous! What a time to be in the right place! Whilst rugby was my life, I also enjoyed going out a lot and experiencing the opportunities London's social scene had to offer. My local watering hole was the Queen's Elm in the Fulham Road, frequented by the actress Julie Christie, the author Laurie Lee, the film director Norman Jewison and the likes, as well as a number of heavy-drinking, jovial Irishmen. One night, and I am embarrassed about this, I was walking home and, bursting for a pee, needed to relieve myself in the street. I was caught, spent the night in a cell at Chelsea nick and appeared at Marlborough Magistrates' Court on Saturday morning. I pleaded guilty, was fined ten shillings (only 50p, but it meant a lot more back then!) and made my way post-haste to Wasps in time for the kick-off. I seem to remember I had quite a good game despite the penury and privation of my reduced circumstances the previous night. (That was another thing you could do back then: have a bit of privacy – there was no media interest or intrusion.)

Eventually, I was selected for England and then the Lions. By this time known as 'Lurch' (of Munster family fame!), I started the 1974 tour to South Africa with a severe bout of flu, having given up cigarettes for 20 Villager cigars a day. During the match against the Quaggas, both of my crowned top teeth were damaged. After the match, I was taken to Pretoria Dental Hospital, whereupon a young student experimented by removing all of my upper gums whilst supplying me with two new crowns. It was no surprise that within a few hours I had an abscess. Luckily, we were travelling to East London, and although I endured the pain for 36 hours I was finally relieved of the agony by a dentist who took both top front teeth out, roots and crowns.

That afternoon, having lost a considerable amount of blood in the dentist's chair, I willingly declared myself fit to play against the all-black side calling themselves the Leopards. For the first time I wore a gum shield, but because it was so uncomfortable and we were winning easily I put it in my pocket at half-time.

Sod's law: the first lineout of the second half, one M. Burton upsets his opposite number to such an extent that he swings a punch. Burton ducks. As I return to terra firma after jumping for the ball, my jaw lands on the end of the opposition prop's fist.

My next recollection is of Willie John sitting on the end of my bed, puffing on his pipe. 'Chris, it's good to see you've recovered,' he said. He paused, puffed on his pipe again and continued, 'Could I ask if you've enjoyed this tour so far?' I'm sure Willie John can embellish the tale. It was quite funny looking back on it, even if at the time I was not terribly amused . . . but that's another story!

I finally retired in 1987 having played for Richmond for more than 20 years. I made many, many friends in the game – they were good friends then and they still are now. I would not have changed anything. I had a wonderful time, with rugby the backbone of my life. I now go to games with my old mates – Andy Ripley, Tony Neary, Roger Uttley, Jan Webster, et al. – and watch a sport that is unrecognisable to the one I played. The new game has players who are fantastically fit, and the hits are much harder. Like all old farts, we just sum it up by saying, 'It wasn't like that in our day,' then enjoy a few pints and disappear into the night.

HOUSE RULES

STEWART McKINNEY

Anyone seeking a life of tranquillity should never buy a house next to a rugby club. When I was coaching Askeans Rugby Club, I had the chance to buy 60 Broad Walk, and the rugby club was at 60A Broad Walk. An 8-foot fence, high enough to repel normal invaders, separated the driveway to the club from the back garden. There was also a stout back door leading from the drive into the utility room. So, in my wisdom, I bought the house – it would be so handy for coaching, being just a 30-yard walk to the clubhouse.

The problem was Saturday nights. The high fence and the back door proved no problem to my young charges. It was like the Somme every Saturday night as the more sober ones came over the top and the more inebriated or less fit by the door. An early Sunday morning reconnaissance might find up to 16 bodies sleeping downstairs – every square foot of carpet or settee would be taken up. That in itself was not the problem, but when the 'guests' arrived they were usually hungry – especially the New Zealanders and in particular one Michael Dowd, an excellent loose-head prop from North Harbour. He had the appetite of a trencherman, and after the Sunday roast disappeared and the door of the icebox had been pulled from its hinges, my wife laid down some ground rules.

The back door would be left open, as the fence was becoming dilapidated by the weekly assaults, and food would be left on the dining table for the starving marauders – trays of sandwiches, chicken legs, sausages, etc. – but on no account was anyone to go near the fridge and go raiding! This system seemed to work well: lads could arrive, avail themselves of the hospitality and kip on the floor, safe and fed.

One Saturday evening, I was enjoying the company of the front-row union in the Coach and Horses in Greenwich, and after closing time Steve Peet, the hooker, decided to give 'Mad Dog' Mark Beckett a lift back to Broad Walk in the back of a furniture-removal van, as he was moving house at the time. On the way up to Blackheath, Mad Dog asked me if I thought he'd be good enough to play for England. Now, a coach has got to know his charges – some need a cuddle and reassurance, others a motivational kick up the arse – and I knew that if I told Dog that he might be good enough, there was a good chance he wouldn't turn up for training, as he'd go out and celebrate my plaudits. Instead, I told him I'd probably drop him the next week (reverse psychology and all that), and he got really upset. I'm glad the Dog didn't turn on me and savage me – he was one brute of a man.

By the time we reached the clubhouse, I'd reassessed the situation in view of Dog's response, and as Peety let us out of the back of the van I relented somewhat, feeling sorry for my harshness. 'I'll tell you what,' I said. 'If you can drive this van around the three pitches in the next ninety seconds, you'll play next week.' He was back in 85 seconds, but he'd taken a short cut across the cricket square, which led to a major enquiry and tales of a police chase the next morning. (That's another story.)

Mark Beckett was now well pleased with himself, and we entered the house, where the usual Saturday-night gathering was scattered on the floors. However, the food appeared to be all gone, and on fear of a quick death the following morning we didn't dare go near the fridge. On the cooker was a huge pot, still warm, and I said, 'Isn't Siobhan very thoughtful. She's left us a pot of broth.' I ladled out a bowl each, and we found two remaining heels of bread that the ransacking piranhas had missed – perhaps they were mouldy.

Anyway, we tucked into our repast, and I remember remarking to the Dog that there wasn't as much body to the soup as usual. He couldn't have cared less – he was going to be playing for the first XV the following Saturday. We wiped the bowls clean with our stale bread and retired, me to bed and Dog to the floor.

The next morning Siobhan was up early and made her way to the kitchen for her caffeine fix but came straight back upstairs and quizzed me about what we had eaten the night before. She had a strange look on her face, but I knew we hadn't broken any of the rules, so I told her, 'We had bowls of the broth that you left for us.'

'You bollox! I was boiling dishcloths!' she managed to splurt out between giggles.

Dog went on to have a distinguished career with Waterloo, and Siobhan ran a successful restaurant in the Bar du Musée. He was quite a good player, and she is quite a good cook.

LA BELLE ÉPOQUE

PETER WHEELER
HOOKER Leicester
ENGLAND 1975–84, 41 caps
LIONS TOURS '77, '80, 7 Test matches

My first introduction to the world of Stewart McKinney was on a trip to France to play for an invitation team put together by John Reason of the *Daily Telegraph*, in what I think was called the Guy Boniface Memorial Match. This was, I would guess, some time in the mid-1970s, and the game was played in the lovely town of Saint-Jean-Pied-de-Port, or something like that, which was situated in the foothills of the Pyrenees, or somewhere like that.

My memory of the detail is a bit hazy, partly because it was over 30 years ago, but mostly because although John Reason was a pretty shrewd judge of a rugby player, he was a bit of a novice at selecting a group of players who were going to make his job as manager easy. For not only had he selected Stewart McKinney, he'd also chosen Fergus Slattery, of Ireland and the '74 Lions, as his sidekick. I had previously toured with Fergus, so I knew his form, but the pairing of him with Stewart was a very heady mix that wasn't to be recommended, except in the most extreme circumstances, like a World War for example.

We travelled down by coach from the airport in Bordeaux and spent the Friday trying to play pelota in the town square. When match day came, with the town band at full throttle and the mayor kicking off the game in torrential rain, you could just see a gleam begin to appear in the eyes of the dastardly duo.

I can't remember the score, but we all embarked on an evening of great hospitality from the French, with endless bottles of wine and singing those songs when you all have to stand up and sit down. By about four in the morning, we lost Fergus and Stewart, who went off on a secret mission, which usually meant they would be having a lash with the local Catholic priest. The next time I saw them was at about 8.30 a.m. I looked out of the hotel bedroom window to see the pair of them trying to catch a couple of horses in the field. Stewart spent half an hour chasing a carthorse and trying to jump onto its back like a demented Apache Indian. Of course, if he did get on, he slid straight back off again, but it kept his teammates in stitches watching from the hotel. They soon disappeared again only to turn up at lunchtime for a quick farewell snifter with the mayor before we left for the airport.

Stewart McKinney – a great player, a great tourist, a great man to have on your side and a man who always has time for another.

LEAVING YOUR MARK AND HIGHS AND LOWS

TONY BOND
CENTRE Sale, Askeans
ENGLAND 1978–82, 6 caps

Leaving Your Mark

I was playing for Broughton Park against Gloucester at home in the late 1970s. This was always a heavily contested fixture, particularly up front, with two very well-matched sets of forwards. There had been a few flare-ups in this particular game, and 'Burto' (Mike Burton) from Glos was involved in most of those, as was 'Nero' (Tony Neary) from Park.

Being a three-quarter, all I could do was watch them get on with it until I saw an opportunity. A maul had set up just in front of where I was standing, and I noticed Burto's head was hanging out. I looked around – the ref was on the other side – so I ran in and smacked Burto and returned back to my position unnoticed apart from a few teammates. When the maul broke up, you could see Burto looking around for his assailant. None the wiser, the game continued until the final whistle.

We were in the bar after the match. One of the great things about rugby back then was that you would socialise with the other team and have a beer with your opposite number. That is until Kevin O'Brien (our full-back who played for Ireland) came up and said to Burto, 'Hey, Burto. That was a great punch that Bondy got you with!' As I went red, you could see Burto taking note while (allegedly) laughing it off. We had a few beers that evening, and then the Glos team jumped on their coach home.

The next season we were playing at Glos, and it was a great game, as they always were. I took a crash ball back and went to ground, laying the ball on our side. It was then that I felt the letters 'M' and 'B' being written on my back. I looked up to see Burto's smiling face! He had not forgotten, and we just laughed at one another and shook hands. That was the great thing about rugby – we were now even.

Highs and Lows

In 1979 I was part of the North of England team that beat the All Blacks at Otley, and it was the highlight of my career. I remember looking around the dressing-room at my teammates and thinking there was no way we could lose the game. There was Fran Cotton and Bill Beaumont, and the best back row that never played for England: Peter Dixon, Roger Uttley and Tony Neary. The half-backs were Steve Smith, who had a tremendous game, and the best fly-half I ever played with, Alan Old. The other centre was Tony Wright, my teammate from Sale, who should also have played for England – he had the best sidestep, straight from rugby league. The wingers were 'Slem' (Mike Slemen) and J.C. (John Carleton), both outstanding, and then Kevin O'Brien, who played himself into the Ireland team, was at full-back.

It was just outstanding. The forwards blew away the All Blacks, the half-backs kept the pack going forward and we scored four tries. We then had to drive to Leicester the next day for a training session prior to the England v. New Zealand game the following Saturday. On arrival we were congratulated on a great result, and then the team was announced for the following week's match. The side did not reflect the result we had just had, and the feeling was not there in the dressing-room come match day. We lost 10–9.

What a difference a week makes!

RUGBY CELEBRITIES

BOBBY WINDSOR

Some players today . . . well, they want to grow up, don't they? They act like silly boys half the time. A lot of them seem to forget where they come from. You know the sort of thing. They're super-duper stars, and mind you don't forget. They try to carry that on once they've finished playing – there's not much humility about them. They're playing a game we *loved*. We played it because we *loved* it, and a lot of these boys are playing rugby for what they get out of it, you know, which is a different way of playing the game, I think. The rugby I played, I'd have played seven days a week. These boys, they only play one game a week now, and they're crying if they get bruised or some bloody bullshit, you know. I think you should play rugby for the love of the game, and some of them play rugby for what they get out of it.

A LAND OF TRADITION

JEFF PROBYN
PROP Askeans, Streatham, Wasps
ENGLAND 1988–93, 37 caps

When you play against the Ireland rugby team, they embody all of the stereotypical characteristics of that wonderful nation. You arrive in the country to a greeting as friendly as a family gathering; every person you meet can't do enough for you. You drive through beautiful countryside to the city of Dublin, then on to a historic hotel perched on a majestic coastline. The next day it's off to Blackrock College's training pitches for the press session, which is followed by one of the strangest traditions in the game: tea with the ladies of Blackrock. There's a final light training session on Friday and then back to the hotel to wait for Saturday's game. Then, at around 7.30 p.m., there is the forwards' walk, a tradition introduced to me by my mate Paul Rendall.

On the first occasion, I refused when he said come for a walk, but he insisted, saying that it was a long-held tradition that the forwards go for a stroll together alone without the coaches as part of the team-building process before the game, so I relented and got ready.

At around 7.30 p.m. we gathered in the foyer and set off out of the hotel and up the hill. About 400 yards up the road we turned right, crossed the road and went into a pub, where there was 12 pints of Guinness sitting on the bar. Two quick pints and a swift stroll back: the perfect set-up for the next day's match.

Arrive at the ground, the match kicks off and you get hit by a whirlwind of fists, knees, feet and heads followed by scrums that pressure you until you squeak and lineouts that resemble a scrap in the jungle, ending with the tallest man standing winning the ball. Then the game ends, and it's into the stand for tea and biscuits.

The formal dinner in the evening is always an eclectic mix of formal black-tie dinner and sitting at Willie Anderson's table and eating your meal without hands, then it's off into the night to finally stumble home as the sun rises above Trinity College.

Of all the countries that play rugby, only Ireland offers this heady mix, win or lose.

CUB

COLIN PATTERSON
SCRUM-HALF Instonians, Ulster
IRELAND 1978–80, 11 caps
LIONS TOUR '80, 3 Test matches

Jimmy Davidson was as pleasant a friend as one could have. He always had a smile on his face and was always ready for an amiable chat on most any subject that you wished to discuss. But not when it came to rugby football. On that subject he was very passionate, both as a player and as a coach.

To say Jimmy was an intense player will bring a smirk to the faces of most of the players who faced him. To be honest, he was a pest and a terror. He was invariably offside. He had his hands in every illegal place that they could be, and if proof were needed that this was true, then one look at Jimmy's face would confirm it.

He must have had stitches on top of stitches over the years, but nothing could deter him from playing his brand of rugby. Capped many times for Ireland, he was truly a tearaway flanker. He probably had the advantage of playing alongside Stewart McKinney in the Dungannon, Ulster and Ireland teams, and together they were formidable. If Jimmy missed you, Stewart wouldn't.

I will always remember Jimmy for his kindness to me when in 1976, having just finished university in Bristol in June, I was selected to play for the full Ulster XV the following season. This selection was a shock to some people. Forwards especially do not like shocks when it comes to the scrum-half who is to stand behind them. Jimmy named me 'Cub', and from then always referred to me by that moniker. For me it was a great confidence boost. If one of the most respected forwards thought I was worthy of the nickname 'Cub', then at least I had a chance. He might have called many other players by the same nickname, but as far as I am concerned it was and is mine alone. I have now in the fullness of time named my own son Cub, and he seems to like it, too.

It was no surprise to me that Jimmy became such a great coach and took the Ulster team to new heights. He made everyone around him believe in themselves, and he brought the best out in them. He was a unique package.

Small, yes. Young, yes. Naive, no. I was scared witless for my first game against Dungannon in 1976. I arrived and made my way into the changing-rooms at Stevenson Park, hoping to see a friendly face but none appeared. I recovered some composure, but upon taking the field it evaporated. Due to the size of the Dungannon men in their blue-and-white hoops, their obvious demeanour showing clearly on their faces, I decided in the best interests of my children, who were not to be born until some ten to fifteen years later, that the best form of defence against these giants was retreat. The game got under way, with life preservation my main objective. After ten or fifteen minutes, our pack seemed to be doing quite well. I rallied my confidence a little and started to play my natural game. The fear subsided.

Then a huge up-and-under was launched towards our backfield. As I ran back I thought only of catching the ball and clearing it. I accomplished the first part of the plan and caught the ball. But then I fell over. I heard the whistle sound to bring the game to a halt just as I was preparing to protect the ball until my forwards arrived.

I rolled over to get up to my feet, and there, six inches in front of me, was a pair of blue-and-white-hooped socks. I looked up to see Stewart smiling a wicked smile. After a little pause, he said, 'You're a lucky boy! I need you next week for Ulster!' He then turned and ran away. From then on, I knew what a near-death experience felt like.

This experience was further etched on my mind the following year when we played away from home against Yorkshire. Dave Caplin, the Yorkshire full-back, had just been picked to play for England. My great friend Adrian Goodrich from Ballymena launched a huge up-and-under, and Dave, the poor fellow, stood motionless in the face of the onrushing Ulstermen. He caught the ball, only to be felled by Alan McLean, also from Ballymena. Stewart arrived next, immediately followed by Harry Steele and the rest of the Ulster pack. Dave must have thought a combine harvester was running over him. The next thing I saw was Stewart coming back around the ruck and going in again to ask him once more to release the ball, as we had need of it . . . or something like that.

At the next scrum the back row of McLean, Steele and McKinney had rather satisfied smiles on their faces. Unluckily for Dave Caplin, they didn't need him for Ulster the following week.

MORE TO LIFE THAN JUST RUGBY

DAVID IRWIN
CENTRE Queen's University, Instonians, Ulster
IRELAND 1979–90, 25 caps
LIONS TOUR '83, 3 Test matches

There was great expectation and excitement during the months leading up to the first Rugby World Cup in Australia and New Zealand in 1987.

As I had done many times over the years, I was driving to Dublin, on this occasion for one of Ireland's pre-World Cup training sessions, with two of my Ulster teammates, Nigel Carr and Phillip Rainey. It was no different to any other early morning start across the border, a journey that all of us had undertaken many times before.

I distinctly remember listening to the radio while chatting to the lads when suddenly there was a blinding white flash, an explosive 'boom' and a feeling of intense heat. Immediately, I thought a roadside bomb had accidentally blown us up. 'Why us? This must be a mistake!'

I found myself still sitting in the driver's seat and still in lane facing towards Dublin. I stared to my immediate right at a huge crater in the road. There was an odour of burning in the air, and we were surrounded by an unforgettable scene of devastation.

My initial instinct was to check that my own body was intact before turning to Nigel, who was semi-conscious and bleeding profusely from head wounds. Phillip was lying motionless across the back seat. I explained to Nigel what had happened and that he would be OK but I had to get him out of the car. As I made my way round to Nigel's door, I noticed the 'supposed' target of the bomb: another vehicle beside my own. Its interior was an inferno, with two vague shadows still sitting in the two front seats. 'God help them,' I thought.

Nigel was complaining of pain in his thigh. 'A possible fractured femur,' I thought, and I worried about his prospects of making the World Cup . . . only six weeks away. Gladly, Phillip, aka 'Chipper', was starting to move in the back seat. Concerned that the petrol tank of the nearby car would explode, I managed to pull Nigel from his trainers, which were trapped under the dashboard, and carry him up the road to safety before returning to help Chipper from the car.

Having recovered one of our kitbags from 60 yards up the road (amazingly catapulted from my boot during the impact of the explosion and collision), I was then taken to Newry police station – Nigel and

Chipper were already en route to Daisy Hill Hospital. I found out that the unfortunate innocent victims were Lord Chief Justice Gibson and his wife, returning via Dublin from their annual holiday. After arriving at Newry police station, I soon phoned all our respective parents and next of kin to inform and reassure them of our well-being.

Soon after, I made my way to the hospital. Phillip was recovering from severe concussion. Nigel's femur was not fractured, but, unfortunately, his other injuries deprived him of the opportunity to take part in the first Rugby World Cup, a once-in-a-lifetime chance. More importantly, however, we were all alive!

The news hit the squad hard. In fact, Syd Millar, our team manager, Trevor Ringland, Hugo McNeill and Keith Crossan had been travelling five minutes behind my car and were diverted around the incident, not realising that their teammates were involved.

I enjoyed the World Cup, probably more than most in the squad. The lesson I learned and live by to this day is that rugby is truly a great sport – in fact, one of the best – but life and good health are the most important possessions we have.

I would like to dedicate this 'rugby story' to a great friend, Jimmy Davidson, and our coach at that World Cup, Mick Doyle. Both loved rugby but enjoyed and lived life to the full.

THE ENTENTE CORDIALE

STEWART McKINNEY

I played representative rugby for ten years, and in that time I'm sure I participated in an additional hundred matches: centenary games, openings of new grounds, games for badly injured players, the annual Tom Kiernan match at Ballymena and, if you were lucky enough to get an invitation, the St Patrick's Day game in Bermuda. There was never any money involved, but those games were great fun and gave you the chance to meet the lads again, not only from Ireland but the other home countries, too. Of course, the drink was free!

I happened upon an exhibition game in France in a very odd way. Ulster were playing Beglais out of season in June 1976. I didn't really know why we were playing, but it turned into a real battle. After the game, who should come into the dressing-room but Andy Ripley and Roger Shackleton. Rips asked me if I would play the next day in the Boniface Memorial game held each year in a different Basque village.

The Ulster team took the bus to the game, and just as they had a great time off the pitch, especially the late Tom Kane from Ballymena, I enjoyed one of the most fabulous exhibition games of my career. Jo Maso, the George Best of French rugby and the most gifted centre I ever played against, used every trick in his repertoire. The craic was mighty afterwards, and I was invited back the following year, as long as I brought Slattery.

Slats and I flew to Bordeaux the next time, and who should be there at the airport but Messrs Peter Wheeler, John Scott, Paul Dodge and Tony Bond with tour leader John Reason from the *Daily Telegraph*. There was never a chance of John organising Slats and me, as he hadn't been very complimentary about the '74 Lions tour and was never complimentary about Ireland.

The minibus took us to a beautiful town called Saint-Jean-Pied-de-Port in the Pyrenees. We arrived late in the evening, but the whole town was there to greet us, and after sampling the most delicious local dishes and huge amounts of wine the sing-song started. Slats and I sang a Basque song he'd taught me, so the two of us were off to a flying start. The game itself ended up in a 46–46 draw, and the result hadn't been contrived.

After the match, John told us to go back to the hotel, where we would be picked up for the mayor's reception. Slats and I had different ideas. We had spotted a bar just outside the ground, and when we entered the Dax band that had played during the game recognised us, gave us a red beret each and thrust a pastis into our hands. (Not the best tipple for dehydration, but we were off and 'out of trap one', as Slats would say.) After about eight more pastis, they informed 'Slatt-ary' and 'Mc-Kinn-ay' they would be parading around the town for us . . . we were meant to be with the mayor on the balcony of the *mairie* (town hall) for the march past.

Once again, Slats and I had different ideas. I took the big drum and Slats selected a trombone. Fortified with pastis, we did our best in the parade around the town. The English lads and John Reason, who were on the mayor's balcony, doubled up with laughter when they saw us. However, the mayor had noticed us, too. As we entered his parlour, he hugged us excitedly and announced that 'Slatt-ary and Mc-Kinn-ay are Basques' . . . and then he gave us more wine.

I don't know what time that reception finished, but the mayor had organised some locals to take his newly recruited Basques away. So, away and away we went, further and further into the Pyrenees.

The people of each village we passed through turned out to meet us, offering us more pâté and more wine. Slats must have thought he was still in New Zealand in 1971, because he started to hang upside down from peculiar places. As I drunkenly tried to focus on a view through a bar window, there he'd be, upside down, looking back at me.

By seven o'clock the next morning, we had reached the top of the mountains, with France on one side and Spain on the other. Through the window, I noticed a small car zigzagging its way up the steep incline. 'For tomorrow,' they said. 'We tired. We go home.' It was the relief squad – fresh bodies! We were now in big trouble.

Ten minutes later, I thought we were in even bigger trouble. Breakfast had been ordered for the nightshift, the dayshift and us too, of course. There was a lot of mucking around and messing about. One of our Basque friends light-heartedly stole some bacon from my plate but dropped it on the table. As I tried to spear it before he could have a second go at it, he stuck out his hand, and my knife stabbed through the fleshy part near his thumb.

The end of *entente cordiale*? Not at all! They all creased up with laughter, got a camera and took snaps of us all with our arms around each other, except for the man with his hand still pinned to the table.

John Reason and the English lads caught up with us at about one o'clock in the afternoon, and by then Slats was riding a horse, not hanging upside down.

I loved exhibition games!

MISTAKEN IDENTITY

WILLIE ANDERSON
LOCK King's Scholars, Dungannon, Ulster
IRELAND 1984–90, 27 caps

My story starts during the final round of games during the Five Nations Championship in 1985. Ireland, under Mick Doyle, had drawn with France and beaten Scotland and Wales to give us an opportunity to secure the Triple Crown and also win the championship. England were the team to beat on our home territory, Lansdowne Road.

The game was a very tight affair, and we were certainly very nervous, what with the home crowd's high expectations and us wanting another Triple Crown to celebrate in the early 1980s. We got to the last ten minutes, and, lo and behold, I gave away a penalty just outside the twenty-two-yard line. With the score at 10–10, I knew this could be our downfall. However, I was delighted when Rob Andrews did Ireland and me a great favour and missed his kick. With about five or six minutes to go, I remember getting into a scrum and asking the referee how long there was to go. The referee on that occasion was Jim Fleming from Scotland. In response to my question, he winked, and I therefore presumed we still had enough time to snatch victory.

We *did* win that day, in normal time, with some magnificent work from Brian Spillane and Donal Lenihan giving a great platform to Michael Kiernan to drop a goal and not only seal the match, but secure the championship, too. As the ball hit the ground on the other side of the posts, the referee blew for full time.

This was only part of the story. The rest of it involved my wife Heather, who came down on the morning of the game with some friends, did a bit of shopping and then went for a drink – as you do! When Heather was in a well-known establishment, she saw Elvis Costello and met Marie Heaney, Seamus Heaney's wife. As Heather is an English teacher, she had much to talk to Marie about, having also studied Seamus's work.

About six weeks later, at the end of the season, Heather and I were invited to a dinner and to stay the evening in Dublin at a very prominent hotel. It was the same night as Barry McGuigan was fighting for the lightweight title of the world, and the fight was on as the dinner was taking place. I had met Barry on several occasions before, and we had become good friends, so there was no way I was missing the fight. Consequently, I periodically went up to my room to get up to date with the action. It was when I had gone upstairs to see the end of the fight that Heather got into conversation with Ciaran Fitzgerald, and he asked her about her day on the occasion of the Triple Crown game. Heather being nervous about speaking with the great captain explained how she had gone for a drink before the game and that she had met *James Joyce's* wife. Ciaran held back his mirth at this strange response, leaned back in his chair and asked Hugo McNeill, our team's literary genius, what age James Joyce's wife would be, to which Hugo replied, 'Er, about 125!' My embarrassed wife made a hasty exit!

As you can imagine, Heather was mortified, and even though Barry McGuigan won his fight I wasn't allowed to leave her side for the rest of the evening.

GETTING EVEN

NOEL MURPHY
FLANKER Cork Constitution, Garryowen, Munster
IRELAND 1958–69, 41 caps
LIONS TOURS '59, '66, 8 Test matches

On 23 January 1965, Ireland were to run out against France at Lansdowne Road with high hopes that this would be the match that would see us spoil the French run of five wins against us. While the 55,000 crowd shivered in the stands and on the terraces, the Ireland team captain, Ray McLoughlin, was in the changing-rooms trying to fire up the boys for a performance that would prove to France that a visit to Lansdowne Road was no walk in the park. Armed with a copy of the *Daily Mail*, in which the correspondent had scathingly written that France were a team of 'thoroughbreds' and Ireland only a team of 'hacks', basically suggesting that we didn't have a chance in hell of beating their Gallic grace, McLoughlin called upon a concerted team effort from us. One way to weaken the French, he declared, was to get them riled up and arguing amongst themselves – cause dissent in their ranks and spoil their fluency, flair and finesse.

The five new caps about to debut, Roger Young, Sean MacHale, Ken Kennedy, Mick Doyle and Ronnie Lamont, were hanging intently on his every word, absorbing the motivational oration, keen to give a good account of themselves and secure selection the next time round.

Ronnie Lamont, playing at flanker, was keen to impress and had quickly thought about how best to cause friction for France from early on. Young, green and strong, when it came to the first lineout and the ball went long, Lamont only went and flattened Walter Spanghero! Monsieur Spanghero was renowned (quite probably notorious) – a fierce man, feared by players from all nations. He was a mighty Basque, with the biggest hands ever seen in this world. This had surely been an act of madness, not bravery!

The referee, Mr Walters from Wales, quite rightly awarded a penalty to France, and while we were walking back the obligatory 10 yards McBride, shaking his head and talking to no one in particular, though I suspect his words were aimed at young Lamont, muttered darkly, 'Why him? What on earth did you have to hit *him* for? Now we're *all* for it!'

Whether the daring whack to the Basque giant took the wind out of their sails or whether Ireland just managed to match them on the day, the result was a 3–3 draw, which might not have been the win we had hoped for, but we got even and didn't lose.

THE AUCTIONEER'S COAT

STEWART McKINNEY

I started to play rugby for Dungannon during the 1968–69 season in what were difficult times for Northern Ireland, and it is a great tribute to Irish club rugby that there were no cancellations of fixtures in the succeeding 11 seasons before I left for London. Blackrock, Wanderers, Highfield, Shannon, Old Crescent, Palmerston, Terenure, Clontarf, UCD and Galwegians all travelled north, and we travelled south.

Blackrock came to play Dungannon in the mid-1970s when the Troubles were at their worst. The 'Miami Showband' murders had just occurred, and what was thought to be a tit-for-tat murder of a young Portadown disc jockey, Norman Kerr, had followed. Feelings were high. Blackrock had travelled strong, with Willie Duggan and Fergus Slattery in the starting line-up and Mick 'Bomber' Browne captain. As the train had long ago stopped running to Dungannon, a fleet of cars picked up the Blackrock players and alickadoos from Portadown station, including Rosa, a lovely old woman who was the chairwoman of the ladies' committee.

After the game and the Dungannon hospitality, the fleet of cars set off back to Portadown. However, there was bad news: a bomb had been discovered on the line between Lisburn and Belfast, thus delaying departure for an hour. 'Oh, God! We'll all be killed!' cried Rosa.

'Not at all,' Ainsley Harrison and I, the only two Dungannon men remaining, replied reassuringly. 'Let's go to McKeever's.' This was a pub around the corner in Woodhouse Street.

The hour had nearly elapsed in good humour when the barman asked who was in charge. The Bomber looked around and reluctantly accepted responsibility for the gathered reprobates, as he was captain. Before Bomber could respond, the barman again asked who was in charge. There was an edge to his voice as he told Bomber that it was time to get the Blackrock team back to the station, and with that he pointed to the window and added urgently, 'Look across the road!'

A mob had gathered, as word had gotten round that a team of 'Free Staters' was in McKeever's. For once, Willie Duggan took the situation seriously, and we hightailed it back to the station. 'Oh, God! We'll all be killed!' Rosa cried again.

'Not at all,' said Ainsley and I (with a touch of déjà vu), secretly fearing that something nasty might take place this time after all. I was really scared that the mob would follow us into the station, and as the train was still two minutes away there was time for all sorts of unimaginable horrors to take place. At this point, Slattery made his announcement: 'I've left my auctioneer's coat in the pub.' Now, it was a fine coat, the sort of coat Bobby Windsor would have nicked, but, at the end of the day, it was just a bloody coat! I don't know whether it was the Guinness or the adrenalin, but from somewhere a surge of bravado coursed through me, and I told Slats to stay where he was and that I would retrieve the blessed article.

I could hear the sound of breaking glass as the mob began putting in the windows of McKeever's. Before I had travelled 20 yards, the barman came running up the street carrying the auctioneer's coat. Situation averted!

Blackrock, despite this scary sectarian skirmish, and the southern clubs kept the club game alive in Ireland, as did the northern clubs who travelled south. Rugby, thankfully, is beyond politics and religious difference, and bonds are made regardless of boundaries or borders.

BREAKFAST WITH S. McK

PHILIP ORR
PROP Old Wesley
IRELAND 1975–88, 58 caps
LIONS TOURS '77, '80, 1 Test match

I have an abiding memory of Saturday, 7 February 1976, and not because it was the day I got my first cap, playing for Ireland against France at the Parc des Princes. Unfortunately, we lost the match 26–3, but, strangely enough, I will never forget the way I received my breakfast in the hotel that morning.

The team were staying in the Hotel Concorde Saint-Lazare in the centre of Paris, and I had the honour of having Stewart McKinney as my roommate that weekend. To put it another way, the Irish Rugby Football Union, in their wisdom, had given Stewart the job of keeping an eye on the new prop forward who was getting his first cap.

VOICES FROM THE BACK OF THE BUS

Like all rugby teams in France years ago, we had to adapt to the French food and their customs, and, of course, getting anything resembling an Irish breakfast was extremely difficult; however, the hotel did their best, and it was possible to get a reasonable breakfast in the dining room.

On the Friday night before the match Stewart told me that he always had breakfast in bed the morning of a game, so he filled in the order for breakfast for both of us and hung it outside on the door handle before we went to bed that night. I must admit that I was surprised at his trust that the breakfast order would reach its correct destination, but I had to accept that he was much more experienced at international rugby, having been on the Lions Tour in South Africa in 1974.

The next morning we waited for our breakfast, which, of course, did not appear at the appointed time. A phone call to room service gave us the information that they were very busy. Stewart then left the hotel room door open to see if he could spot the room-service waiter who was looking after our floor and try and persuade him to bring our breakfast next. He spotted the waiter and told him (I doubt if the man spoke English) that we were still waiting for our breakfast.

The waiter passed our door again ten minutes later with breakfast for another room, and Stewart again told him that we were still waiting for ours. The same thing happened fifteen minutes later. Stewart was extremely annoyed at this stage. The next time the waiter appeared with a breakfast tray Stewart was ready. He relieved him of the tray, quickly retreated into the room and closed the door. This incident helped take my mind off the game and had the added value of stirring up Stewart's aggression.

I cannot remember what was on that tray, but I do remember it was not to my liking, although I didn't have the nerve to tell Stewart. Since that day I have never ordered my breakfast to be delivered to my room – I much prefer to have it in the dining room.

BRICKING IT!

JEREMY GUSCOTT
CENTRE Bath
ENGLAND 1989–99, 65 caps
LIONS TOURS '89, '93, '97, 8 Test matches

It was the first time that Australia was to host a Lions tour on its own since 1899 and the first visit for us Down Under since 1971. As it turned out, the 1989 tour was also the penultimate Lions tour of the amateur era, 1993 seeing the last of them.

Much was expected from the tour. Managed by Clive Rowlands, Finlay Calder led the team, and under the watchful eyes of Roger Uttley and Ian McGeechan, who probably knew a bit about touring from their South African experience in 1974, the squad faced their first Test in Sydney.

The earlier matches against the state teams had resulted in wins, some of them impressive, some of them not so, but spirits were high and expectations, too. However, the first Test match wasn't the dream result we had hoped for – we lost 30–12. We regrouped, beat ACT 41–5 and changes were made for the second Test at Ballymore Stadium in Brisbane. We had to win.

The Australians are always desperately competitive, and a pretty dour encounter was punctuated with the odd fisticuffs, not unusual in the 'old' days. During the last quarter of the match, I was given the chance to make an opportunist grubber kick, following up to score a cheeky try against the run of play. I'll never forget that moment. In the seconds it took for me to touch down, I managed to replay every single try I had scored in my entire rugby career, from mini-rugby and school to my time at Bath. Every player who had been alongside me for each of those tries played their role in out-of-focus slow motion as I grounded the ball for what turned out to be the score that won us the match. Savouring the moment, enjoying the thrill of the score and putting our team into the lead, I felt like a true hero out of a *Boy's Own* comic story.

Grinning and delighted with my performance, our physio Kevin Murphy brought me abruptly out of my reverie when he said, 'I tell you now, *he'll* never lay another brick again!' I hadn't considered that the tour would end and that we would all be going back to our usual jobs, even though they were of the sort that might imperil a blossoming rugby career. I had only just arrived on the international scene after my debut in Romania a couple of months earlier, and the camaraderie of touring had already seeped into my skin. Strange the way things turn out, isn't it?

AND JUDGEMENT WAS PASSED

PETER ROSSBOROUGH
FULL-BACK Coventry
ENGLAND 1971–5, 7 caps

We had taken an England A team to Australia in 1995 whilst the World Cup was being played in South Africa. This was a dual-purpose tour: to develop future international players, and to have our standby players in the southern hemisphere in case of emergency.

We had two hookers: the irrepressible Mark 'Ronnie' Regan and Gareth Adams, a very successful flanker trying to convert to hooker. In what was a very happy and hard-working tour party, our only problem was stopping the full-blown fights that erupted in every training session between Ronnie and Gareth, each of whom was desperate for the starting hooker spot. It eventually got too much and was spoiling the quality of our sessions, distracting the players and frustrating the coaches, Mike Slemen and Keith Richardson.

In time-honoured fashion a players' court was convened to sort out the problem, as Gareth and Ronnie were actually coming close to injuring each other. We might have ended up with no hooker. Cases were presented by the players' advocates and judgement handed down by 'Hanging Judge' Gareth Archer. In his wisdom he decided that Ronnie and Gareth should be handcuffed together for 24 hours, requiring them to do everything – and it meant everything! – in one another's company. The logic was that this would surely make them help each other, get to like each other and even become (whisper it) friends! So far, so good.

The second part of the judgement was that in addition to being handcuffed, they should wear a boxing glove each on their free hand. Again, the logic was impeccable: they would be forced to help each other in all sorts of interesting ways. Then the logic fell apart because for Gareth and Ronnie there was only one thing to do with a boxing glove, and they set about each other with an aggression worthy of Joe Calzaghe! Cue mayhem. Sublime!

PLUS ÇA CHANGE

STEWART McKINNEY

Willie John always protected his players, no matter their size, whether on or off the pitch, whether home or away. On the occasion of Moss Keane's first cap in Paris, Willie was determined to make sure that the temptations and excesses of the city didn't get him into trouble and that he would get home safely.

Moss is a big bloke with a healthy appetite that requires constant feeding. He is always hungry, and on the way home to their rooms Willie even bought him chips to keep him placated. (So far, so good.) Unfortunately, the route back to the hotel took them through the Pigalle, where ladies of the night and their pimps, not renowned for their manners or their morals, hang out. One such gentleman stole the chips from Moss. Wrong move! You didn't mess with Moss's food, especially food that was a gift! Despite having the looks of an ex-boxer and probably the street nous to get down and dirty in any ordinary brawl, the pimp had never met the match of an enraged Moss. Moss sideswiped him a powerful blow, an almighty whack akin to a bear cuffing with its paw, so that the pimp immediately stumbled and fell directly into the gutter.

This wasn't the Irish boys' territory, and soon a crowd of locals had gathered, not pleased that one of their own had been dishonoured with such a loss of dignity on their own turf. Their mood turned nasty, and the crowd quickly became a mob baying for blood, wanting to defend the reputation of their neighbourhood and restore the perverse status of the pimp in the street hierarchy.

Moss and Willie stood back to back, ready to take on all-comers. This is Sparta! By the time the gendarmes had arrived, it was clear that a battle had taken place. The two giants, leviathans, had scattered bodies and piled them high in a traditional Irish rugby defence: attack!

'They started it. That man stole my chips!' the man-mountains offered the men of the law.

The gendarmes quickly reassured them, 'But, messieurs, we didn't come to arrest you. We came to save the mob!'

A FAIR TEST

JOHN TAYLOR
FLANKER London Welsh
WALES 1966–73, 26 caps
LIONS TOUR '68, '71, 4 Test matches

I have to smile when I hear modern players complaining about referees – they don't know how lucky they are! Whenever we played in South Africa, New Zealand or Australia, we always had a home referee – and they were, without fail, real 'homers'.

Worst of the lot was an Australian called Craig Ferguson, who almost cost Wales victory at the Sydney Cricket Ground in 1969. With a couple of minutes to go, we were leading 19–11 when Australia mounted a last desperate attack. Maurice Richards, our left wing, comfortably, so he and we thought, tackled Wallaby full-back Arthur McGill into touch short of the line, but McGill stretched out, got the ball down and Ferguson awarded the try. Richards swore – for the only time in his life, I think – and Ferguson awarded a restart penalty on halfway after McGill landed the conversion. They went for goal but, fortunately, the kick fell short and we scraped home 19–16.

In the bar I collared Ferguson and bluntly asked what he thought he was playing at. I naively thought he might have felt a bit guilty, but not a bit of it. 'Listen, mate,' he said. 'Down here union is the fourth code – you've got rules, you've got league, you've got soccer and then you've got union. Our blokes need all the help they can get, and I'm the man to do it.'

Two years later I arrived back in Sydney with the Lions, and as I stepped off the plane there was a guy on the tarmac waiting to shake my hand. 'Welcome back,' he said. 'Craig Ferguson. Remember me? I'm still a cheating bastard, and I'm refereeing on Saturday!'

CON HOULIHAN AND GRANDSTANDS

TONY ENSOR
FULL-BACK Wanderers, Leinster
IRELAND 1972–8, 22 caps

Con Houlihan, who I understand is now in his 80s and to the best of my knowledge still sports his long straggly white hair and who without doubt has absolutely no idea who I am, has featured in my life on two particular occasions. One of the occasions took place during my playing days and the other during my commentating days.

I was often teased about the fact that when I played rugby I always wore the collar of my jersey up, as was the fashion in those days, my flowing hair falling below the collar. WAGs and some of my friends would comment that most of the time my collar was still up at the end of the match, which only confirmed what everybody knew: that I was the only full-back in Ireland who could get through a match without making a single tackle. I had to accept this opinion of my physical commitment to the game, as I had a similar one. I think I was as conscious of what was going on off the field as on it.

The first incident related to a final trial in Donnybrook in or around 1972. I was the incumbent full-back on the Leinster team at the time, and trials were therefore to be avoided at all costs. You could, after all, only lose your place! However, on this particular occasion, not being daring enough to feign an injury, which I am sure the unscrupulous Willie Duggan had done, I turned out in front of a vast crowd of about 100 people, made up mostly of mothers and grandmothers (fathers and grandfathers had to work, as these matches were played on a Wednesday afternoon) and the odd sports journalist whose editor couldn't send him to a more attractive sports fixture.

I was, like most young buffs playing rugby in those days, always on the lookout for a lovely D4 babe, the Irish equivalent of a Sloan Ranger or Chelsea Girl (apologies to Ross O'Carroll-Kelly). During the trial match, I did cast an eye up to the now redeveloped old grandstand to see if I could perhaps pick out some particularly attractive young girl. I was, of course, oblivious to the fact that a wily old sports journalist from Castleisland had been focusing on me for some time.

The following day in the *Evening Press* I read, and I paraphrase:

> If Tony Ensor spent more time watching the rugby ball than
> looking up into the grandstand, it might impress the selectors
> more, and I hasten to suggest that the birds he was looking at
> were not the hundreds of pigeons fluttering their way around
> the eaves of the grandstand but of another kind altogether!!

I must admit that that particular comment endeared me to Con Houlihan
for evermore, even though I cannot say that my mother was equally
impressed! I often wondered what the selectors thought when they read
the article.

The next incident also involved the learned fellow and a grandstand
but in altogether different circumstances. Before recounting that story, I
would like to explain how I first discovered my serious problem with
vertigo, which dominated my second encounter with Con Houlihan.

I was in Paris in 1971. Dublin were playing Paris in a pre-season
friendly. Part of the itinerary, intended to keep us out of the café bars,
was a visit to the Eiffel Tower. In those days each of the four pillars
from ground level to the first platform from which the lift commenced
had a metal staircase within it. We proceeded to climb up those stairs,
and when I reached the first platform I was suddenly struck by a
stomach-wrenching feeling that I was going to fall over. Some people,
I understand, feel an irresistible urge to jump off, but I can assure
you that was not my reaction. I slipped into the crowd, allowed my
co-players to get into the lift and then went back to the metal stairs,
where I proceeded in a state of absolute fear and trepidation to sit down
and work my way down, step by step, on my backside, which caused
much amusement, as you can imagine, to those who were ascending
the stairs.

Just as I reached the bottom and was preparing to run to the nearest
bar for a nerve-settling beer, I looked across at one of the other pillars.
Whom did I see emerging on his backside but the captain of Dublin,
Tom Grace. As we had caught one another out, we came to an instant
pact that nobody would ever hear about this. I am not breaching my
undertaking with him now, because after a few beers he could not resist
telling the story that very night. For those of you who know Tom Grace,
you will realise that this was a record. To actually admit his failings rather
than slag others for theirs was unheard of. Ask Vinnie Becker.

In any event, back to Con Houlihan and to Edinburgh in 1983. I
had been given the grand task of doing what was then known as the
inter-round commentaries with Jim Sherwin for RTE, and we were
preparing to take our place in the commentary box an hour before the

kick-off when to my horror we reached the end of what can only be described as a gangplank. This metal structure was suspended from the roof of the upper grandstand in Murrayfield, and I realised that I had to cross over this to get to the commentary position. I completely froze and refused point-blank to move an inch further. To ensure I would take my place, Jim Sherwin simply shouted at me not to be such a fool and get over it. I could not convince him that it really was not possible for me to continue. I got down on my hands and knees, eyes firmly closed, and crawled along the gangplank over the thousands of people taking their seats below me.

When I eventually reached the commentary place, I realised that we were hanging from the roof of the grandstand, almost out over the pitch itself. I shook uncontrollably throughout the match, and I desperately tried not to think of what I would do after the final whistle blew.

The match having taken its course and the crowd having left the ground and all of my co-commentators from the BBC and other radio stations having left the commentary box, I simply sat there in an effort to pluck up enough courage to crawl my way back to terra firma. I looked around, and to my amazement there was another body still left. It was the aforementioned Con Houlihan. Naturally, I assumed he was typing his copy for the following Monday's *Evening Press*. However, I soon discovered, by the ashen look on his face, matching his white wispy hair, that he, like me, was frozen to the spot.

We instantly acquainted each other with our forms of illness, and with the benefit of shared Dutch courage produced from his flask crawled our way to the back of the grandstand and down onto the tarmac at the back of the stand. Friends for life, born of adversity.

As we strolled leisurely to the nearest taverna, I mentioned to him that I had long admired the comment he had made about me watching the birds in the grandstand in Donnybrook, and he said, in his inimitable way, that if he had been on the pitch that day, playing that match, he would have been much more interested in watching girls, too. He could recall that it was one of the most boring experiences of his rather interesting life.

THE LONDON IRISH

PAT PARFREY
COACH/DOCTOR UCC, London Irish, Munster
IRELAND 1974, 1 CAP

In my days (1976–82) London Irish was a melting pot, where immigrants from the north and south of Ireland mixed with the children of exiles while pursuing their future in various parts of London. Despite the political troubles in Ulster being at their zenith, nationalistic southern Catholic rugby players and Protestant players from the Loyalist community endeavoured to create the best rugby team they could and beat the best the English had to offer. Yes, accents could identify the provenance of each individual, but their actions were identical. The small 'p' politics of the rugby club dominated the large 'P' politics of the island of Ireland.

The pleasure of playing in, and partying with, a team of friends was unalloyed. Sunbury was the place where the McKibbens (Roger and Alistair), that fucker Kennedy (as Ken was usually called), the acerbic and gracious Guy Beringer, the fun-loving Dave Donovan, the quietly spoken and affectionate Walter Jones, the trusty prop Alex Newbury, the outlandish and outstanding Stewart McKinney were friends with the enveloping Michael Gabriel Molloy, the shrewd Mick Mahony, the welcoming Mick Smythe, the tough and resourceful Geno McCarthy and the Dublinesque Duncan Leopold. Fortunately, London Irish depended on the descendents of exiles, leavened by the British public-school system, to provide a sense of culture (not history) . . . but this lasted no longer than the first ruck on the park and certainly lasted no longer than the first pint in the bar! As the cultured ambience was no more than veneer, the recent immigrants bonded easily with the exiles. John O'Driscoll (of Lions fame but a party lunatic), the graceful Hugh Condon, the happy Barry Murphy, the elfin John Casalaspro, the dynamic Les White and the engaging Paul Crotty all added skill to the spirited Irish concoction.

In the later years of this era English players, with no Irish connection, joined the club, and the social cohesion of London Irish was unimpaired. Three doctors, skilled rugby practitioners, Peter Enevoldson, Clive Meanwell and Tony Watkinson, became our friends and initiated the London Irish outreach to the English game, culminating in the internationalisation of the professional status.

Winning is the currency of sporting success, celebration the motivation to retain interest in it. Consequently, social cohesion is critical to optimise team performance. We were brothers, and we loved each other (except Kennedy, who didn't love any of us).

We won big games in the premier England competitions, and we lost some, too, but throughout these times we enjoyed each other's company. We felt we were achieving our potential on the playing field, and we certainly achieved it, playing, off the field. London Irish and its players live in my heart.

A LARGE BILL

STEWART McKINNEY

Ballynahinch Rugby Club was one of the junior clubs in Ireland when I was at Stranmillis College, playing for King's Scholars. Extremely fit PE students made up 90 per cent of our team, so the tactics of Ballynahinch and other opposition sides were to slow us down, by whatever means they thought appropriate – all is fair in love and war, and necessity is the mother of invention!

We usually played Ballynahinch on a Wednesday night. Both sides changed at the back of the White Horse pub. The cows were chased off the pitch, and the battle would begin. There was no such thing as a 'learning curve', that much-hackneyed phrase, playing against the likes of Willie Vance, Ian Alexander or Arthur Gibson.

Intimidation from the touchline was coarse, to say the least, and the repartee simple, direct and lacking in subtlety. The first time I had my nose broken was against Ballynahinch, and as I lay in a red haze all I could hear was, 'Take him away to the vet's!'

However, back at the White Horse, as the teams washed away the mud and blood from the encounter at the taps behind the pub, Ballynahinch prepared, as always, to fill us full of hospitality, regardless of the result. We'd have a terrific night, and they'd send us away with crates of Guinness, as us poor wee students were always hard up! Ballynahinch was a wonderful grounding for the bigger battles to come in Port Elizabeth and Christchurch.

So, I had no hesitation when in 1976 that great stalwart of the 'Hinch', Joe Carlisle, asked me to bring a team to open their new pitch. I was so proud – Stewart McKinney's International XV! By then

Ballynahinch had fantastic facilities, but the hospitality of the White Horse remained the same.

I was in Malone Rugby Club about six years ago when I met 'Wee' Joe Carlisle, and he informed me he had a bill to show me. From his wallet he took a dishevelled piece of paper, the bill for Stewart McKinney's International XV. The total was £26. It was an itemised account, and my £4 stuck out like a sore thumb amongst the other lads, such as Ian McIlrath, who had claimed perhaps a pound or two. 'Joe,' I said, 'don't forget I had the extra expense of making the telephone calls!'

I wonder how much it would cost to take an international team to Ballynahinch today?

BLEEP TESTS, QUESTIONNAIRES AND AFFECTIONATE GREETINGS

JIMMY McCOY
PROP Dungannon, Bangor, Ulster
IRELAND 1983–90, 16 caps

It was the first Saturday in September 1977. After having joined Dungannon Rugby Club and trained with them during August, at the tender age of 19 I was ready to make my debut for the first XV against local rivals Portadown in the world famous Beattie Cup. I had certainly heard of Jimmy D. and had watched him play for Ireland on the good old black–and–white television, but the legend had not appeared at pre-season training.

The kick-off was at 2.30 p.m., and we were due to meet in the changing-room at 2 p.m. I wanted to make a favourable impression and was there at 1.45 p.m. to find it empty; however, by 2 p.m. most of the team had arrived, and at about five past two in sauntered Jimmy D., greeting everybody with his customary big smile and handing out sheets of paper. He came over to me and said, 'All right, Cub? Fill out this questionnaire.' He smiled a big broad smile and moved on.

I don't actually recall much about my debut that day, for my mind was taken over with concern about Jimmy D.'s questionnaire and the leading questions it contained, such as 'How much alcohol do you drink during the week?' and 'How much alcohol do you drink on a Friday night before a game?' Most worryingly of all, 'Would you ever not have a drink after a game on Saturday?'

Jimmy D. was not a regular for the Dungannon first XV at the end of the 1970s, which was disappointing for me, as I did not often get the opportunity to turn out with him. It was also a blessing in disguise and somewhat of a relief, because any time he did play he always had another questionnaire . . . and some of the questions were getting more detailed: 'How much fruit would you eat during a day?' and 'How often would you do weight training?'

Jimmy D. moved on from Dungannon into coaching and eventually became Ulster coach in 1983. I was a regular in the Ulster team at that time, and I didn't know whether to laugh or cry when I heard that Jimmy D. was going to be coach. I was dreading the inevitable questionnaires and what further enquiries he would make about our personal habits over the years to come.

On his first training evening with the Ulster squad at Ravenhill, he came into the changing-room and greeted all the players. Upon meeting me, he gave me the usual greeting, 'All right, Cub?' There was no hint of a questionnaire – he just moved on. I need not have worried – or maybe I should have.

Jimmy D. was buzzing with excitement about the Ulster squad and wanted to make us the best club side in the world. Everything was going well for me after his arrival until he phoned me one day requesting that I come up to Queen's University to do a 'bleep test'. My first thought was that it must be some sort of new after-match drinking game to replace 'Fizz Buzz' and 'One Red Hen' and that he was asking me to test this new game out as I was undefeated champion at the other two!

Oh, how wrong could I have been? He went into great detail about the requirements and the benefits of the bleep test, enthusing almost evangelically about this latest assessment of fitness. Luckily for me, and probably even luckier for Jimmy D., I was always busy at work (keeping the peace) whenever the beep tests were taking place. He could see how disappointed I was at missing them!

After raising the standard of coaching to a completely new level with Ulster, Jimmy D. was appointed Ireland coach in 1987. I was in the Ireland squad at this time, and when he met us for the first time at Lansdowne Road I was greeted with the usual, 'All right, Cub?' Jimmy D. wanted the Ireland players fitter, stronger and faster, and it was to this end that one Saturday on the back pitch at Lansdowne Road he had us in groups sprinting up and down to analyse our techniques – in just our shorts and boots, with Feidlim recording the session on video. It was hilarious to watch players such as Willie Anderson and Trevor

Ringland trying to sprint whilst holding their bellies in. Nigel Carr and I had no such problems! It has been stated by numerous players, coaches and observers of the game that Jimmy D. was ahead of his time, and of that there is no doubt.

I have to say that I saw Jimmy D. really drunk only the one time, and that was one night in Dungannon Rugby Club when he turned the fire hose on the alickadoos and soaked them all – sorry, sorry, that wasn't Jimmy D., that was Stewart McKinney.

I met Jimmy D. at various events over the years, and he was always bubbly – he oozed enthusiasm and positivity – asking about work and the family, and always with the same Jimmy D. greeting, 'All right, Cub?'

WELL REMEMBERED

OLLIE CAMPBELL
FLY-HALF Old Belvedere, Leinster
IRELAND 1975–84, 22 caps
LIONS TOURS '80, '83, 7 Test matches

As I was weaned on the exploits of the 1948–49 Ireland Grand Slam (Ooh, we've had another one – it's been a long time coming) and Triple Crown-winning teams, the highlight of my rugby career was being on the Triple Crown-winning team of 1982. Ireland had not won the Triple Crown since '49, nor had they ever won it at Lansdowne Road. One of the unexpected bonuses of this historic victory was that it suddenly seemed as if my great rival for the fly-half spot, Tony Ward, had never existed. It was a very good time to be Ollie Campbell, and the proceeding months were perhaps the happiest and most fulfilling of my life. It was probably the defining day of my life, too, and during that time I just didn't have a care in the world.

At the end of the season I spent the May bank holiday with friends in Westport, County Mayo. As I was heading home on the beautiful Monday morning, I picked up an elderly woman who was thumbing a lift on the outskirts of Westport. It turned out she was visiting a friend in Castlebar Hospital, only ten miles away.

In the course of our conversation she told me about St Patrick ridding all the snakes from Croagh Patrick and thus from Ireland. We talked a bit about business, and then she asked whether I played any sport. I said I did. 'Is it Gaelic you play?' she asked.

'No,' I said with pride. 'Rugby's my game.'

With that she unexpectedly went silent and only spoke as we were pulling into Castlebar. Talking more to herself than to me and shaking her head slightly as she spoke, she said that there was only one thing about rugby she did not understand. I asked her what that was, as I might be able to help. With a weary, resigned and low voice she eventually said that the only thing she did not understand about rugby was why Tony Ward was not in the Ireland team!

Ten years later I told that story at the end of a radio interview that Jimmy Magee did with Tony and me for RTE. Tony was nearly sick laughing. When I got home that night, there was a message on my answering machine from a Margaret McMenamin (with an accompanying address in Westport). She had heard the interview and admitted that she was the culprit.

To her eternal credit, despite a few placatory visits to her home, Christmas cards, boxes of chocolates and even some flowers, she remained a firm Tony Ward fan to the end of her days. Naturally, I have never taken the risk of picking up anyone thumbing a lift since, and all these years later I am still waiting to have a conversation with someone, anyone, anywhere, who does not mention the name Tony Ward!

OLD DOGS AND NEW TRICKS

ROGER CLEGG
PROP King's Scholars, Bangor, Old Crescent, Ulster
IRELAND 1972–5, 5 caps

Many and humorous were the tales at the back of the bus; mine, however, relates to more recent times, as one's memory fades as one gets older – or so my wife says!

In March 2007 my son Jamie had finished his final season of rugby at school and had been asked to play at number 8 for Bangor's third XV at Ballynahinch. Mother and father dutifully went to support their son and the Bangor team. After 25 minutes, Jamie pulled his hamstring, and Bangor were down to 14 men, as no substitutes had been brought.

However, this old codger, in his 58th year and still thinking himself mightily fit (you know what I mean), decided to take the field. I put on Jamie's togs, complete with the number 8 jersey, which was where I was certain I would play. I wouldn't have offered my services otherwise, suffering as I was with a prop's stiff neck and not wanting it any stiffer.

The Bangor captain decided, however, that the scrum was weak, and I reluctantly agreed to play prop until half-time. The first scrum was called, and I, as had been customary, immediately engaged the opposition, to the sounds of squealing. I remembered a bit about the 'new rules', disengaged, apologised and listened to the ref: crouch, touch, pause, engage.

After five minutes, there was another scrum. Once again, I did what came naturally; once again, there was a squeal from the opposition. I broke up from the scrum realising I was under severe scrutiny from the ref. What could I say other than, 'Sorry, I haven't played under the new rules.' Considering I hadn't played since 1991 in a celebration match to mark the retirement of my former coach at King's Scholars, Jos Lapsley, that was a bit of an understatement. The referee became quite agitated and spoke to me severely. 'This is a safety issue. Have you ever played at prop before?'

(How could he be expected to know that some 30-odd years before this old boy had played with Willie John McBride, Mike Gibson and the like. Some of the Bangor lads had that week been watching the ESPN Classic channel, and by chance the rugby match being screened had been Ireland v. France in 1973, my first cap for Ireland, when two Bangor lads had played, Dick Milliken and me. So, thankfully, there were some chuckles from behind. Thank you, God, that *someone* knew.)

My reply to the referee's question was, 'Once or twice!'

CONDITIONS JUST ABOUT PERFECT HERE AT TWICKENHAM

MARK BROMAGE
UTILITY BACK Askeans

The words of the great Bill McLaren came to mind as I arrived down at the London Eye to meet my host Hugh McHardy and the rest of the group who were about to embark upon a top-notch corporate jolly – a boat trip on the Thames in a vintage cruiser, with a champagne reception followed by a five-course lunch accompanied by fine wines, after which we were scheduled to disembark at Richmond into limos that would whisk us on to Twickenham itself, where we had seats for the autumn international between England and the All Blacks.

It was a gloriously crisp, sunny late October day, and as I was introduced to my fellow passengers the sense of excitement was tangible – what a day's entertainment lay in prospect for us all. We were a disparate bunch for sure: with me I had an American client, whose first trip to a rugby match this was, and his number two, a keen rugby man originally from Belfast but now living in Atlanta; there was a Kiwi couple, who again had never been to Twickers but who were both big into rugby – additionally, she was huge with child; there were two hooray bond-dealer types, who looked like they were big into booze (and probably other substances, too), judging by their appearance on arrival; and there was a 'couple' from Birmingham, both in their 40s and married (albeit to other people), and they seemed more and more interested in examining each other's tonsils as events unfolded.

With our genial host Hugh making a total of ten people, this was the merry band that walked up the gangplank onto *The Edwardian*, a splendidly restored early-twentieth-century motor cruiser, at around 10.30 a.m. Glasses of bubbly were thrust into waiting hands and off we set, heading east to start with for a bit of sightseeing, as we had time aplenty. There was not a breath of wind on the Thames, making it virtually shirtsleeve weather, and people conversed easily as we passed various London landmarks before eventually turning around at Tower Bridge and proceeding back westwards towards our eventual disembarkation point near the ground.

In chatting to Hugh we discovered that this was his first venture into corporate rugby entertainment on this scale and that the event was very much his idea – we could only applaud his decision as we tucked into our splendid luncheon around a grand dining table in the oak-panelled stateroom of the boat. Our glasses were regularly topped up with Montrachet or Saint Emilion, administered by pretty, friendly Eastern European waitresses. All the while we cruised up the Thames, and the Houses of Parliament and the MI5 building eventually gave way to quieter stretches of river as we continued our serene progress past Putney Bridge and beyond.

A heaving cheeseboard and vintage port were then served up, and with the group having fully bonded the next thing we knew the table was in full song, with each of us taking a turn at doing our 'party piece'. This was followed by short speeches – largely in praise of our fine host – whilst the boat sailed on towards our destination, by now in splendid isolation on the water apart from the occasional rowing crew passing by with a friendly wave in the beautiful late-autumn sunshine.

We eventually repaired onto the deck to ready ourselves for offloading, but as the boat neared Richmond Bridge it slowed almost to a halt in midstream – I thought to avoid ploughing into the large number of birds who strangely seemed to be walking on water. This was followed by a worrying grating sound, and it quickly became apparent that we had run aground. As a result of the outgoing tide, the river was about one-inch deep at that point, and the birds were actually standing on the river bed! We could see our cars waiting by the right-hand side of the bridge, but there was no way of getting across to them, and although this seemed like a highly amusing situation to start with the realisation quickly spread that unless an urgent solution was found we might be stranded in the middle of the river until the tide turned several hours later.

Our friendly skipper weighed up the options and eventually proposed an attempt to get the boat across to the left-hand side, where there was a rusty metal ladder against a piece of concrete banking that he thought we might be able to get up. We were asked to sign a disclaimer form in case of any mishap, and to the accompaniment of much nervous laughter he gingerly manoeuvred the good ship to port. With the horrid sound of metal scraping on gravel, we inched painfully toward the bank. Through great skill and seamanship (and despite being shouted at by a lock-keeper, who was telling us in no uncertain terms that we were breaking the law and that he was going to report us) our crew got us close enough to lash the boat against the ladder, and one by one the party tipsily clambered up the ladder onto the very muddy grass bank above – without mishap, apart from mud-splattered clothing and shoes. A great cheer went up, and our happy band strolled over the bridge to the cars.

I waited for Hugh, who had not yet disembarked, as he was sorting things out with the skipper. When he appeared at the top of the ladder, his ashen face was a giveaway that something was badly amiss, and when I politely enquired as to what the problem might be he mumbled something about having lost the tickets. I asked him to repeat himself (assuming he was joking), at which point he started hyperventilating – eventually getting himself together sufficiently to say, 'What are we going to do?' I realised he was serious and proposed searching his bag, his jacket and the boat again, but he was pretty convinced that he remembered what he'd done with the tickets: he'd left them on his hall table, where he'd put them so he wouldn't forget them. He then told me to put things in perspective. 'This is not the Somme in 1915 – nobody's died here,' were his useful words. He then somehow persuaded me that I should go and tell the others, as he was in no fit state to do it – so I walked in something of a daze over Richmond footbridge, where I imparted the news to the slightly dishevelled, muddy group, with Hugh a safe distance behind.

At this point, the two City bankers departed in disgust, the Kiwi girl burst into tears and her hubby started babbling incoherently, my two clients were somewhat taken aback – and even the face-suckers looked a little gobsmacked. Hugh joined the remaining team (once he thought it was safe to do so) and apologised profusely, promising that we would somehow still get to see the game. At this point, I suggested we get the cars to the ground and go to the ticket office in the hope that we could get duplicates for the tickets languishing on the hall table. Time was moving on, so we got into the cars and crawled through the traffic to the ground. On pulling up behind the East stand, we jumped out and told our tale of woe to a Rugby Football Union ticket lady. She was very understanding but couldn't help us unless we knew the ticket numbers – not a lot of use and a bit of a catch-22, because the numbers were on the tickets, which were in Hugh's flat, so we had to think again.

By then there was about ten minutes to go until kick-off, so our situation was becoming desperate. Hugh had been phoning rugby mates of his in the vain hope that somebody might have spares when suddenly his mobile went off, and after a brief moment he set off running in the direction of The Stoop, shouting, 'I've got three. Stay there. I'll be back in ten!' We stood in the shadow of the stand, hearing the strains of the anthems and the haka. While waiting, we decided amongst ourselves that the couple from New Zealand should have two of the tickets and my American client the other one. A very sweaty and out-of-breath host reappeared after about ten minutes, waving some tickets, which were handed out to the three lucky recipients, and the rest of us followed Hugh back to The Stoop, where he had procured seats at a big-screen showing of the game for the rest of us, which was better than nothing, but somewhat frustrating. As we moved further from the stadium, we could hear the roars of the crowd and sense the atmosphere within.

Needless to say, it was a cracking match, which England narrowly lost but should have won, and we ended up having a brilliant night out in Twickenham and Richmond, although we never saw the Kiwi couple again – it had all been too emotional for them. The unconcerned couple just kept on snogging, coming up for air and a quick drink every now and then, and my American client told me that it was the biggest sporting adventure he'd ever been on.

The story of the forgotten tickets seemed to have spread through the rugby cognoscenti, and a fine footnote to the tale came in The Sun at Richmond much later on in the evening when Jason Leonard spotted our host across the heaving bar and yelled out to him, 'Oi, McHardy! I'm a prop, but even I know that if you're doing corporate hospitality for an international, you need effing tickets, you mute!' This prompted a belly laugh from the entire pub and rounded off the occasion of the best match at Twickenham that I didn't go to. Conditions just about perfect . . .

THE BIG GREEN GIANT

GARETH EDWARDS
SCRUM-HALF Cardiff
WALES 1966–78, 53 caps
LIONS TOURS '71, '74, 10 Test matches

Over the course of ten Tests played on the same side as Willie John McBride for the British and Irish Lions I learned to respect, fear and cherish his presence. His incredible work rate, allied to his fearsome physical presence, made him the perfect player to have on your side. I loved the fact that he was one of my 'brothers in arms' in South Africa and New Zealand, always taking good care of me – and anyone who dared to get near me!

On the other hand, over the course of seven Five Nations clashes for Wales against Ireland, I witnessed the warrior in a different guise. Not only Willie John, but anyone wearing the green jersey! It was never a pleasant experience seeing the 'other' side of those players on whom you had relied for survival with the Lions when you came up against them in the championship. There is a wonderfully raw edge to Irish rugby and Irish players. Yes, they have great skill, but they also possess other qualities that are not always found in such great abundance in players from other nations.

It was some of those latter qualities that forced me to take my life into my own hands at Lansdowne Road in 1974 when I was leading

Wales against Willie John's Ireland in the Five Nations. It was my third visit to the home of Irish rugby in a Wales jersey, and I was still waiting for my first win.

My first visit in 1968 was bizarre in the extreme, as the English referee Mike Titcomb awarded a drop goal to me that didn't go over the bar. This led to a mini-invasion – and a huge backlash from Tom Kiernan's side that ended with them winning 9–6. Two years later we were supposed to make it back-to-back Triple Crowns in Dublin, although obviously somebody forgot to tell Tom's men that they were supposed to roll over for us. We lost 14–0, and, as they say, we were lucky to get nil! Those two matches taught me to expect the unexpected at Lansdowne Road – and to expect to be called on to meet fire with fire.

So, back to 1974. I'd been reinstated as captain of Wales, and we'd struggled to beat Scotland 6–0 at home in our opening game. Next stop was Lansdowne Road. Wales were in the process of rebuilding from the 1971 Grand Slam side into the team that would add two more Slams and four Triple Crowns before the end of the decade. Not that I had a pack of shrinking violets in front of me. Tough as teak Glyn Shaw joined Bobby Windsor and Walter Williams in the front row, Geoff Wheel and Allan Martin were kicking off their record partnership in the second row and Dai Morris, Merv 'the Swerve' Davies and Terry Cobner formed the back row. I felt comfortable and quietly confident, but those are terrible feelings to take into a game in Dublin. Perhaps I should have taken a closer look at an Ireland pack containing five players with whom I had toured with the Lions.

Sean Lynch, Ken Kennedy and Ray McLoughlin were in the front row, Willie John was captain of the side in the second row alongside a young Moss Keane, and my old mate Fergus Slattery joined Seamus Deering and Terry Moore in the back row. I say 'old mate' when referring to Slats, but that was only when we were playing on the same side. When he was in green and I was in red, he was a complete pain in the arse.

And it was Slats who was at the heart of my difficulties in Dublin in 1974. Like a good traditional Irish back-row forward, he was taking no prisoners and being very physical and confrontational. His lead was enthusiastically followed by everyone else. The only bonus for us was that one of his major partners in crime on the rugby field, Stewart McKinney, missed the game because of injury! Not that the nice young man from Kerry, Moss Keane, was slow to pick up the gist of things on his first championship game on home soil. After all, he had the master of the dark arts of forward play, Willie John, alongside him.

We scored a smart try through J.J. Williams and seemed to be in good shape going into the second half with the scores level at 9–9 and a strong Lansdowne Road breeze behind us. But the Irish like nothing more than a challenge, to feel their backs being pressed hard against the wall.

Well, the more we pressed, the more we suffered. Outside of J.P.R. Williams at full-back and Phil Bennett at outside-half, we had a pretty inexperienced back division. The more they got the ball, the more Slats and co. terrorised them. Nothing went right for us in that second half, and every time we won the ball it led to trouble. Willie John's men tackled us early and late, with the ball and without it – they simply smashed down anything in red.

It led to a few scuffles and a lot of moaning in the captain's ear. Finally, Bobby Windsor told me I had to do something when yet another Wales player was laid out flat. It was then that the red mist finally glazed over my eyes. We won the ball at a lineout, moved it sweetly down our back line and looked to be threatening. At the breakdown the English referee Ken Pattinson blew his whistle and penalised us again. I turned to look back across the field, and three of my players were lying prone on the ground with blood gushing from various wounds.

'You must be joking, ref. Look at my players,' I bellowed at him. With that, he blew his whistle and summoned Willie John over for a midfield captains' conference. He laid down the law to both of us, and I couldn't help myself from shouting at him again, saying, 'You must be joking.'

Throughout our collective bollocking, Willie John just looked at me bemused without saying anything. It was then that I completely flipped. Rising up to my full height of 5 ft 8 in., I glared at Willie John and roared, 'C'mon, McBride, pull your team together.'

Again, he just looked at me with that little gleam in his eye. 'What are you on about?' he asked.

'OK, then, McBride. If that's the way you want it, that's the way you'll have it.' I stormed back to my players, and the game continued – in exactly the same vein as it had done before the referee had called us over!

We failed to take advantage of the wind, and the game remained scoreless in the second half, giving Ireland a point that enabled them to win the championship that season. And it meant I had to wait until 1976 to get my first taste of victory on Irish soil.

After the match, friendship and sanity resumed. Willie John was no longer a monster in green, but the epitome of geniality. As we stood together at the post-match dinner, with pint of Guinness in one hand and pipe in the other, he looked down at me and asked, 'Gar, were you really threatening me out there this afternoon, little fella?' I didn't need to reply. We laughed about it and got on with a great night.

Two years later at Lansdowne Road it was business as usual. Could it ever be any different against Ireland?

PLAYING TO INSTRUCTIONS

STEWART McKINNEY

I think Willie Duggan has as strong an aversion to writing as he had to training in his heyday. He had many theories to back up his hatred of over-taxing himself prior to a big match. 'I might peak too soon' or 'You wouldn't expect a Derby horse to train like this the day before the big race!' On the pitch was a different matter, and he was as brave and hard a man as I ever played with. Importantly, he was behind me in the lineout, and for years he watched my back – literally. You never know, I might still receive a story, but in the meantime . . .

Dungannon played Wanderers one Saturday in Dublin, enjoyed their hospitality and three of us, Kieran O'Loane, Willie Anderson and I, headed off in Willie Anderson's car to Kilkenny to stay with Willie Duggan and Ned Byrne, Willie's cousin. We were all playing for Fergus Slattery's International XV against a Waterford Select XV to open a new pavilion or some other occasion. As Kilkenny was quite close to Waterford, a relaxing night with Ned and Willie seemed like a good idea.

Willie Anderson was particularly keen to meet the 'Doog', as he was a young and upcoming number 8. Except Willie Duggan didn't turn up. We were in Ned's pub. Nine o'clock passed, ten o'clock, eleven o'clock. Willie Anderson was desperately disappointed, but at 11.15 p.m. in trooped the Doog. 'Sorry, lads, I fell asleep. What are you having?'

We went to bed in the wee small hours and agreed to meet at eleven o'clock that morning to drive the 35 miles to Waterford. Willie didn't arrive till noon, and for once he was in a rush. 'Quick, lads, I've another game to play first!' He drove like a maniac through the Kilkenny countryside until we reached a country lane, where there were hundreds of cars parked. He drove past them all to get to a gate by a Gaelic-football pitch and blocked the entrance. Frantically, he began to change, but an official challenged him, asked him what the hell he was doing and told him to move the car. 'I'm playing. I'm not moving the car and bollocks off!'

The official said that there was only 15 minutes of the match left. 'That'll be enough!' Willie replied as he ran to a priest on the touchline, who lit him a fag, whispered some instructions in his ear and made a substitution. The great number 8 was now a full forward, and within 30 seconds there was a big high ball into the goalmouth. The opposition goalkeeper, ball and all, landed in the net, and the unfortunate last line of defence didn't look too grand. Willie ran back to the priest, retrieved the remnants of the fag, jogged to his car and changed again. 'I told you it wouldn't take too long!' he said to the bemused gateman, and off we set to Waterford.

YOU'RE MY FIRST, YOU'RE MY LAST . . . MY EVERYTHING!

STEVEN HUTTON
SECOND ROW Irish Schools, NIFC

When Stewart phoned me a while ago to ask me to make a contribution to his book and to keep it clean enough to be published, I panicked, wondering how I would manage that! As I've known Stewart for nearly 40 years, I decided to recap some of my experiences with him, ones that hopefully won't cause any offence.

While I was a pupil at Abbotts Cross Primary School, Stewart introduced me to what was to become a lifelong passion for rugby football (mind you, a lot of the referees in Ulster rugby would say he has a lot to answer for). At the time, Stewart was teaching there, and he was at the height of his playing career, having been selected for the 1974 British Lions. I can remember the whole school having to do projects on South Africa. He managed to get me all the touring players' autographs (probably worth something on eBay now, but I won't be selling). I'm not sure if he recalls but in that same year he also coached us to the final of the Ulster Schools mini-rugby tournament held at Ravenhill (unheard of in those days for a school like ours).

It was many years later that our paths were to cross again when Stewart was invited to take up the coaching position at NIFC, or

'North' as we were better known. This is where it gets really hard to try and keep things clean!

Before I recount anything further about him, I should probably set the scene. Most of the stories are about the North away trips, which always seemed to follow a familiar pattern: get to the venue, play the match as hard as possible and then overindulge in the post-match revelries. The away trips became part of our club's folklore. I have to admit I learned a lot about life on these trips; for example, lobsters don't survive in chlorine, certain shoes and kit bags can float in hotel pools, when everyone in the team wears the same club-coloured cravat strange things can happen to you in Cork on a Saturday night, and when you go to a Chinese restaurant in the south of Ireland always ensure there are wine glasses to drink from, otherwise you are likely to be ejected from the premises!

On one of our many journeys home, Stewart came out with one of his classic lines. It was a pissing-wet Sunday afternoon, and we were travelling back from the west of Ireland rather the worse for wear. During a back-of-the-bus court session, he looked out the window (you couldn't see two feet in front for rain and fog) and said, 'Jeez, boys will ya look at that! Isn't Ireland the most beautiful country in the world?' A fitting punishment ensued. You must forgive me, as my memory at this stage was somewhat blurry, but I can recall that shortly afterwards we were to witness Stewart's unusual use of club ties. (I'm reliably informed that Kleenex are not looking to exploit this particular function!)

Another memorable trip was on the train home from Limerick. Again, I should probably set the scene. It was a Sunday morning after a big win, and the North guys were doing what came naturally: having a pre-journey drink home (to settle the nerves, of course). By the time we boarded the train, spirits were high. Taking over the bar carriage and holding court, the craic was mighty, and we were joined by a charming young couple from America who had just started their honeymoon. Joining in with the banter, they had great fun listening to all the old stories as we entertained the entire carriage. When we reached Limerick Junction and they left the train, another classic was heard: 'Nice guy, but the wife's a horse!' Once the ensuing laughter had died down, we were again to witness Stewart's unusual use of his club tie, this time on the exact spot where he had been dropped from the Ireland team 25 years previously!

I was also fortunate enough to captain our club when Stewart was coach, and we led the team on a pre-season tour to Canada. Having gone to great lengths to ensure we got to see as much of Canada as possible, part of our trip involved travelling through the Rockies by bus from Calgary to Vancouver. The scenery was spectacular, probably one of the natural wonders of the world, certainly a site of scientific interest and great natural beauty. (Hey, they do documentaries about this!) We had been on the road for a few hours when Stewart decided he would brighten things up by asking one of our front-row forwards what they thought of the spectacular scenery, to which the said gentleman replied, 'You've seen one fucking tree and mountain, you've seen all of them!' Needless to say, he wasn't in contention to be our cultural attaché for the rest of the trip!

The tour turned out to be a great success, setting us up for an incredible season, in which we went on to win our league, the first time an Ulster club team had achieved such a feat. However, that year was not without its amusing moments. If memory serves, the North bus had to leave Ballinasloe rather rapidly one Sunday morning, as Stewart had not settled his bill with the local gypsies for a horse he had allegedly bought the night before at the Ballinasloe horse fair. On another of our trips, returning to Belfast on a Sunday afternoon (rather the worse for wear again), one of the lads spotted a woman out running and piped up with, 'God, boys, will you look at the ass on that female jogger,' only for our winger to pipe up with, 'That's actually my wife!'

I can also recall on another occasion taking a prop forward from England (a new recruit) to Cork, his drink of choice being cider. On the way down it was explained that they didn't consume cider in Cork, stout being the preferred tipple. By the time the match was over and we made it to the bar, it transpired that the club was, in fact, sponsored by Bulmer's cider! Our prop was last seen disappearing into the president's room to finish off a case of it!

I was very lucky to play when I did, while the guys today have to do things differently to my generation. I know the team I played for would always refuse to return home on a Saturday night from Cork, Limerick or Galway. I was also lucky to have been coached by Stewart, always a great motivator, even in the latter days of my playing career. I guess not too many guys can say that their first coach from primary school was also the final coach they had as a senior player.

FRENCH LEAVE

STEWART McKINNEY

When playing against France, the Ireland team used to stay in the Hotel Concorde Saint-Lazare on the periphery of the Pigalle, the red-light district of Paris. The district has its own subculture and is inhabited by locals who have grown to love the sleaze associated with their area, the familiarity of the street vendors and the amusement provided by the tourists and strays who venture into their world. Petty crime is commonplace, and there is a frisson of suspicion in the air when an outsider ventures into this milieu.

Now, rugby players are human. Strong young men have their needs and desires, and in searching for his appetite to be satisfied one Feidlim McLoughlin found himself in confrontation with a street seller. Overcome by desire, Feidlim couldn't stop himself from reaching out for the tempting wares openly displayed by the alleyway kerb. He knew it was wrong, he knew his mother wouldn't be proud but surely he wouldn't be found out here in Paris. God, those sausages smelled good!

Feidlim sidled up surreptitiously to the object of his desire, checked that he was unobserved and with the stealth and skill of a street urchin trained by Fagin slipped the sausage into his pocket. He strolled on nonchalantly without a glance, totally focused on the corner in front of him where he would be able to turn and indulge himself unseen.

Mission accomplished, Feidlim was anticipating sinking his teeth into the exotic charcuterie when there was a great commotion behind him. The shouting interrupted his thoughts, and he turned to see what all the fuss was about. To his horror, it was the sausage seller waving his arms, shouting and remonstrating with Gallic fervour. '*Arrête! Arrête!*' he cried, pointing at Feidlim. '*Mes saucissons!*' Feidlim knew he'd been rumbled but couldn't understand how. He was sure he'd gotten away with the perfect crime . . . until he noticed the chain of sausages linked behind him. *C'est la vie!*

SPEED OF THOUGHT

CLIFF MORGAN
FLY-HALF Cardiff, Bective Rangers
WALES 1951–8, 29 caps
LIONS TOUR '55, 4 Test matches

I have always loved the quick, amusing comments of rugby players. I remember the great British and Irish Lions wing Tony O'Reilly being chastised by one of his teammates on using an excess of embrocation. O'Reilly's excuse was that even if you were not fit, you should try to smell fit!

For some reason, I always made friends with front-row forwards; for example, Ray Prosser of Pontypool and Wales – and he was a Lion, too. After I retired from playing in 1958, I wrote a regular column in the *Sunday Times*. One Sunday I happened to pick the subject of forward play. The following Saturday I arrived at the Wales trial at Newport, where Ray said to me, 'Hey, Cliffie, what is all that rubbish you wrote in that thick paper? You know nothing about us up front. You were one of those prima donnas in the backs!'

One prop forward I adored in the 1950s was Cliff Davies of Wales and the British and Irish Lions. He was a man of many parts and for me the epitome of all that is good and wholesome about rugby. He was a coal miner, singer, poet and part-time undertaker, loved by people all over the rugby world. He had a true sense of values. One of his stories that captures perfectly the near-religious fervour of the game concerned the young minister who was ordained in Cliff's local chapel one Thursday, played his first game for the local club on the Saturday and preached his first sermon on the Sunday morning. The entire rugby team went to the service. Afterwards they asked Cliff what he thought of the new minister. He replied, 'Powerful in prayer but bloody hopeless in the lineout!'

Doing his job as a part-time undertaker, he was asked one day how much a coffin would cost. 'Forty-eight pounds,' he replied.

'That's a bit steep. I could get one from the Co-op.'

Cliff then puffed on his pipe and said, 'Well, take that one if you like, but pitch-pine it will be, and your arse will be through it in six months!'

Lansdowne Road, Dublin, has wonderful, haunting memories for me. I remember during the Ireland v. Wales match in 1952 my father lost his teeth – and he wasn't even playing!

What actually happened was that just after half-time my dad saw his only son work a scissors with Ken Jones, who then ran 50 yards to score a Triple Crown-winning try. My dad leaped to his feet and shouted with joy, spitting out his false teeth 20 rows in front of him! They were lost for ever. Some time later I was telling this story on Irish television with Tony O'Reilly, and he added, 'I know a farmer from Limerick who is still wearing them!'

THE SAFE PERIOD

STEWART McKINNEY

Ken Kennedy is a fantastic doctor and his wife Farida a brilliant physiotherapist. Ever the consummate professional, rugby is never far from his mind. Rumour has it that during a gynaecology lecture he was at, he was asked, 'When is the safe period?' Unblinkingly, he retorted, 'Half-time when Wales play Ireland at Cardiff Arms Park.' Whether he was the lecturer or the student is unclear, but the reply is mustard nonetheless.

GETTING THE CRAIC STARTED

STEWART McKINNEY

At the beginning of our tour in '74 there was a certain reserve amongst us, but one night in Stilfontein, a sleepy little West Transvaal town, the ice was well and truly broken. The management called a choir practice to organise a repertoire of songs for after-match functions. After half an hour of feet shuffling and averting of eyes, not a single song had been sung. We were all too shy.

It was an unmitigated disaster, and to rescue the situation Gareth asked Bobby Windsor to tell us a few jokes. The next hour was the funniest I've ever experienced as the Duke told jokes about nuthouses, owls and parrots. As if by magic, the singing began. Billy Steele sang 'Flower of Scotland', Willie John 'The Green Glens' and Slats 'Monto'.

After that happy evening, the characters of the team emerged. Mike Burton could mimic every member of the party and was especially good at Ulster accents. He had Willie John off to a T, right down to his crooked index finger.

Ralston drolly related his tour misfortunes, Grace was full of mischief and Andy Ripley fostered stray animals, gave away his kit, composed poetry and dressed improperly on every occasion. Phil Bennett was CAMRA's representative on tour and Fran Cotton . . . champion kipper.

HIP, HIP HOORAY

STEWART McKINNEY

Gareth Edwards could think so quickly on a rugby pitch. Cork Constitution were celebrating a new clubhouse or ground, I can't remember which, and a lot of the Wales boys, including Gareth, had come over to play for the International Invitation XV. These occasions are usually upbeat: there's a healthy spirit of competition and the players love having the opportunity to play with those whom they might not normally have the opportunity to play alongside. Boots are on and boundaries are down. It is a welcome diversion to catch up with characters only considered in terms of victory or vanquish when facing them as opponents, whereas invitation exhibition games allow them to be comrades in arms.

On the Sunday the weather changed. It became unbelievably foul, lashing stair rods of rain, howling a gale-force wind and so utterly bone-freezing cold that the usual celebratory mood present at such a game had perished. Neither the players nor the shivering spectators were any longer enjoying the match.

Ten minutes into the second half the ball went into touch and the referee blew his whistle for a lineout. Fifty minutes of unrelenting, unrepentant and unpleasant weather was enough. 'Hip-hip!' shouted Gareth, who was captain. 'Hooray!' we immediately responded and ran off, followed by Cork Con, who echoed the hurrahs, leaving a bemused referee shaking his head and looking at his watch. Conditions in the bar of the clubhouse were much more conducive to rugby relations!

PREPARATION AND PRESENTATION

ROGER YOUNG
SCRUM-HALF Queen's University, Collegians, Hamiltons
(Cape Town), Ulster
IRELAND 1965–71, 26 caps
LIONS TOURS '66, '68, 4 Test matches

I played with two Irish Kens, Kennedy and Goodall, and each of them was a master of his position. Ken Kennedy was a perfectionist when it came to preparation for an international. He was meticulous in the detail of his schedule, a player with a professional approach in what was the amateur era. He could also become extremely fractious when anyone interfered with his pre-match routine.

In March 1970 I had the misfortune to be his roommate prior to the Ireland v. Wales game. It was a great Wales team, containing many of their legends – J.P.R. Williams, Stuart Watkins, John Dawes, Barry John, Jeff Young, Delme Thomas, Dai Morris, Mervyn Davies and Gareth Edwards as captain.

We retired early, a good night's sleep being considered a prerequisite for a good performance the following day. Except the peace was shattered when, at midnight, the phone rang. It was my girlfriend Jennifer – now my dear wife – ringing to wish me all the best from Montreal. (Jennifer had forgotten about the time difference.) Kennedy was furious at the interruption and beside himself with rage. Well, the ringing had already caused a disturbance, and the call had been answered, so to minimise any further disruption I burrowed under the duvet to take the call and keep the conversation as quiet as possible. I quickly went back to sleep afterwards, but Ken was still muttering threats and recriminations as I dozed off. An hour later we were wakened again by rapping at the door. 'Who the fuck is it for you *this* time?' screamed Kennedy. 'Open the door!'

The culprit was the great man from the city of Derry, Ken Goodall. 'I'm a bit restless. I've come for a cigarette,' drawled Ken G. Ken K. went berserk.

The next day, having been up after midnight smoking to settle himself, Goodall, the great number 8, starred in a 14–0 win over the immensely talented Wales side, scoring one of the greatest individual tries ever seen at Lansdowne Road: a chip ahead, a gather and a run-in from 50 yards.

A few minutes later I fed a scrum. Ken Kennedy struck it cleanly, and the ball was quickly channelled to Goodall's feet, where he held it.

'Give me the ball, Ken!' I demanded.

'Say please.'

'Give me the ball, Ken. McGann wants to drop a goal,' I pleaded.

'Say please.'

'*Please*, Ken, give me the fucking ball!' And he did.

What would he have done to Wales with a good night's sleep behind him?

THE WHISTLER

STEWART McKINNEY

Ernie Davis, a hooker for King's Scholars, CIYMS and Ulster, was a total enigma and an inspiration to many young rugby players in Ulster who came through the Boys' Model School in Belfast during the 1960s and '70s. He is remembered fondly, even though many of his charges have still-vivid recollections of him 'taking lumps out of the boys' – he only wanted the best for them. He was dedicated to the teaching profession and his beloved club CIYMS.

Poetry was one of his great loves, too. He knew by heart epic poems, ballads and doggerel verse, and he could recite a stanza for any occasion. He promised me a story and said he'd explain why he played hooker (something to do with his rival being blind in his left eye), relate the story behind the orange boots, tell me about lining up his schoolboy team to dispense spoonfuls of cod-liver oil and elaborate on why he provided boots for the boys who couldn't afford them to give them the best chance of winning the highly prized and much coveted Schools Cup trophy. Sadly, he passed away before I could mine the stories from him. The 'wee man in the white mac' died – in probably a rugby player's dream exit – while watching his old club team CIYMS playing a Saturday fixture at their home ground, Belmont, before the final whistle made its sound. It seems fitting, therefore, to pay tribute to Ernie with his own poem – about a certain well-known international referee's whistle. (Thanks for letting me use it, Stephen. I know it's not all true!)

> When Stephen was a wee, wee lad
> He got a present from his dad
> Which set his heart alight with glee

It was a whistle – and a pea!
Wee Stephen blew with all his might
Half the day and half the night
He blew and blew with might and main
And sent the neighbours half insane.
Only Stephen's mum and dad
Thought the world of their wee lad
Thought he'd make a fine musician
Sent him for an audition –
To the London Philharmonic
But the noise he made was chronic!
The conductor said that he should take his whistle and his pea,
'Go back home across the sea – and be a rugby referee!'
Wee Stephen was enthusiastic
Bought some shorts with strong elastic
Joined the union for a start
Learned every single law by heart.
He refereed with such devotion
Quickly gained himself promotion
Till they let him have a go
At handling an interpro
And then a game between two nations
But still some had their reservations.
All agreed that he was able
But was he also fully stable?
When Stephen blew to start the game
Something snapped inside his brain
He blew and blew so long and hard
That the players and the crowd
Thought it was a symphony
Composed for whistle and a pea.
He penalised the lock for lifting
He told the full-back off for rifting
Sent the hooker off for fighting
And the tight-head off for biting
Awarded penalties galore
And ever higher rose the score.
To argue back meant quick dismissal
With one blast of Stephen's whistle
Tackles aimed above the thigh
He blew them up for going high
What a day it was for kickers
Nothing like it seen at Twickers.
From every angle near and far
They banged the ball across the bar

VOICES FROM THE BACK OF THE BUS

From the left and from the right
They kicked them over with delight.
Steve ne'er took a moment's rest
He whistled like a man possessed
He whistled high, he whistled low
Largo and adagio,
Syncopation, blues and bop
Country Western, jazz and pop
He puffed and blew in sharps and flats
He caterwauled like forty cats
The fans were speechless – stunned – amazed
They stood and watched completely dazed
While Stephen in that awesome hush
Whistled like a love-sick thrush.
That was Stephen's hour of glory
Often told in song and story
On that memorable day
Thirty took the field of play
But when the final whistle blew
There were only – twenty-two
Escorted home by forty coppers
To save him from the knives and choppers
(Of sixty thousand maddened fans
Escorted by ten armoured vans)
In a bullet-proof Land Rover.
Alas, Steve's refereeing days seemed over
That game between the Rose and Thistle
Immortalised by Stephen's whistle
That England lost in extra time
By 98–99!

LIST OF AUTHORS